MILTON KEYNES, MORE THAN CONCRETE COWS

REAL ANIMALS AND PLANTS TOO

records compiled by
Milton Keynes Natural History Society
for the years 1987 - 1999

ISBN 0 9538787 0 8

Published by Milton Keynes Natural History Society
The Hanson Environmental Study Centre,
Wolverton Road, Great Linford,
Milton Keynes, MK14 5AH

Printed by City Print (Milton Keynes) Ltd.
17 Denbigh Hall, Bletchley, Milton Keynes

Front cover: Robin, Great Linford, Small Tortoiseshell Butterfly, Bee Orchid, Shaggy Pholiota fungus

Back cover: Kitten looking at Southern Hawker dragonfly

Contents

Contents 3

Foreword 5

Acknowledgements 5

Introduction 6

    Area 7

    Geology 7

    Altitude 7

    Habitats 7

Contributors 9

    Society Contributors 9

    Non-society Contributors 9

    Major Authors 9

Gazetteer 12

Vascular Plants 14

    Ferns and Horsetails 15

    Conifers 15

    Flowering Plants 15

        Dicotyledons 15

        Monocotyledons 29

        Grasses 31

Bryophytes 34

    Liverworts 34

    Mosses 35

Fungi 38

    Gill Fungi 39

    Bracket Fungi *etc.* 41

    Cup Fungi *etc.* 42

    Puff-balls, Earth Stars *etc.* 43

    Jelly Fungi *etc.* 43

    Hyphomycetes, Phycomycetes *etc.* 43

    Slime Moulds 44

    Rusts and Smuts 44

Lichens 46

Mammals 49

Birds 51

Reptiles 56

Amphibians 56

Fish 56

Invertebrates 57

Slugs and Snails 58

    Slugs 58

    Snails 58

    Bivalves 59

Arthropods 60

Waterfleas, Woodlice and Fresh-water Shrimps 60

Millipedes 61

Centipedes 61

Spiders, Harvestmen, Ticks and Mites 61
   Spiders 61
   Harvestmen 62
   Ticks and Mites 62
Insects 63
   Bristletails, Two-tailed Bristletails and Springtails 63
   Mayflies 63
   Dragonflies and Damselflies 63
   Grasshoppers and Crickets 64
   Earwigs 65
   Cockroaches 65
   Booklice 65
   Sucking Lice 65
   True Bugs 65
   Lacewings and Alder Flies 66
   Scorpion Flies 66
   Butterflies and Moths 67
      Butterflies 67
      Moths 68
   True Flies 83
   Fleas 86
   Sawflies, Ants, Bees and Wasps 87
   Beetles 88
Earthworms and Leeches 94
Rotifers 94

Foreword

In the early 1970's, when bulldozers and other massive earth-moving equipment were making inroads (and laying the foundations for roads) into the agricultural lands surrounding the soon-to-be engulfed villages of the Milton Keynes area, one wondered how wildlife could possibly survive such an onslaught. With the subsequent influx of some 200,000 people with their motor cars, and also other transport necessary to support an ever-expanding development, what hope was there for the native trees and wild flowers, and the birds, mammals and insects dependent on them?

At first sight, it seemed that the only vegetation in the new town would be the almost overgenerous plantings of ornamental shrubs and trees lining the vast network of roadside verges and the unending series of roundabouts with, in summer, their splashes of bright colour from thousands of rose bushes.

However, in this special publication, the naturalists of the now well-established Milton Keynes have clearly demonstrated that such a pessimistic view of the most famous (infamous!) of England's new towns is far from correct. They have shown to the community that amongst its citizens there is a vigorous body of wildlife enthusiasts supporting a lively Natural History Society. Also, the membership of the Society has demonstrated that it has wide-ranging talents and knowledge by the very fact that it has brought together in this volume a remarkable (and heartening) catalogue of almost all the major groups of flora and fauna of the area. In so doing, it has shown that first impressions can be misleading and that all is far from lost following the inevitable "march of progress" as the new town has grown. Equally important is the fact that this publication will provide a valuable benchmark for future naturalists anxious to continue to monitor, in the coming years, the survival of the area's wildlife resource. It is a notable achievement.

Alan J Brook

Acknowledgements

The production of this book would not have been possible without the help of a large number of people. Society members were the main source of records and information, but we are also much indebted to others for their contributions, without whom some of the lists would have been most inadequate.

The appearance of the book has been enhanced by the use of drawings and photographs provided by members and friends. The text has all been typed by volunteers and the task of preparing it as camera-ready copy was undertaken by George Mahoney. We are grateful to all of these participants.

We have also been fortunate to receive financial support from:
- **Milton Keynes Council,**
- **English Partnerships,**
- **Milton Keynes Parks Trust,**
- **Anglian Water Environmental Partnership with funds provided by Cleanaway Limited under the Landfill Tax Credit scheme,**
- **the Millennium Festival Awards for All**
- and **Professor Alan Brook.**

Without help from these sources and a generous donation from the Society itself we could neither have produced such a comprehensive book nor yet so many copies to reach such a wide audience. We should all be most grateful.

Introduction

Since its formation in March 1968, Milton Keynes Natural History Society has, in addition to providing information and discussion opportunities at its weekly meetings and various other activities, always sought to address wider aspects of natural history. Included among these other activities have been the conduct of surveys or projects associated with particular sites and habitats often in co-operation with similar organisations and the publication of various booklets. Among the latter have been the occasional Journals written by Society members and, in particular, a summary detailing the significant events and anecdotes *of 'MKNHS - The First Twenty-Five Years 1968 - 1993'*. In keeping with this outlook, the Society felt that seven years after the latter booklet and as we now move into a new millennium, it would be appropriate to prepare a current list of the species of organisms found in Milton Keynes.

This list would cover not just the popular birds, plants and butterflies, but also other invertebrates, mosses, liverworts, lichens, fungi, mammals, fish, reptiles and amphibians, although we shall stop short of including bacteria, viruses and the like, By its very nature, being compiled from the observations of many individuals having different objectives and methods of assessment when making their recordings, the list will not be comprehensive nor reflect an equal emphasis between or within the various groups of organisms. However, it will act as a reference to some of the features of the fauna and flora of Milton Keynes noted during the years 1987 - 1999 inclusive, against which records from past and future years could be assessed. This is particularly important as it is only recently that Milton Keynes has been designated a Unitary Authority and thus is now responsible for local government administration in an area of North Bucks separate from the remainder of the county of Buckinghamshire. The area has, of course, seen drastic changes in landscape and natural habitat during the last 30 years, as development of the new town has progressed and this will inevitably continue for some time yet. As the urban area expands, greater emphasis will be given within the planning process to the conservation of important habitats and sites of interest. For this, consideration will need to be given to the known or presumed biodiversity at any given site or habitat and here the list will provide a small, but significant, part of the information to be utilised.

The records have originated from many sites of interest on both public and private property (in the latter case only after permission to enter had been obtained from the owner). Some of the sites have been specifically declared to be of wildlife importance, such as Site of Special Scientific Interest (SSSI), Local Nature Reserve (LNR), Wildlife Trust Nature Reserve (the local Trust being the Berks, Bucks and Oxon. Wildlife Trust - formerly BBONT) and Site of Importance for Nature Conservation (SINC). Sites and habitats comprise Woods and Hedgerows, Water and Wetlands, Grassland and Arable, Churchyards and their boundaries and Urban Greenspace. Because of the limitations of space, few of the records in this book are listed as being present at a specific site but in many cases an indication of the type of habitat in which the organism may be found is indicated. None of the records is attributed to a specific recorder, but acknowledgement is given by name to all who individually made a contribution.

The record of each species is comprised of a number of elements, mostly occupying just a single line of text. A scientific (Latin) name is always given, a common (English) name where possible and some indication of habit or habitat. Other information which may be included will depend on the type of organism and may include: frequency in Bucks and/or Milton Keynes, native or introduced, time and duration when the organism may be seen *etc.*

Whilst every effort has been made to include all records known to us during the period 1987 - 1999, there will be omissions and other lists which may be available should also be consulted *e.g.* those at the Buckinghamshire Environmental Records Office, the Milton Keynes Environmental Records Office and the North Bucks Bird Club monthly lists.

It should be borne in mind that recording is a continuous process and the Society welcomes all contributions to augment this list. Who knows, it may be appropriate to produce another in five years time! Such contributions should be sent to the Society c/o The Hanson Environmental Study Centre, Wolverton Road, Great Linford, Milton Keynes, MK14 5AH with the name of the organism, date of observation, precise location (with 6-figure grid reference) and name of recorder, together with some verification, if possible, and any other information relevant to the organism.

Area

The area covered by the lists is that part of Buckinghamshire which now comprises the administrative area of the Borough of Milton Keynes, together with that small part of Salcey Forest which was, until recently, a part of the county.

Geology

The northern part of Milton Keynes has the oldest rocks in Buckinghamshire and, as one moves south, younger rocks are present. Most are covered with recent, superficial drift deposits. Outcrops run roughly north-east to south-west across Milton Keynes, but few are fully exposed being mostly covered with Boulder Clay. The soils derived from the rocks impart differences in pH (acidity/alkalinity), though most are neutral or alkaline; only in the Brickhills does one encounter noticeably acid soils.

The most northerly areas have Boulder Clay and Lias Clay with Great Oolite to their south. This is a hard limestone and is close to the surface in places so imparts a highly calcareous nature to the soils (high pH values). It has been quarried in several places and used for building purposes, including boundary walls. Where Oxford Clay has been extracted (to the south of the limestone), bricks were made and used locally.

The rivers Great Ouse and Ouzel have cut courses through the limestone or clay and their valleys have Alluvium and Glacial Gravels, the latter having been extracted from a number of sites. In a few places the clay and limestone are separated by a narrow band of Cornbrash (a mixture of rubbly limestones), very suitable for growing corn crops.

The escarpment on which Bow Brickhill and Little Brickhill stands is of Lower Greensand, a substrate which is so different from all other formations in that it supports an acid soil and the rock itself is an acid sandstone.

Altitude

Almost the whole of Milton Keynes is below 150m in height, except the hills above Bow Brickhill which rise to 171m to the east of the church. The northern clay areas around Hanslope to the west and Hardmead to the east are next in height, but rarely exceed 100m. The River Great Ouse west of Turvey is at 45m above sea level, so the whole of Milton Keynes can be considered as lowland.

Habitats

Woodlands and Hedgerows

Much of the previously extensive areas of woodland have been cleared, though important remnants remain and have a rich and varied flora, together with their associated faunas. Apart from the coniferous woods on the Lower Greensand ridge on which Bow and Little Brickhills stand, the other woods are mainly deciduous, but sometimes with conifers. The conifers, of course, are all planted but there are special plants and animals which are native to the area and only found in such woods.

The main deciduous woods were all, probably, parts of the larger Salcey Forest and Whaddon Chase. Some have had coniferous trees planted in places but, in the main, natural woodland remains. In the north are The Straits (an erstwhile BBONT reserve and part of the area still known as Salcey Forest), Great Wood and Dinglederry. These two are part of Yardley Chase and privately owned. Salcey has free access along many rides. Stokepark Wood has access along some splendidly wide rides; Little Linford Wood is being restored (by BBOWT) to its former glory after a spell of disastrous felling. Hollington Wood, Gayhurst Wood and Moulsoe Woods are all privately owned but have interesting plants and animals. Similarly, Hoo Wood which was bisected during construction of the M1.

Howe Park Wood, Linford Wood and Shenley Wood all lie within the original boundary of the area designated for Milton Keynes development and are good examples of oak/ash woodlands on damp clay soils. In springtime, between them, are fine displays of Bluebells, Wood Anemones, Primroses and Violets, together with rarer species of orchids and Herb-Paris.

Much of Oakhill Wood is planted with conifers but, again, it is private property. Of recent interest is the area known as Hazeley Wood which has had hundreds of Oak, Hornbeam and Silver Birch trees planted. It will take hundreds (at least!) of years for mature woodland to be formed, but MKNHS is helping to monitor the changes which are taking place.

The other main woody features of the area are the hedgerows. These form field boundaries and often separate the highway from the surrounding land. A few are very old and represent remnants left when woodland was felled. These, assart hedges, are the richest in species and the most valuable for wildlife, providing food and shelter for birds and a wide variety of butterflies and other insects.

Water

The River Tove forms part of the north-western boundary of Milton Keynes, the River Great Ouse, more or less, bisects it from the west at Stony Stratford to the north-east at Turvey and, towards its eastern end, the River Ouzel flows north to join it at Newport Pagnell. Part of this river has been canalised as, for example, near Willen, but its banks have become quite well vegetated. Another long-standing, but man-made waterway is the Grand Union Canal which is accessible, via its towpath, along its whole length through Milton Keynes. All of these are important habitats for increasing biodiversity and some of our most interesting plants and animals are to be found in the water or marginal vegetation.

What are now extremely valuable water bodies for wildlife are the disused gravel pits, now water-filled, along the river Great Ouse - at Stony Stratford, Great Linford, Newport Pagnell and Emberton. As well as for wildlife, use of the lakes has also been made for fishing, boating and as an added amenity attraction at Emberton Park. The Blue Lagoon Local Nature Reserve has been developed around another mineral extraction site. Its pits are deep, and were formed as clay was taken for the making of Fletton bricks.

Other, artificially created, water bodies are the balancing lakes so characteristic of Milton Keynes. Their utilitarian function is to take excessive run-off water from the built-up area and release it 'gently' into the main river system. However, Willen Lake, in particular, has become an excellent site for birds (and their watchers!) and is said to be the best site in Buckinghamshire for bird watching. The fluctuating water level means that the marginal vegetation is not as good as it is by rivers or even ponds, but the exposed mud with its rich small animal life is attractive to birds. Only a few ponds remain in the area, though, at one time, most pastures had one. There is a wide network of small ditches and streams in the area, but their value for wildlife varies with the management they receive.

Grassland

Cattle and sheep rearing and grazing were once the main activities on many of the local farms. The fodder came from grass, most of which had been sown after ploughing - so-called "improved grassland". On the whole it is of low value for wildlife but there are still a few places (especially on the limestone) where 'improvement' has not taken place and the plant and animal diversity is high. Drainage and flood-alleviation measures of low-lying land, especially close to the rivers, have taken their toll on the species-rich hay meadows which once occurred. It is believed that there is now only one small area of fen vegetation left in the whole Borough, though there are a few places with wet grassland.

The other main places with grasses are the arable fields - usually acres of monoculture wheat or barley. Headlands and field margins used to be havens for a wide range of insects and other small animals, but these have now all-but disappeared. So, too, have many of the cornfield weeds and, it is well-known, there has been a steady decline in farmland birds like lapwings and skylarks over the last few decades.

Churchyards

From the wildlife point-of-view, churchyards are often the only places left in a village or town where there is unimproved grassland. There has been disturbance over the years and necessary management, but these have often maintained a rich variety of plants like Bird's-foot-trefoil, Burnet Saxifrage, Cowslips and Celandines and, rarely, Meadow Saxifrage, and consequently good insects (like butterflies) and birds.

In the north of Milton Keynes, many of the churchyards are surrounded by walls made from locally quarried limestone. These make splendid sites for mosses, lichens, spiders and woodlice for example. We have no natural rock exposures in the whole area, so these walls (also found in other parts of some of the villages) make unique sites. The use of a wide variety of rocks for making tombstones has, over the years, increased diversity of species, especially of lichens, which grow on them.

Churchyards off the limestone tend to be surrounded by hedges and these, too, add habitat diversity to the sites - and a different diversity to the Borough's wildlife as a whole.

Urban Greenspace

Within the built-up areas there is a wide range of nooks and crannies where plants and animals may find a home. Some are in well defined habitats (as those above), but there are other places like pavement cracks, footpaths across fields and other odd corners where wild plants and animals thrive. Larger areas are those like clumps of trees, the play parks and areas around sports fields which all play their part in providing a place for something to live. Among the outstanding features of Milton Keynes are the verges along the grid roads (and, to a lesser extent, on some of the estates) which are planted with many horticultural species, as a landscape amenity. These provide 'wildlife corridors' which may assist, directly or indirectly, in the dispersal of many species.

Contributors

Society Contributors

Gerry Baker, Charlie Blake, Len Bourne, Alistair Baxter, Steve Brady, Philip Brown, Chris Coppock, John Davis, John Day, Bernard Frewin, George and Anne Grove, George and Frances Higgs, Les Hill, Beryl Hulbert, Mike Killeby, Martin Kincaid, Nick Jarvis, Wally and Joan Lancaster, Paul Lund, Clare Mahaddie, George Mahoney, Sue Marie, Roy Maycock, Linda Murphy, Alan Nelson, Martin Oliver, Linda Piggott, Audrey and John Prince, Viola Read, Pat and Margaret Reynolds, Derek Schafer, Andy Shaw, Matthew Slaymaker, Bob Stott, Jean Varley, Jeff and Jenny Watt, Carol Watts, Arthur Whitehouse, John and Margaret Wickham, Tony Wood, Aaron Woods.

Non-society Contributors

Bryan Brown (Bat parasites), Rachel Burton (Art work), Tom Chester (Lichens), Andy Clarke (Butterflies), Jerry Cooper (Fungi), Rai Darke (Butterflies), Andy Harding (Birds), Eric Hollowday (Rotifers),Theresa Howard (Bat flea), John Mander (Butterflies), Bernice Mann (Butterflies), David Manning (Micro-moths), Charlotte Matthews (Art work), Reg Mead (Butterflies), Ian Middlebrook (Beetles & Butterflies), Harriet Milner (Butterflies), Geoff Moss (Butterflies & Macro-moths), Andy Patmore (Butterflies), Colin Plant (Beetles), Gordon Redford (Butterflies), Colin Savage (Macro-moths), George Solt (Butterflies), Keith Stapleton (Butterflies), Andrew Stephenson (Invertebrates), Mike Street (Fish), Norman Stone (Butterflies)

Major Authors

Vascular plants	Roy Maycock and Aaron Woods
Mosses & Liverworts	Frances Higgs
Fungi	Derek Schafer
Lichens	Tom Chester
Mammals	Bernard Frewin and Linda Piggott
Birds	Alan Nelson and Martin Oliver
Invertebrates (general)	Steve Brady and John Wickham
Slugs & Snails	Aaron Woods
Dragonflies & Damselflies	George Mahoney
Butterflies	Mike Killeby
Moths	George and Frances Higgs

Steve Brady

Steve Brady has a degree in Zoology, specialising in Entomology. He joined the Society in 1985 and has served as its Secretary since 1992. He maintains a long standing interest in entomology, especially Hymenoptera and lesser Orders (*e.g.* Booklice), as well as terrestrial invertebrates. He records locally when time permits, particularly as part of the Hazeley Wood Study Group. He is a member of the British Entomological and Natural History Society and the Amateur Entomological Society.

Tom Chester

Tom Chester graduated in Geography and Geology, the latter proving particularly useful in his study of Lichens and their association with tombstones and walls. His original natural history interest was in birds, but this changed to lichens a number of years ago. He is now the co-ordinator for the British Lichen Society's national churchyard survey. He has given a number of talks and practical sessions to the Society.

Bernard Frewin

Bernard Frewin is one of the original group of four who helped to found the Society in 1968. At that time, he was interested in taxidermy so decided that, to get lifelike specimens, he ought to know more about the creatures he was stuffing. This increase in knowledge became more and more important and so began studies of small mammals in a variety of habitats. Badgers soon became part of his studies and the field experience he has gained has put him in the forefront of badger conservation. His services for badgers are frequently called upon.

George Higgs

George Higgs joined the Society in 1986 to meet, learn and share expertise with like-minded people. He has a great love of the countryside and interest in natural history in general, but feels that his main interest is in Butterflies and Moths. He is a member of the British Entomological and Natural History Society and the Amateur Entomological Society. He has carried out regular moth recording at a number of Milton Keynes venues, as well as other parts of the United Kingdom. He was responsible for adding a number of species to the Guernsey moth list and added the White Letter Hairstreak to the Alderney list. All of his records are submitted to the appropriate county recorders and other interested organisations, such as the Forestry Commission.

Frances Higgs

Frances Higgs also joined the Society in 1986 and begun studying Bryophytes in 1987. She joined the British Bryological Society in 1989 and regularly submits records to the Buckinghamshire and Northamptonshire county recorders. She has given a number of talks and practical sessions to the Society and points out that the mosses and liverworts are much under-recorded, so provide an excellent opportunity for people to get involved.

Mike Killeby

Mike Killeby has been watching and studying butterflies in the United Kingdom and abroad since moving to Milton Keynes in 1976. He has also been breeding some species in a dedicated plastic tunnel which he built for the purpose. He joined the Society in the mid 80's and has served as its Chairman. His interest in butterflies developed into a passion for moths, which he has been recording since 1992. During the late 90's he co-ordinated the Milton Keynes records for the Millennium Butterfly Atlas.

George Mahoney

George Mahoney was interested in natural history whilst at school, but became more serious when he joined the Society in 1973, starting off by trying to identify the True Bugs. They were very difficult so, some 13 years ago, swapped allegiance to the dragonflies and damselflies and is now very proficient at identifying them. He is a member of the Dragonfly Society and maintains their web site. Other interests include animal behaviour and evolution and photography (particularly wildlife). He is a past Chairman of the Society.

Roy Maycock

Roy Maycock was one of the four founder members of the Society in 1968 and is currently its President. He became interested in wild flowers in his late teens and joined the Botanical Society of the British Isles whilst at University. He was involved in the survey of Buckinghamshire plants for a proposed county Flora but, regrettably, it has never been published. Since 1986 he has been the BSBI's recorder for the county. After early retirement from teaching, he carried out a botanical survey of all churchyards in Bucks and then repeated the exercise in Oxfordshire. He was employed for six years by BBOWT, firstly to lead a team training in field survey work skills and subsequently as an assistant county officer.

Alan Nelson

Alan Nelson joined the Society in 1994 and has a wide range of interests, particularly birds, orchids, dragonflies, butterflies and their photography. He is a licensed ringer for the British Trust for Ornithology, has carried out survey work for them and is a member of two Ringing Groups. He is a member of the RSPB and leader of the local Phoenix and Young Ornithologists Groups. Other active involvement is with Bat Conservation, the British Dragonfly Society (where he is helping to set up a Buckinghamshire branch) and regularly carrying out recording survey for these societies. He is currently Chairman of the Society.

Martin Oliver

Martin Oliver joined the Society in 1998. He was already a keen birder and involved in the running of the local Phoenix and Young Ornithologists Groups of the RSPB. Recently, his natural history interests have included dragonflies, butterflies and now moths.

Linda Piggott

Linda Piggott has been a member of the Society since 1982. She is a voluntary bat warden for English Nature and surveys wild bat populations for the Bat Conservation Trust. She also cares for sick, injured and orphaned bats, rehabilitating and releasing them whenever possible.

Derek Schafer

Derek Schafer trained as a chemist at Oxford University. He is an amateur mycologist whose interest in fungi came later in his career and he has recently been making a special study of Ink Caps. He is also involved in the British Mycological Society and a member of the editorial panel of 'Field Mycology'. He joined the Society in 1999 and has already led several forays for us.

John Wickham

John Wickham joined Bletchley Natural History Society, as it was then, early in 1968 after visiting as a speaker. He was Chairman for seven years and is currently a Vice-President. His interest in natural history and, in particular, entomology is driven by a desire to identify and understand the distinguishing characteristics and life histories of organisms. He has been co-ordinator of the Hazeley Wood Study Group since its inception in 1993.

Aaron Woods

Aaron Woods had an interest in wild flowers from a very young age. He was identifying specimens from the age of six and joined the Wildflower Society at the age of 12. Two years later he won its junior members prize. He joined this Society when he was 13 and rapidly developed his field identification skills to gain an extensive knowledge of wild and garden plants. He is a member of the Botanical Society of the British Isles. From seaside shell collecting, he developed an interest in slugs and snails and, by being actively involved with various recording projects, has extended his interests to include birds, insects, mosses and liverworts.

Gazetteer

Each place name is followed by a 4-figure grid reference so that it can be located within a 1 km square. Linear sites do not fit into single 1 km squares. They include: Ouse Valley Park, Ouzel Valley Park, River Great Ouse, River Ouzel, River Tove, Water Hall Park, North Loughton Valley Park, Grand Union Canal, Disused railway lines, Railway Walk, North Buckinghamshire Way, Swan's Way and Redway system.

Sites marked * have no public access (but please check other places too).

Astwood	9547	Haversham	8242
Back Wood	9033	* Haversham Lake	8342
Bell's Copse	9233	Hazeley Wood	8136
* Blackhorse Lake	8442	Heelands	8440
* Bletchley Park	8635	Hill Barns	9034
Blue Lagoon Park	8632	Hills and Hollows	8339
Bow Brickhill	9034	* Hollington Wood	8948
*Bow Brickhill Heath	9134	* Hoo Wood	8445
Bow Brickhill Park	9134	Howe Park Wood	8334
* Bozenham Mill	7648	* Jubilee Pit	8631
Bradwell Abbey	8239	Kiln Ground	9133
Bradwell Common	8439	* Kilwick Wood	8653
* Bradwell Lake	8342	Lathbury	8745
Brandon's Wood	9146	Lavendon	9153
Broomhills Wood	9132	* Lavendon Wood	9255
Broughton	8940	Linford Wood	8440
Brown's Wood	9134	Little Brickhill	9032
(*) Buttermilk Wood	9231	Little Brickhill Copse	9232
Caldecotte Lake	8935	Little Linford Wood	8345
Calverton	7939	Lodge Lake	8338
Campbell Park	8639	Long Street	7948
Castlethorpe	7944	Loughton	8337
Central Milton Keynes	8438	Lower Weald	7838
Chicheley	9045	* Lower Wood	9241
Clifton Reynes	9051	Manor Park	8542
* Clifton Spinney	9250	Middle Weald	7938
CMK Bus Station	8438	Milton Keynes Bowl	8536
Cold Brayfield	9252	Milton Keynes village	8839
* Dinglederry	8552	Moulsoe	9041
Down Covert	9033	* Moulsoe Old Wood	9242
Emberton	8849	Mount Farm Lake	8735
Emberton Park	8850	Mount Farm Park	8735
Filgrave	8748	* New Covert	9039
Fishermead	8638	Newfoundout	8633
Furzton Lake	8436	Newton Blossomville	9251
Galley Hill	7940	* Newton Wood	9250
Gayhurst	8446	North Crawley	9244
* Gayhurst Wood	8346	* Nun Wood	9231
Giffard Park	8542	* Oakhill Wood	8135
Great Linford Park	8542	* Old Covert	9140
* Great Wood	8452	Old Wolverton	8141
Hanslope	8046	Old Wolverton church	8041
Hanson Environmental Centre	8342	Olney	8851
Hardmead	9347	Olney churchyard	8951

* Open University	8837
Ouse Valley Park car park	8142
Plysu Pits	9236
Ravenstone	8550
Ravenstone Mill	8548
* Redhouse Lake	8542
Salcey Forest	8150
* Seven Acre Covert	9048
Shenley Church End	8336
Shenley Wood	8236
Sherington	8946
* Snip Wood	9253
Stanton Low church	8342
Stanton Wood	8439
Stantonbury Lake	8343
Stoke Goldington	8348
Stokepark Wood	8249
Stonebridge	8241
Stony Stratford	7940
Stony Stratford Nature Reserve	7881
Teardrop Lakes	8437
The Heath	9133
The Warren	9133
* Thickthorn Wood	9147
* Threeshire Wood	9155
* Tickford End Pits	8844
Tongwell Lake	8642
Two Mile Ash	8138
Tyringham	8546
Walton Lake	8837
Walton Oxbow	8837
Wavendon	9037
Wavendon Wood	9135
Weeks Wood	9034
Weston Underwood	8650
Willen Lake, north	8740
Willen Lake, south	8739
Willen Village	8839
Woburn Sands	9235
Wolverton	8140
Wolverton Balancing Lakes	8040
Wolverton Mill	7941
Woolstone	8739
Woughton-on-the-Green	8737

Vascular Plants

Bee Orchid

Vascular plants are those which have tissues to conduct food and water and include Pteridophytes (ferns and horsetails) and Spermatophytes - the Gymnosperms (conifers and yew) and Angiosperms (all the flowering plants). Each of these groups is listed separately and, to make access easier the flowering plants are further divided into Dicotyledons (those, usually, with broad leaves with net-like veins) and Monocotyledons (those with narrow leaves and parallel veins). Grasses are Monocots, but here are also listed separately.

The lists which follow each have five columns - the first with scientific names, the second with common names (arranged alphabetically), the third whether the plant is native to the British Isles or introduced, the fourth (when present) stating whether the plant is rare or very rare within Buckinghamshire as a whole. The final column may give some indication of a plant's frequency in Milton Keynes and the sort of places where it may be found. Identification of the plants listed has virtually always been possible to the species level and, quite often, to the sub-species level where such exists. Only one common name has been used for each species, so sometimes it may not be the one which is recognised *e.g. Cardamine pratensis* is listed as Cuckooflower, though it may also called Lady's-smock. Similarly, *Arum maculatum* is Lords-and-Ladies but may also be Cuckoo-pint or Parson-in-the-pulpit or Bobbins or any one of over a hundred others!

Within the area of the development of the new town, a tremendous amount of planting of non-native plants has taken place. Some of them have reproduced and spread, others have not. Most of the introduced species listed will have produced seedlings at least; very few are listed where they are only known as being planted.

The native species in the lists include all the familiar plants, as well as those which are less common but which make up the 'wild' landscape. Again, within the development area there has been planting of some native species so their present distribution may not reflect the distribution before development.

The prediction (in 1926) that Brookweed would turn up in Buckinghamshire was realised in 1991 and the discovery of Grass-poly in 1999 was most unexpected. Other plants new to the area have come in with seed mixes - most spectacularly the first British record in 1978 of Californian Lobelia. It did not survive! Bird seed, too, has been the origin of several alien species and the habit of rejecting plants from gardens has given rise to more records.

Records made to compile the lists have come from a large number of people, to whom we are most grateful. All of those records are maintained on a tetrad (*i.e.* 2km x 2km square) basis, though these are not shown here. More details of the more interesting species are also kept.

Key

I	=	Introduced into the British Isles
N	=	Native to the British Isles (not necessarily so in Milton Keynes)
R	=	Rare in Buckinghamshire
VR	=	Very Rare in Buckinghamshire
U	=	Previously unrecorded for Buckinghamshire
Parentheses ( )		signify doubt

References and Further Reading

Blamey, M. and Grey-Wilson, C. (1989). The Illustrated Flora of Britain and Northern Europe. Hodder & Stoughton

Garrard, I. and Streeter, D. (1983). The Wild Flowers of the British Isles. Macmillan.

Martin, W.K. (1981) The New Concise British Flora in Colour (3rd ed.). Michael Joseph & Ebury Press

Rose, F. (1981). The Wildflower Key for the British Isles - North-west Europe. Warne

Rose, F. (1989). Colour Identification Guide to the Grasses, Sedges, Rushes and Ferns of the British Isles and North-western Europe. Viking.

Stace, C.A. (1997). New Flora of the British Isles (2nd ed.). Cambridge

Ferns and Horsetails

Ophioglossum vulgatum	Adder's-tongue	N	Very rare; old grassland
Pteridium aquilinum			
ssp. *aquilinum*	Bracken	N	Scattered in the less alkaline areas
Dryopteris dilatata	Buckler-fern, Broad	N	Woods
Dryopteris carthusiana	Buckler-fern, Narrow	N	Uncommon; woods
Blechnum spicant	Fern, Hard	N R	A few sites on the Brickhills; very rare
Athyrium filix-femina	Fern, Lady	N	Wet woods
Azolla filiculoides	Fern, Water	I R	River Ouse; spreading; quantities vary yearly
Phyllitis scolopendrium	Hart's-tongue	N	Walls, away from direct sunlight; drains
Dryopteris filix-mas	Male-fern	N	Common; woods, base of walls; churchyards
Dryopteris affinis			
ssp. *borreri*	Male-fern, Scaly	N R	Only record is from Little Linford Wood
Polypodium vulgare	Polypody	N R	Walls, epiphyte on trees
Polypodium interjectum	Polypody, Intermediate	N	Walls; probably under-recorded
Polystichum aculeatum	Shield-fern, Hard	N R	In one wood in north MK
Asplenium adiantum-nigrum	Spleenwort, Black	N	Rare; on a wall at Calverton
Asplenium trichomanes			
ssp. *quadrivalens*	Spleenwort, Maidenhair	N R	Walls; often on railway bridges
Asplenium ruta-muraria	Wall-rue	N	Walls; with the above
Equisetum arvense	Horsetail, Field	N	Rough grassy places, bare ground; weed
Equisetum telmateia	Horsetail, Great	N R	Damp woods and banks on acid soils
Equisetum palustre	Horsetail, Marsh	N	Rare; damp places/fens, watersides
Equisetum x litorale	Horsetail, Shore	N VR	Linford Pits
Equisetum fluviatile	Horsetail, Water	N R	Very rare; lake

Conifers

Taxodium distichum	Cypress, Swamp	I	Planted in Ouzel Valley & Campbell Parks
Larix decidua	Larch, European	I	Planted; occasional in woods, churchyards
Larix x marschlinsii	Larch, Hybrid	I	Planted
Larix kaempferi	Larch, Japanese	I	Planted
Pinus nigra			
ssp. *laricio*	Pine, Corsican	I	Planted
Pinus sylvestris	Pine, Scots	N	Planted; very occasionally self-sown
Metasequoia glyptostroboides	Redwood, Dawn	I	Planted nr. the Water Gardens & Gt. Linford
Picea abies	Spruce, Norway	I	Planted; woods, plantations
Picea sitchensis	Spruce, Sitka	I	Planted as a crop; Crownhill near H4
Sequoiadendron giganteum	Wellingtonia	I	Parks, gardens; few in the Woolstones
Taxus baccata	Yew	N	Churchyards, woods; planted, may self-set

Flowering Plants

Dicotyledons

Trachystemon orientalis	Abraham-Isaac-Jacob	I	May survive from gardens or as throwouts
Eranthis hyemalis	Aconite, Winter	I	Naturalised: gardens, churchyards, under trees
Agrimonia eupatoria	Agrimony	N	Grassy verges and uncut areas
Alnus glutinosa	Alder	N	Uncommon; riversides; also planted

Scientific name	Common name	Status	Notes
Alnus incana	Alder, Grey	I	Planted; rarely seeding
Alnus cordata	Alder, Italian	I	Planted by MKDC etc.; rarely seeding
Alyssum saxatile	Alison, Golden	I	Garden origin; walls, where it persists
Lobularia maritima	Alison, Sweet	I	Garden origin; frequent casual
Amaranthus retroflexus	Amaranth, Common	I	Waste places, (bird-seed origin)
Amaranthus hybridus	Amaranth, Green	I	Waste places, (bird-seed origin)
Anemone blanda	Anemone, Balkan	I	Garden origin; occasional escape
Anemone x hybrida	Anemone, Japanese	I	Garden origin; rare escape
Anemone nemorosa	Anemone, Wood	N	Woods; mostly in open areas under trees
Angelica sylvestris	Angelica, Wild	N	Wet woods, ditches, water-sides
Aralia chinensis	Angelica-tree, Chinese	I	Occasionally planted; rarely self-setting
Malus sylvestris	Apple, Crab	N	Woodland, hedgerows; much over-recorded
Malus domestica	Apple, Cultivated	I	Relict of cultivation, hedges, wood margins
Mentha x villosa	Apple-mint	I	Garden origin
Arabis caucasica	Arabis, Garden	I	Planted on rockeries etc., fragments survive
Lamiastrum galeobdolon			
ssp. argentatum	Archangel, Yellow	I	Gardens & shrubberies; may cover lrg areas
ssp. montanum	Archangel, Yellow	N	Woods; uncommon but may cover lrg areas
Fraxinus excelsior	Ash	N	Woods, hedges
Asparagus officinalis			
ssp. officinalis	Asparagus, Garden	I	Garden origin; occasional escape
Populus tremula	Aspen	N	Woods
Cosmos bipinnatus	Aster, Mexican	I	Garden origin; may seed and persist
Aubrieta deltoidea	Aubretia	I	Garden origin; walls
Geum urbanum	Avens, Wood	N	Woods, shady hedgerows
Melissa officinalis	Balm	I	Herb of garden origin
Populus x jackii	Balm-of-Gilead	I	Occasionally planted
Impatiens glandulifera	Balsam, Indian	I	Riverside, ditches; becoming persistent
Impatiens capensis	Balsam, Orange	I	Canalsides, rarely by ponds; Caldecotte Lk.
Impatiens parviflora	Balsam, Small	I R	Uncommon on waste places or in gardens
Populus trichocarpa	Balsam-poplar, Western	I	Rare; planted by streams and other places
Pseudosasa japonica	Bamboo, Arrow	I	Garden origin, may persist
Berberis vulgaris	Barberry	(I)	Found in a few old hedgerows
Berberis julianae	Barberry, Chinese	I	Planted; rarely seeding
Berberis darwinii	Barberry, Darwin's	I	Planted; hedges, rarely seeding
Berberis x stenophylla	Barberry, Hedge	I	Planted; brookside, walls, occasionally seeding
Berberis thunbergii	Barberry, Thunberg's	I	Commonly planted; seedlings frequent
Epimedium sp(p).	Barrenwort	I	Rare; garden origin
Odontites vernus			
ssp. serotinus	Bartsia, Red	N	Short grassy places
Clinopodium vulgare	Basil, Wild	N	Short turf on calcareous soils
Galium uliginosum	Bedstraw, Fen	N R	Base-rich fens
Galium saxatile	Bedstraw, Heath	N	Rare; short grassland on greensand
Galium mollugo			
ssp. mollugo	Bedstraw, Hedge	N	Grassland, hedgerows
ssp. erectum	Bedstraw, Hedge	N	As above, but usually on drier soils
Galium verum	Bedstraw, Lady's	N	Dry grassy places
Fagus sylvatica	Beech	N	Specimen trees & woods on the Greensand
Beta vulgaris			
ssp. vulgaris	Beet, Root	N	Garden origin; throw-out
Bidens frondosa	Beggar-ticks	I VR	Single sighting by lake; likely to spread
Campanula takesimana	Bellflower	I	Only seen as an escape at North Crawley
Campanula portenschlagiana	Bellflower, Adria	I	Garden origin; on walls
Campanula latifolia	Bellflower, Giant	N R	Rare; woods in the north
Campanula persicifolia	Bellflower, Peach-leaved	I	Garden origin; occasional escape
Campanula rapunculus	Bellflower, Rampion	I	A rare casual
Campanula poscharskyana	Bellflower, Trailing	I	Garden origin; on walls
Stachys officinalis	Betony	N	Old, wet meadows
Vaccinium myrtillus	Bilberry	N VR	On sandy soils of the Brickhills
Convolvulus arvensis	Bindweed, Field	N	Grassy places; garden weed
Calystegia sepium			
ssp. sepium	Bindweed, Hedge	N	Hedgerow scrambler, urban weed

Calystegia silvatica	Bindweed, Large	I	Hedgerow scrambler, urban weed
Betula pubescens			
ssp. *pubescens*	Birch, Downy	N	Woods on sand; less common than next sp.
Betula pendula	Birch, Silver	N	Woods on sand; often planted
Corydalis solida	Bird-in-the-bush	I	Garden origin; park in Newport Pagnell
Ornithopus perpusillus	Bird's-foot	N R	Light, sandy soils
Lotus corniculatus	Bird's-foot-trefoil, Common	N	Grassy places, churchyards
Lotus pedunculatus	Bird's-foot-trefoil, Greater	N	Wet places; grassland, woods
Lotus glaber	Bird's-foot-trefoil, Narrow-leaved	N R	On open clay, rare elsewhere
Persicaria amphibia	Bistort, Amphibious	N	In or by water; damp grassland
Persicaria amplexicaulis	Bistort, Red	I	Garden origin
Cardamine hirsuta	Bitter-cress, Hairy	N	Common weed of open areas *e.g.* in gardens
Cardamine amara	Bitter-cress, Large	N VR	Very rare; single record from canalside
Cardamine flexuosa	Bitter-cress, Wavy	N	Damp woodland rides, bare ground
Solanum dulcamara	Bittersweet	N	Woods, hedges, ditches, ponds, rough areas
Fallopia convolvulus	Black-bindweed	N	Cultivated land
Populus x canadensis	Black-poplar, Hybrid	I	Planted in woods, by river
Populus nigra			
ssp. *betulifolia*	Black-poplar, Native	N	Rare; by rivers
Prunus spinosa	Blackthorn	N	Woods, thickets, hedgerows
Colutea arborescens	Bladder-senna	I	Occasionally planted and may seed
Montia fontana	Blinks	N VR	Very rare in wet places on acid soils
Borago officinalis	Borage	I	Of casual occurrence; garden origin
Buxus sempervirens	Box	N	Always planted; churchyards, hedges
Rubus fruticosus	Bramble	N	Woods, hedgerows, rough ground, gardens
Rubus laciniatus	Bramble, Cut-leaved	I	Of garden or planted origin; escapes
Rubus cockburnianus	Bramble, White-stemmed	I	Garden origin; planted
Vicia faba	Broad Bean	I	Relict of cultivation
Veronica beccabunga	Brooklime	N	Streams, ditches, riversides, canal, marshes
Samolus valerandi	Brookweed	N U	Recently discovered near Little Linford
Cytisus scoparius	Broom	N	Woods, roadsides on the greensand
Cytisus battandieri	Broom, Pineapple	I	Planted; rarely seeding
Orebanche minor	Broomrape, Common	N	Shrub bed at Kingston Centre
Tamus communis	Bryony, Black	N	Hedges, wood margins
Bryonia dioica	Bryony, White	N	Climber; wood margins, hedgerows
Rhamnus cathartica	Buckthorn	N	Hedgerows, scrub, rarely in woods
Hippophae rhamnoides	Buckthorn, Sea	N	Much planted; often suckering
Fagopyrum esculentum	Buckwheat	N	Casual; planted for pheasant food
Ajuga reptans	Bugle	N	Woods; occasionally in damp grassland
Anchusa arvensis	Bugloss	N	Uncommon; sandy soil weed
Prunus domestica			
ssp. *insititia*	Bullace/Damson	I	Hedgerows
Arctium lappa	Burdock, Greater	N	Uncommon; hedges, canalsides, riversides
Arctium minus	Burdock, Lesser	N	Common; woods, hedges, roadsides
Bidens connata	Bur-marigold, London	I VR	Canal and river banks; increasing
Bidens cernua	Bur-marigold, Nodding	N R	Only seen by the Tear Drop lakes
Bidens tripartita	Bur-marigold, Trifid	N	Riversides, canal banks
Sanguisorba officinalis	Burnet, Great	N R	Old, wet meadows
Sanguisorba minor			
ssp. *muricata*	Burnet, Fodder	I	Now rare; formerly grown as a fodder crop
ssp. *minor*	Burnet, Salad	N	Short, calcareous grassland
Pimpinella saxifraga	Burnet-saxifrage	N	Grassland
Pimpinella major	Burnet-saxifrage, Greater	N	Roadside verges, wood borders
Petasites hybridus	Butterbur	N R	By water; female plants very rare
Ranunculus bulbosus	Buttercup, Bulbous	N	Dry grassy places
Ranunculus sceleratus	Buttercup, Celery-leaved	N	Wet mud by water; rare garden weed
Ranunculus arvensis	Buttercup, Corn	N R	Very rare casual now; was an arable weed
Ranunculus repens	Buttercup, Creeping	N	Gdn weed, damp meadows, woods, waterside
Ranunculus auricomus	Buttercup, Goldilocks	N	Woods, churchyards
Ranunculus sardous	Buttercup, Hairy	(N)	(Introduced with grass-seed mix)
	This could be a misidentification	VR	
	for *R. marginatus*		
Ranunculus acris	Buttercup, Meadow	N	Meadows, other grassy places

Buddleja davidii	Butterfly-bush	I	Garden origin; wasteland, urban pavements
Cotula coronopifolia	Button-weed	I **VR**	Rare; flood alleviation overflow at Tongwell
Silene vulgaris			
ssp. *vulgaris*	Campion, Bladder	N	Open grassy places
Silene x *hampeana*	Campion, Pink	N	Roadsides, hedgerows
Silene dioica	Campion, Red	N	Hedgerows, waste land, much planted in MK
Lychnis coronaria	Campion, Rose	I	Garden origin; may seed and/or persist
Silene latifolia			
ssp. *alba*	Campion, White	N	Roadsides, wasteland
Iberis umbellata	Candytuft, Garden	I	Casual as a garden escape
Carum carvi	Caraway	I	Introduced with (bird) seed
Daucus carota			
ssp. *carota*	Carrot, Wild	N	Dry grassy places
Silene armeria	Catchfly, Sweet-William	I	Garden origin
Nepeta cataria	Cat-mint	N	One roadside record from Ravenstone
Nepeta x *faassenii*	Cat-mint, Garden	I	May persist from throwouts
Hypochaeris radicata	Cat's-ear	N	Grassland, churchyards
Chelidonium majus	Celandine, Greater	(N)	Close to habitation; churchyards
Ranunculus ficaria			
ssp. *bulbilifer*	Celandine, Lesser	N	Damp meadows, woods, hedgebanks
ssp. *ficaria*	Celandine, Lesser	N	Damp meadows, woods, hedgebanks
Apium graveolens	Celery	N	Garden origin
Centaurium erythraea	Centaury, Common	N	Open, sunny areas without competition
Anthemis arvensis	Chamomile, Corn	N **R**	Now (always) of planted origin
Anthemis cotula	Chamomile, Stinking	N	Uncommon; cornfield and wasteland weed
Sinapis arvensis	Charlock	(N)	Arable weed, waste places
Prunus padus	Cherry, Bird	N	Planted; of garden origin; railwayside, woods
Prunus avium	Cherry, Wild	N	Rare; woods; also frequently planted
Anthriscus caucalis	Chervil, Bur	N **R**	Rare; field or path sides
Anthriscus cerefolium	Chervil, Garden	I	Seen in one Heelands garden; elsewhere maybe
Chaerophyllum temulum	Chervil, Rough	N	Hedgerows
Castanea sativa	Chestnut, Sweet	I	Uncommon; woods on less alkaline soils
Stellaria media	Chickweed, Common	N	Weed of waste and cultivated land
Myosoton aquaticum	Chickweed, Water	N	Watersides
Cichorium intybus	Chicory	(N)	Roadsides
Dendranthema cv.	Chrysanthemum, Pot	I	Very rare; garden origin/throw-out
Potentilla reptans	Cinquefoil, Creeping	N	Weed of short, grassy places, rough ground
Potentilla norvegica	Cinquefoil, Ternate-leaved	I	Casual; single plant seen once
Salvia verbenaca	Clary, Wild	N	Very rare; churchyard wall (now gone)
Galium aparine	Cleavers	N	Very common weed in many habitats
Clematis montana	Clematis, Himalayan	I	Garden origin
Clematis viticella	Clematis, Purple	I	Seems established at one site by river Ouzel
Trifolium hybridum			
ssp. *hybridum*	Clover, Alsike	I	Naturalised relict of cultivation
Trifolium arvense	Clover, Hare's-foot	N **R**	Dry grassy places on light soils; rare
Trifolium pratense	Clover, Red	N	Grassy places, rough ground
Trifoilium fragiferum			
ssp. *fragiferum*	Clover, Strawberry	N	Short grassy places (on limestone)
Trifolium repens	Clover, White	N	Grassy places, inc. lawns, rough ground
Trifolium medium	Clover, Zigzag	N	Rare; woodland rides
Agrostemma githago	Cockle, Corn	I	Now always planted, often from seed mixes
Crataegus persimilis	Cockspur-thorn, Broad-leaved	I	Planted
Tussilago farfara	Colt's-foot	N	Roadsides and waste places
Symphytum officinale	Comfrey, Common	N	By rivers and streams
Symphytum grandiflorum	Comfrey, Creeping	I	Rare; hedges
Symphytum x *uplandicum*	Comfrey, Russian	I	Roadsides, rough and waste land
Symphytum orientale	Comfrey, White	I	Village roadsides and churchyards
Cardamine bulbifera	Coralroot	N **R**	Escaped from garden planting in Heelands
Centaurea cyanus	Cornflower	N	Not now a cornfield weed; always an escape
Centaurea montana	Cornflower, Perennial	I	Garden origin
Valerianella locusta	Cornsalad, Common	N	Walls, bare ground, grassland
Valerianella carinata	Cornsalad, Keel-fruited	N **VR**	Walls, bare ground, dry banks

Ceratocapnos claviculata	Corydalis, Climbing	N **VR**	Woods and hedges on the greensand
Pseudofumaria lutea	Corydalis, Yellow	I	Garden origin; spreads in urban areas, walls
Cotoneaster simonsii	Cotoneaster, Himalayan	I	Rare; garden origin; disused rly, naturalises
Cotoneaster hjelmqvistii	Cotoneaster, Hjelmqvist's	I	Garden origin; rare escape
Cotoneaster bullatus	Cotoneaster, Hollyberry	I	A planted shrub; rarely seeding
Cotoneaster integrifolius	Cotoneaster, Small-leaved	I	Very rare; garden origin; roadside
Cotoneaster horizontalis	Cotoneaster, Wall	I	Garden origin; self sown in walls, waste places
Cotoneaster x watereri	Cotoneaster, Waterer's	I	Garden origin; commonly escapes
Cotoneaster salicifolius	Cotoneaster, Willow-leaved	I	A planted shrub; rarely seeding
Primula veris	Cowslip	N	Grassy places, roadsides
Geranium dissectum	Crane's-bill, Cut-leaved	N	Cultivated, arable and wasteland, short grass
Geranium molle	Crane's-bill, Dove's-foot	N	Cultivated land, grassland
Geranium x oxonianum	Crane's-bill, Druce's	I	Garden origin but may naturalise
Geranium endressii	Crane's-bill, French	I	Casual; near gardens
Geranium pyrenaicum	Crane's-bill, Hedgerow	(N)	Roadsides, churchyards, hedgerows
Geranium pratense	Crane's-bill, Meadow	N	Grassy banks, roadsides
Geranium macrorrhizum	Crane's-bill, Rock	I	Garden origin
Geranium rotundifolium	Crane's-bill, Round-leaved	N **VR**	Very rare; casual at base of a wall in Bletchley
Geranium lucidum	Crane's-bill, Shining	N	Uncommon; churchyards, walls
Geranium pusillum	Crane's-bill, Small-flowered	N **R**	Waste and grassy places on dry soils
Lysimachia nummularia	Creeping-Jenny	N	Woods, damp grassland, churchyards
Lepidium sativum	Cress, Garden	I	Bird-seed alien
Lepidium draba			
ssp. *draba*	Cress, Hoary	I	Waste places, roadsides; often in large clumps
Arabidopsis thaliana	Cress, Thale	N	Weed in open situations, churchyards
Cruciata laevipes	Crosswort	N **R**	Hedgerows; uncommon
Ranunculus hederaceus	Crowfoot, Ivy-leaved	N **R**	Very rare; acid springs/flushes
Cardamine pratensis	Cuckooflower	N	Marshy grassland, watersides, churchyards
Gnaphalium uliginosum	Cudweed, Marsh	N	Damp, bare places, wet cart ruts
Ribes nigrum	Currant, Black	(I) **R**	Woods, hedgerows, possibly of garden origin
Ribes rubrum	Currant, Red	(I)	Woods, hedgerows, or bird-sown
Bellis perennis	Daisy	N	Abundant; short turf, lawns, churchyards
Leucanthemum vulgare	Daisy, Ox-eye	N	Grassland, roadside verges; much planted
Leucanthemum x superbum	Daisy, Shasta	I	Garden origin; waste places
Taraxacum agg.	Dandelion	N	Ubiquitous weed, but many different species
Lamium hybridum	Dead-nettle, Cut-leaved	N **VR**	Very rare; cultivated and waste ground
Lamium amplexicaule	Dead-nettle, Henbit	N **R**	Weed of cultivation, waste ground
Lamium purpureum	Dead-nettle, Red	N	Weed of cultivation, waste ground
Lamium maculatum	Dead-nettle, Spotted	I	Garden origin; hedges, walls
Lamium album	Dead-nettle, White	N	Common weed of hedgerows, rough ground
Rubus caesius	Dewberry	N	Woods, scrub, hedges
Rumex obtusifolius	Dock, Broad-leaved	N	Weed in waste places, roadsides, grassland
Rumex conglomeratus	Dock, Clustered	N	Damp grassy places by ponds and rivers
Rumex crispus			
ssp. *crispus*	Dock, Curled	N	Weed of waste and cultivated land
Rumex pulcher	Dock, Fiddle	N **R**	Churchyards, dry grassy places
Rumex maritimus	Dock, Golden	N **VR**	Recently discovered on mud by a lake
Rumex hydrolapathum	Dock, Water	N	By the sides of canal and river
Rumex sanguineus	Dock, Wood	N	Damp shady places
Rumex x pratensis	Dock, a Hybrid	N	Rare; with parents
Cuscuta europaea	Dodder, Greater	N **VR**	Rare; parasitic on nettles on river banks
Rosa canina	Dog-rose	N	Hedges, scrub, woods
Viola riviniana	Dog-violet, Common	N	Woods
Viola canina			
ssp. *canina*	Dog-violet, Heath	N **R**	Very rare; heaths and woods in the Brickhills
Cornus sanguinea	Dogwood	N	Woods, hedgerows
Cornus sericea	Dogwood, Red-osier	I	Planted; often by water; seedlings frequent
Cornus alba	Dogwood, White	I	Planted; occasionally seeding
Filipendula vulgaris	Dropwort	N **R**	Marshy or dry calcareous grassland
Lycium barbarum	Duke of Argyll's Teaplant	I	Walls and hedgerows near habitation
Sambucus nigra	Elder	N	Hedges, woods, scrub, churchyards, gardens

Sambucus canadensis	Elder, American	I	Planted for leaf or fruit colour
Ulmus x *hollandica*	Elm, Dutch	N	Suckers frequent in hedgerows
Ulmus procera	Elm, English	N	Woods, hedges
Ulmus x *vegeta*	Elm, Huntingdon	N	Suckers reasonably frequent in hedgerows
Ulmus minor			
ssp. *minor*	Elm, Small-leaved	N R	Woods, hedges
Ulmus glabra			
ssp. *glabra*	Elm, Wych	N	Woods, hedges; trees killed but suckers survive
Circaea lutetiana	Enchanter's-nightshade	I	Woods and a few gardens
Oenothera biennis	Evening-primrose, Common	I	Railway ballast; Bletchley
Oenothera glazioviana	Evening-primrose, Large-flowered	I	Railway ballast, waste land
Lathyrus latifolius	Everlasting-pea, Broad-leaved	I R	Garden escape; hedgerows, rough grass
Lathyrus sylvestris	Everlasting-pea, Narrow-leaved	N R	Grassy woodland rides, hedgebanks
Robinia pseudoacacia	False-acacia	I	Garden origin; may sucker
Chenopodium album	Fat-hen	N	Arable and garden weed
Foeniculum vulgare	Fennel	(I) R	Garden origin; waste places
Tanacetum parthenium	Feverfew	I	Naturalised; waysides and walls near habitation
Rosa arvensis	Field-rose	N	Hedges, scrub, open places
Veronica persica	Field-speedwell, Common	I	Cultivated and waste land
Veronica agrestis	Field-speedwell, Green	N	Cultivated land
Veronica polita	Field-speedwell, Grey	N	Cultivated land
Scrophularia nodosa	Figwort, Common	N	Woods
Scrophularia auriculata	Figwort, Water	N	Damp places, often by water
Pyracantha coccinea	Firethorn	I	Much planted; seedlings frequent; may persist
Linum usitatissimum	Flax, Cultivated	I VR	Relict of cultivation or bird-seed alien
Linum catharticum	Flax, Fairy	N	Uncommon; light, open soils
Erigeron acer	Fleabane, Blue	N R	Dry barish places
Conyza canadensis	Fleabane, Canadian	I	Increasing; urban and waste ground
Pulicaria dysenterica	Fleabane, Common	N	Damp grassland, roadsides
Ageratum houstonianum	Flossflower	I	Of garden origin
Kickxia spuria	Fluellen, Blunt-leaved	N	Arable weed; decreasing
Kickxia elatine	Fluellen, Round-leaved	N	Arable weed; decreasing
Myosotis discolor	Forget-me-not, Changing	N R	Rare; dry, light soils, damp meadows
Myosotis ramosissima	Forget-me-not, Early	N R	On light soils only *e.g.* the Brickhills
Myosotis arvensis	Forget-me-not, Field	N	Arable weed, waste places
Myosotis sylvatica	Forget-me-not, Garden	N	Garden origin; churchyards; no wild records
Brunnera macrophylla	Forget-me-not, Great	I	Garden origin; may persist if established
Myosotis laxa	Forget-me-not, Tufted	N	Watersides
Myosotis scorpioides	Forget-me-not, Water	N	Watersides
Pilosella aurantiaca			
ssp. *carpathicola*	Fox-and-cubs	I	Garden origin; grassland, churchyards
Digitalis purpurea	Foxglove	N	Woods and hedgebanks on the greensand
Tellima grandiflora	Fringe-cups	I	Garden origin
Fumaria officinalis			
ssp. *officinalis*	Fumitory, Common	N	Cultivated land, waste places
Galinsoga parviflora	Gallant-soldier	I	Garden and nursery weed; now rare
Lycopus europaeus	Gipsywort	N	Watersides
Echinops exaltatus	Globe-thistle	I	Garden origin; may establish for short time
Tragopogon pratensis			
ssp. *minor*	Goat's-beard	N	Roadsides, grassy places
Galega officinalis	Goat's-rue	I	Rare; roadside
Solidago canadensis	Goldenrod, Canadian	I	Naturalised in waste places and waysides
Solidago gigantea	Goldenrod, Early	I	Rare; waste places
Chenopodium bonus-henricus	Good-King-Henry	N R	Rare; relict of cultivation; Olney, Stantonbury
Ribes uva-crispa	Gooseberry	(N)	Hedgerows, open scrub, woods, churchyards
Physalis peruviana	Gooseberry, Cape	I	Very rare; garden origin
Chenopodium ficifolium	Goosefoot, Fig-leaved	N	Roadside verges and parks (from seed mix)
Chenopodium polyspermum	Goosefoot, Many-seeded	N	Arable weed
Chenopodium rubrum	Goosefoot, Red	N	Arable weed, manure heaps
Chenopodium urbicum	Goosefoot, Upright	(I)	One casual record only from a building site

Ulex europaeus	Gorse	N	Dry grassy places, scrub; off alkaline soil
Mahonia aquifolium	Grape, Oregon	I	Gdn origin; hedges, waysides, pheasant cover
Vitis vinifera	Grape-vine	I	Casual; originating from wine-making grapes
Lithospermum arvense	Gromwell, Field	N R	Persisting in shrub beds at Heelands
Lythrum hyssopifolia	Grass-poly	N U	Very rare; recently discovered in mud by a lake
Prunus domestica			
ssp. *italica*	Greengage	I	Rare; garden origin
Aegopodium podagraria	Ground-elder	I	Pernicious urban weed
Glechoma hederacea	Ground-ivy	N	Common; woods, hedges, grassland
Senecio vulgaris	Groundsel	N	Weed of cultivated and waste ground
Senecio sylvaticus	Groundsel, Heath	N R	Very rare; heathy places only
Senecio viscosus	Groundsel, Sticky	(N)	Waste and rough ground, railway ballast
Liquidamber styraciflua	Gum, Sweet	I	Planted near the Water Gardens, Woughton
Campanula rotundifolia	Harebell	N	Uncommon; on the greensand
Leontodon autumnalis	Hawkbit, Autumn	N	Grassy places
Leontodon hispidus	Hawkbit, Rough	N	Grassy places, especially where alkaline
Crepis vesicaria			
ssp. *taraxacifolia*	Hawk's-beard, Beaked	I	Roadside verges, rough grassy places
Crepis biennis	Hawk's-beard, Rough	(N)VR	Bradwell Abbey
Crepis capillaris	Hawk's-beard, Smooth	N	Common; grassy places, churchyards
Crataegus monogyna	Hawthorn	N	Very common; woods, hedgerows
Crataegus x media	Hawthorn, Hybrid	N	Woods, hedgerows
Crataegus laevigata	Hawthorn, Midland	N	Woods; very occasionally in hedgerows
Corylus avellana	Hazel	N	Common; woods, hedges
Calluna vulgaris	Heather	N	Rare; only on the greensand
Torilis nodosa	Hedge-parsley, Knotted	N VR	Very rare; fields; Olney, Bradwell Abbey
Torilis japonica	Hedge-parsley, Upright	N	Hedgerows, grassy places
Petasites fragrans	Heliotrope, Winter	I	Garden origin; known to persist for many years
Helleborus foetidus	Hellebore, Stinking	N	Always of garden origin; may persist
Conium maculatum	Hemlock	N	Roadsides, ditch margins
Eupatorium cannabinum	Hemp-agrimony	N	Canal, lake margins, damp grassy places
Galeopsis bifida	Hemp-nettle, Bifid	N	Rough ground, arable, hedges; under-recorded
Galeopsis tetrahit	Hemp-nettle, Common	N	Rough ground, hedges
Hyoscyamus niger	Henbane	N R	Disturbed ground; rarely in same place twice
Geranium robertianum	Herb Robert	N	Woods, hedgerows, walls, churchyards
Heracleum sphondylium			
ssp. *sphondylium*	Hogweed	N	Roadsides, wasteland, open grass, churchyards
Ilex aquifolium	Holly	N	Woods, hedges, gardens; often bird-sown
Alcea rosea	Hollyhock	I	Garden origin; walls, paths, hedgerows
Lunaria annua	Honesty	I	Garden origin; waysides, hedgerows
Lonicera periclymenum	Honeysuckle	N	Woods, hedges
Lonicera pileata	Honeysuckle, Box-leaved	I	Much planted; sometimes seeding
Lonicera henryi	Honeysuckle, Henry's	I	Garden origin; may seed or throwouts survive
Leycesteria formosa	Honeysuckle, Himalayan	I VR	Garden origin; may be bird-sown
Lonicera japonica	Honeysuckle, Japanese	I	Of planted origin
Lonicera nitida	Honeysuckle, Wilson's	I	Much planted to form hedges
Humulus lupulus	Hop	N	Hedgerows
Ballota nigra			
ssp. *meridionalis*	Horehound, Black	N	Hedgerows
Carpinus betulus	Hornbeam	N	Woods; occasional as a specimen tree
Ceratophyllum demersum	Hornwort	N	Uncommon in still or running water
Aesculus hippocastanum	Horse-chestnut	I	Avenues, parks, churchyards
Aesculus carnea	Horse-chestnut, Red	I	Planted as specimen trees; rarely seeding
Armoracia rusticana	Horse-radish	I	Roadsides
Sempervivum tectorum	House-leek	I	Walls, roofs
Sempervivum arachnoideum	House-leek, Cobweb	I	Planted on limestone walls, but persists
Hedera helix			
ssp. *helix*	Ivy	N	On trees, walls, hedgerows; churchyards
Amelanchier lamarkii	Juneberry	I	Planted; woods

Anthyllis vulneraria			
ssp. *polyphylla*	Kidney Vetch	I	Planted *e.g.* Little Brickhill bypass
ssp. *vulneraria*	Kidney Vetch	N	Uncommon; open calcareous areas
Centaurea nigra	Knapweed, Common	N	Dry grassland, especially calcareous
Centauria scabiosa	Knapweed, Greater	N	Dry calcareous grassland
Scleranthus annuus	Knawel, Annual	N VR	Single record from a disturbed roadside verge
Polygonum aviculare	Knotgrass	N	Open ground
Polygonum arenastrum	Knotgrass, Equal-leaved	N	Open ground, field gateways
Fallopia sachalinensis	Knotweed, Giant	I	Very rare; pathside, Campbell Park
Laburnum anagyroides	Laburnum	I	Garden origin; spinneys, self-set in urban sites
Laburnum x *watereri*	Laburnum, Voss's	I	Garden origin; not as common as the above
Alchemilla mollis	Lady's-mantle, Garden	I	Often planted in gardens; seeds freely
Alchemilla filicaulis			
ssp. *vestita*	Lady's-mantle, Hairy	N R	Rare; woodland rides, old damp grassland
Stachys byzantina	Lamb's-ear	I	Garden origin
Physalis alkekengi	Lantern, Chinese	I	Very rare; garden origin
Consolida ajacis	Larkspur	I	Garden origin or planted
Prunus laurocerasus	Laurel, Cherry	I	Much planted; frequently self-sown
Daphne laureola	Laurel, Spurge	N	Uncommon; hedgerows, woods
Viburnum tinus	Laurustinus	I	Garden origin; spinney at Wolverton
Lavandula angustifolia	Lavender	I	Garden origin; may seed or persist as throwout
Doronicum pardalianches	Leopard's-bane	I	Rare; Stonebridge (garden origin)
Lactuca virosa	Lettuce, Great	(N) R	Rare but increasing; waste places
Lactuca serriola	Lettuce, Prickly	(N)	Increasingly common; waste places, open areas
Syringa vulgaris	Lilac	I	Garden origin; hedgerows
Tilia x *vulgaris*	Lime	N	Planted as specimen trees
Tilia platyphyllos	Lime, Large-leaved	N	Occasionally planted as a specimen tree
Tilia cordata	Lime, Small-leaved	N	Always planted in MK; estate roadsides
Astragalus glycyphyllos	Liquorice, Wild	N R	Canalsides; a few grassy places
Lobelia erinus	Lobelia, Garden	I	Garden origin; frequent casual
Lysimachia punctata	Loosestrife, Dotted	I	Garden origin; may appear naturalised
Lythrum salicaria	Loosestrife, Purple	N	Watersides, woods
Lysimachia vulgaris	Loosestrife, Yellow	N R	Rare; river banks
Pedicularis sylvatica			
ssp. *sylvatica*	Lousewort	N VR	Marshy grassland; Little Brickhill
Nigella damascena	Love-in-a-mist	I	Garden origin
Medicago sativa			
ssp. *sativa*	Lucerne	I	Formerly cultivated; grassy and rough places
Pulmonaria officinalis	Lungwort	I	Garden origin; hedgerows
Pulmonaria rubra	Lungwort, Red	I	A rare garden escape; seen at North Crawley
Sherardia arvensis	Madder, Field	N	Short grass, lawns, open waste areas
Malva sylvestris	Mallow, Common	N	Rough grassland, roadsides
Malva neglecta	Mallow, Dwarf	N	Rough areas, waysides, churchyards, gardens
Lavatera trimestris	Mallow, Royal	I	Of garden origin; may escape
Acer campestre	Maple, Field	N	Hedgerows and woods
Acer platanoides	Maple, Norway	I	Planted; parks, churchyards; seeds freely
Acer saccharum	Maple, Silver	I	Occasionally planted
Chrysanthemum segetum	Marigold, Corn	I	Arable weed; road verges on the greensand
Tagetes patula	Marigold, French	I	Occasionally seen as a throwout
Caltha palustris	Marigold, Marsh	N	Marshy grassland, pond margins, streamsides
Calendula officinalis	Marigold, Pot	I	Garden throw-out or self-set; may establish
Galium palustre	Marsh-bedstraw, Common	N	Marshy grassland, watersides
Althaea officinalis	Marsh-mallow	N	Always, but rarely, planted
Hydrocotyle ranunculoides	Marsh-pennywort, Floating	I VR	Tongwell Lake; may not persist
Matricaria recutita	Mayweed, Scented	N	Cultivated places, rough ground
Tripleurospermum inodorum	Mayweed, Scentless	N	Weed of waste and cultivated land
Limnanthes douglasii	Meadow-foam	I	Of garden origin; barely persists
Filipendula ulmaria	Meadowsweet	N	Watersides, damp places
Medicago lupulina	Medick, Black	N	Common; grassy places, rough ground
Medicago arabica	Medick, Spotted	N VR	Rare; short grass
Melilotus officinalis	Melilot, Ribbed	I	Open grass, rough ground

Melilotus altissimus	Melilot, Tall	I	Open grass, rough ground
Melilotus albus	Melilot, White	I R	Very rare; casual by roadsides
Mercurialis annua	Mercury, Annual	(N) R	Rare; garden or flower bed weed
Mercurialis perennis	Mercury, Dog's	N	Woods, old hedges
Aster x *salignus*	Michaelmas-daisy, Common	I	Garden origin; roadsides and wasteland
Aster x *versicolor*	Michaelmas-daisy, Late	I	Garden origin, roadside
Aster lanceolatus	Michaelmas-daisy, Narrow-leaved	I	Garden origin
Reseda lutea	Mignonette, Wild	N	Waste ground where calcareous
Soleirolia soleirolii	Mind-your-own-business	I R	Garden origin; wall bases, possibly increasing
Mentha arvensis	Mint, Corn	N	Fields, woods, by ponds
Mentha aquatica	Mint, Water	N	Watersides
Mentha x *verticillata*	Mint, Whorled	N	Watersides, woods, fields
Viscum album	Mistletoe	N	Very rare; Bow Brickhill, Giffard Park, Willen
Philadelphus coronarius	Mock-orange	I	Garden origin
Cerastium fontanum			
ssp. *vulgare*	Mouse-ear, Common	N	Very common; grassy places
Cerastium semidecandrum	Mouse-ear, Least	N VR	A plant of light soils; rare on the Brickhills
Cerastium diffusum	Mouse-ear, Sea	N VR	Very rare; Newfoundout only
Cerastium glomeratum	Mouse-ear, Sticky	N	Open areas; paths, churchyards
Pilosella officinarum	Mouse-ear-hawkweed	N	Short grassland, railway ballast
Myosurus minimus	Mousetail	N VR	Has occurred in two places around planted trees
Euphorbia amygdaloides			
ssp. *robbiae*	Mrs Robb's Bonnet	I	Garden origin, but establishes freely
Artemisia vulgaris	Mugwort	N	Roadsides, waste places; often in tall vegetation
Verbascum nigrum	Mullein, Dark	N	Known from one disused churchyard
Verbascum densiflorum	Mullein, Dense-flowered	I	Casual by roadside at Upper Weald
Verbascum thapsus	Mullein, Great	N	Walls, waste places esp. on limestone
Malva moschata	Musk-mallow	N	Grassy places
Malva alcea	Musk-mallow, Greater	I	Garden origin
Brassica nigra	Mustard, Black	N	Roadsides, field margins -?decreasing
Brassica juncea	Mustard, Chinese	I	One garden casual; probably under-recorded
Alliaria petiolata	Mustard, Garlic	N	Hedges, roadsides, woods, churchyards
Sisymbrium officinale	Mustard, Hedge	N	Weed of cultivation, waste places, roadsides
Erysimum cheiranthoides	Mustard, Treacle	I	Cultivated and wasteland
Sinapis alba			
ssp. *alba*	Mustard, White	I	Arable weed of calcareous soils
Urtica urens	Nettle, Small	N	Weed of disturbed ground esp. on light soils
Urtica dioica	Nettle, Stinging	N	Ubiquitous weed, especially on rich soils
Solanum nigrum			
ssp. *nigrum*	Nightshade, Black	N	Weed of wasteland and gardens
Atropa belladonna	Nightshade, Deadly	N R	Tyringham churchyard; Woughton Park
Lapsana communis			
ssp. *communis*	Nipplewort	N	Waste places, hedgerows, garden weed
Quercus ilex	Oak, Holm	I	Occasional as a specimen tree
Quercus robur	Oak, Pedunculate	N	Common; woods, hedgerows
Quercus rubra	Oak, Red	I	Planted; woods
Quercus petraea	Oak, Sessile	N	Brickhill Woods
Quercus cerris	Oak, Turkey	I	Planted as specimen trees
Elaeagnus umbellata	Oleaster, Spreading	I	Much planted; seedlings occasional
Atriplex patula	Orache, Common	N	Arable and garden weed
Atriplex prostrata	Orache, Spear-leaved	N	Arable and garden weed
Salix viminalis	Osier	N	Close to rivers and ponds; much planted
Salix x *sericans*	Osier, Broad-leaved	N	Hedgerows, scrub
Salix x *smithiana*	Osier, Silky-leaved	N	Rare; Loughton
Primula elatior	Oxlip	N	Planted at Woolstone
Primula x *polyantha*	Oxlip, False	N	Woods
Primula x *digenea*	Oxlip/primrose hybrid	N	With the planted parents at Woolstone
Picris echioides	Oxtongue, Bristly	(I)	Very common in development areas. MK weed!
Picris hieracioides	Oxtongue, Hawkweed	N	Rare; calcareous grassland
Viola x *wittrockiana*	Pansy, Garden	I	Garden origin, throw-out

Viola tricolor			
ssp. *tricolor*	Pansy, Wild	N R	Rough, open areas
Viola arvensis	Pansy, Field	N	Arable weed, open places
Myriophyllum aquaticum	Parrot's-feather	I VR	Aquarists' throw-out; ponds
Petroselinum segetum	Parsley, Corn	N	Rare; dry banks
Anthriscus sylvestris	Parsley, Cow	N	Roadsides, woods, churchyards; abundant
Aethusa cynapium			
ssp. *cynapium*	Parsley, Fool's	N	Arable and garden weed
Petroselinum crispum	Parsley, Garden	I	Garden origin; occasionally escapes
Sison amomum	Parsley, Stone	N	Hedgebanks
Aphanes arvensis	Parsley-piert	N	Arable fields, short grass
Aphanes australis	Parsley-piert, Slender	N VR	Rare on the acid soils of the Brickhills
Pastinaca sativa	Parsnip, Wild	N	Roadsides, rough ground
Lathyrus odoratus	Pea, Sweet	I	Rare; garden origin; non-persistent
Pyrus communis	Pear	I	Rare; hedges, spinneys
Sagina apetala			
ssp. *apetala*	Pearlwort, Annual	N	Walls, dry bare ground
ssp. *erecta*	Pearlwort, Annual	N	As above but more common; also on paths
Sagina procumbens	Pearlwort, Procumbent	N	Paths, lawns, short turf, garden weed
Parietaria judaica	Pellitory-of-the-wall	N R	On and by walls, especially of limestone
Thlaspi arvense	Penny-cress, Field	(N)	Waste and arable land
Paeonia officinalis	Peony, Garden	I	Garden relict
Mentha x piperita	Peppermint	N	Streamsides; Castlethorpe
Lepidium campestre	Pepperwort, Field	N R	Rare; rough grassland, bare ground
Lepidium ruderale	Pepperwort, Narrow-leaved	(I) VR	Of uncertain persistence by roads
Vinca major	Periwinkle, Greater	I	Garden origin; hedgebanks
Vinca minor	Periwinkle, Lesser	(I)	Garden origin; hedgebanks, copses
Persicaria lapathifolia	Persicaria, Pale	N	Damp waste and arable land
Petunia x hybrida	Petunia	I	Garden origin; rare escape
Pontederia cordata	Pickerelweed	I	Few plants planted in Loughton Brook
Crassula helmsii	Pigmyweed, New Zealand	I	An invasive species of ponds; increasing
Anagallis arvensis			
ssp. *arvensis*	Pimpernel, Scarlet	N	Arable weed, churchyards, gardens
Matricaria discoidea	Pineappleweed	I	Common; bare places, paths, pavements
Oxalis articulata	Pink-sorrel	I	Garden origin
Oxalis debilis	Pink-sorrel, Large-flowered	I	Rare; churchyard
Oxalis incarnata	Pink-sorrel, Pale	I	Garden origin
Platanus x hybrida	Plane, London	I	Planted; Caldecotte Lake, CMK, Bletchley
Plantago coronopus	Plantain, Buck's-horn	N VR	Very rare; in a few places on dry sandy soil
Plantago major			
ssp. *intermedia*	Plantain, Greater	N	Rough open places or grassland
ssp. *major*	Plantain, Greater	N	As above, but the more frequent ssp.
Plantago media	Plantain, Hoary	N	Calcareous grassland
Plantago lanceolata	Plantain, Ribwort	N	Rough grassy places
Prunus domestica			
ssp. *domestica*	Plum	I	Occasional in hedgerows
Prunus cerasifera	Plum, Cherry	I	Planted, especially in development area
Populus x canescens	Poplar, Grey	I	Woods
Populus nigra 'Italica'	Poplar, Lombardy	I	Planted; by canal, field margins
Populus alba	Poplar, White	I	Woods, hedgerows, by river
Papaver atlanticum	Poppy, Atlas	I	A rare garden escape
Eschscholzia californica	Poppy, Californian	I	Garden origin; seeds fairly freely
Papaver rhoeas	Poppy, Common	N	Arable weed, roadsides
Papaver dubium			
ssp. *dubium*	Poppy, Long-headed	(N)	Arable weed, waste ground, roadsides
Papaver somniferum	Poppy, Opium	I	Garden origin; common as a casual
Papaver pseudoorientale	Poppy, Oriental	I	An uncommon garden escape; North Crawley
Papaver dubium			
ssp. *lecoqii*	Poppy, Yellow-juiced	(N) R	Arable weed, waste ground, roadsides
Solanum tuberosum	Potato	I	Casual as a throwout and on rubbish tips
Primula vulgaris	Primrose	N	Woods
Amaranthus hypochondriacus	Prince's-feather	I	Casual garden weed in Bletchley
Ligustrum ovalifolium	Privet, Garden	I	Planted; hedges, spinneys

Ligustrum vulgare	Privet, Wild	N	Hedgerows, woods
Chaenomeles speciosa	Quince, Japanese	I	Garden origin
Raphanus sativus	Radish, Garden	I	Bird-seed alien
Raphanus raphanistrum	Radish, Wild	(I)	Rough ground, arable weed
Lychnis flos-cuculi	Ragged-Robin	N	Wet grassland, woods
Senecio jacobaea	Ragwort, Common	N	Grassland, roadsides, wasteland
Senecio erucifolius	Ragwort, Hoary	N	Wasteland, open grassy places
Senecio squalidus	Ragwort, Oxford	I	Railway ballast, waste ground, walls
Senecio cineraria	Ragwort, Silver	I	Garden origin; occasional escape
Brassica napus ssp. *oleifera*	Rape, Oil-seed	I	Common; roadsides, field-margins
Rubus idaeus	Raspberry	N	Woods, heaths; the Brickhills
Nothofagus nervosa	Rauli	I	Planted in Linford Wood
Persicaria maculosa	Redshank	N	Waste and cultivated land
Phragmites australis	Reed, Common	N	By water; often forming large stands
Ononis repens	Restharrow, Common	N	By canal and in alkaline grassland
Ononis spinosa	Restharrow, Spiny	N R	Rare; grassy places on clay
Rhododendron ponticum	Rhododendron	I R	Weed in the Brickhills, particularly in woods
Sisymbrium orientale	Rocket, Eastern	I VR	Rare; naturalised in urban waste places
Sisymbrium altissimum	Rocket, Tall	I R	Rare; casual in waste places
Rosa pimpinellifolia	Rose, Burnet	N	Garden origin; spreads readily
Viburnum opulus	Rose, Guelder	N	Hedgerows, woods
Rosa rugosa	Rose, Japanese	I	Frequently planted; frequently established
Rosa multiflora	Rose, Many-flowered	I	Much planted on some estates
Rosa ferruginea	Rose, Red-leaved	N	Planted, maybe for its leaf colour
Rosa virginiana	Rose, Virginian	I	Much planted; occasionally seeding
Rosa 'Nozomi'	a Rose cultivar	I	Planted
Hypericum calycinum	Rose-of-Sharon	I	Of garden origin
Sorbus aucuparia	Rowan	N	Woods on the greensand; introduced elsewhere
Fallopia baldschuanica	Russian-vine	I	Hedges, gardens
Carthamus tinctoria	Safflower, Downy	I	Bird-seed origin in one Heelands garden
Salvia patens	Sage, Gentian	I	One plant seen once near Milton Keynes village
Teucrium scorodonia	Sage, Wood	N R	Woods and waysides on the Brickhills
Onobrychis viciifolia	Sainfoin	I	One plant seen once at Caldecotte Lake
Tragopogon porrifolius	Salsify	I	Occasionally planted; may escape
Arenaria serpyllifolia ssp. *leptoclados*	Sandwort, Slender	N R	Walls
Moehringia trinervia	Sandwort, Three-veined	N	Woods
Arenaria serpyllifolia ssp. *serpyllifolia*	Sandwort, Thyme-leaved	N	Walls, bare paths
Sanicula europaea	Sanicle	N	Woods
Serratula tinctoria	Saw-wort	N R	Stokepark Wood
Saxifraga cymbalaria	Saxifrage, Celandine	I	Garden origin
Saxifraga granulata	Saxifrage, Meadow	N R	Very rare; greensand meadows and churchyards
Silaum silaus	Saxifrage, Pepper	N	Old, damp grassland
Saxifraga tridactylites	Saxifrage, Rue-leaved	N R	Limestone walls
Knautia arvensis	Scabious, Field	N	Alkaline grassland
Prunella vulgaris	Selfheal	N	Short grassy areas, lawns
Sorbus torminalis	Service-tree, Wild	N	Planted; Linford Wood, Campbell Park
Galinsoga quadriradiata	Shaggy-soldier	I	Garden weed, urban footpaths; now rare
Jasione montana	Sheep's-bit	N VR	Very rare; heathland, Bow Brickhill
Capsella bursa-pastoris	Shepherd's-purse	N	Widespread weed of open soils
Potentilla anserina	Silverweed	N	Woodland rides, roadsides, grassland
Scutellaria galericulata	Skullcap	N	By water; canal walls and locks
Cotinus coggygria	Smoke-tree	I	Common in gardens; seedlings rarely seen
Antirrhinum majus	Snapdragon	I	Garden origin; persists in walls
Achillea ptarmica	Sneezewort	N R	Rare; fens, riversides
Symphoricarpos albus	Snowberry	I	Very commonly planted; hedges,woods,gardens
Symphoricarpos x *chenaultii*	Snowberry, Pink	I	Much city planting; occasionally escapes
Cerastium tomentosum	Snow-in-summer	I	Garden origin; may persist

Saponaria officinalis	Soapwort	(I)	Roadsides; often double-flowered
Sorbaria sorbifolia	Sorbaria	I	Occasionally planted; may seed
Rumex acetosa			
ssp. *acetosa*	Sorrel, Common	N	Grassland
Rumex acetosella	Sorrel, Sheep's	N	Heathy places, light acid soils
Oxalis acetosella	Sorrel, Wood	N	Woods
Sonchus arvensis	Sow-thistle, Perennial	N	Arable fields, waste places, river banks
Sonchus asper	Sow-thistle, Prickly	N	Waste places, roadsides, cultivated ground
Sonchus oleraceus	Sow-thistle, Smooth	N	As above, but often near habitation
Mentha spicata	Spearmint	I	Garden origin; naturalises
Ranunculus lingua	Spearwort, Greater	N VR	Planted; ponds, lakes
Veronica chamaedrys	Speedwell, Germander	N	Common; grassy places, churchyards
Veronica hederifolia			
ssp. *hederifolia*	Speedwell, Ivy-leaved	N	Open places and cultivated ground
ssp. *lucorum*	Speedwell, Ivy-leaved	N	Shady places *e.g.* hedgerows, open woods
Veronica filiformis	Speedwell, Slender	I	Lawns, churchyards, gang-mown fields
Veronica serpyllifolia			
ssp. *serpyllifolia*	Speedwell, Thyme-leaved	N	Damp grassy places including lawns and paths
Veronica arvensis	Speedwell, Wall	N	Walls, open ground, cultivated land
Spinacia oleracea	Spinach	I	Rare; garden origin
Spiraea japonica	Spiraea, Japanese	I	Rare; garden origin
Aucuba japonica	Spotted-laurel	I	Planted in shrubberies and churchyards
Inula conyzae	Spikenard, Ploughman's	N	Dry scrubby grassland (on limestone)
Euonymus europaeus	Spindle	N	Woods, hedges; sometimes planted
Euonymus japonicus	Spindle, Evergreen	I	Relict of cultivation; planted in one spinney
Spiraea japonica	Spiraea, Japanese	I	Rare; garden origin, rarely seeding
Claytonia perfoliata	Spring Beauty	I R	Roadsides, gardens, churchyards on greensand
Euphorbia myrsinites	Spurge, Blue	I	Garden origin
Euphorbia platyphyllos	Spurge, Broad-leaved	N	Very rare; cultivated ground, casual
Euphorbia lathyris	Spurge, Caper	(N)	Naturalised in gardens and waste places
Euphorbia cyparissias	Spurge, Cypress	(N)	Rare; garden origin, spinney at Wolverton
Euphorbia exigua	Spurge, Dwarf	(N)	Arable weed
Euphorbia characias	Spurge, Mediterranean	I	CMK shrubberies; often self-sown
Euphorbia peplus	Spurge, Petty	N	Cultivated ground, waste places
Euphorbia helioscopia	Spurge, Sun	N	Cultivated ground, waste places
Euphorbia dulcis	Spurge, Sweet	I	Rare; garden centre weed
Spergula arvensis	Spurrey, Corn	N	Arable or waste land on light (sandy) soil
Spergularia rubra	Spurrey, Sand	N R	Very rare on the Brickhill sands
Hypericum hirsutum	St John's-wort, Hairy	N	Woods, especially along rides
Hypericum maculatum			
ssp. *obtusiusculum*	St John's-wort, Imperforate	N R	Very rare; grassy places
Hypericum perforatum	St John's-wort, Perforate	N	Woods, grassland, railway ballast
Hypericum pulchrum	St John's-wort, Slender	N	Open areas of Brickhill Woods
Hypericum tetrapterum	St John's-wort, Square-stalked	N	Wet places, including woodland rides
Stellaria holostea	Stitchwort, Greater	N	Hedges, woods
Stellaria graminea	Stitchwort, Lesser	N	Grassy places
Sedum acre	Stonecrop, Biting	N	Walls, gravelly places especially near habitation
Sedum spurium	Stonecrop, Caucasian	I	Garden origin; walls, graves
Sedum rupestre	Stonecrop, Reflexed	I	Garden origin; churchyards, walls, banks
Sedum dasyphyllum	Stonecrop, Thick-leaved	I	Rare; walls near habitation
Sedum album	Stonecrop, White	(I) R	Walls near habitation; churchyards
Erodium cicutarium	Stork's-bill, Common	N R	Lawns, rough grass
Potentilla sterilis	Strawberry, Barren	N	Woods; along rides
Fragaria x *ananassa*	Strawberry, Garden	I	Garden origin; waste places
Fragaria vesca	Strawberry, Wild	N	Woods; along rides
Rhus typhina	Sumach, Stag's-horn	I	Garden origin; suckers freely
Helianthus annuus	Sunflower	I	Casual
Rosa rubiginosa	Sweet-briar	N VR	Very rare; hedges; MKDC planted
Rosa micrantha	Sweet-briar, Small-flowered	N VR	Very rare; hedges
Coronopus squamatus	Swine-cress	N	Farmyard gateways, pathways, bare ground
Coronopus didymus	Swine-cress, Lesser	I R	Uncommon; waste ground
Acer pseudoplatanus	Sycamore	I	Common; woods, parks, gardens; seeds freely

Tanacetum vulgare	Tansy	N	Grassy and rough places
Vicia hirsuta	Tare, Hairy	N	Rough grassy places
Vicia parviflora	Tare, Slender	N VR	Very rare; grassy banks Heelands (now gone)
Vicia tetrasperma	Tare, Smooth	N	Grassy places
Dipsacus fullonum	Teasel	N	Riversides, roadsides, churchyards
Dipsacus pilosus	Teasel, Small	N VR	A roadside on the Northants border; long known
Onopordum acanthium	Thistle, Cotton	I	Casual; roadsides, waste places
Cirsium arvense	Thistle, Creeping	N	Widespread weed
Cirsium acaule	Thistle, Dwarf	N	Uncommon; short calcareous turf
Cirsium palustre	Thistle, Marsh	N	Woods, wet grassland, watersides
Silybum marianum	Thistle, Milk	I	Casual
Carduus nutans	Thistle, Musk	N	Uncommon; calcareous grassland
Cirsium vulgare	Thistle, Spear	N	Common weed
Carduus crispus	Thistle, Welted	N	Grassy places; roadsides
Cirsium eriophorum	Thistle, Woolly	N R	Limestone turf
Carduus x stangii	Thistle, a Hybrid	N	A rare plant; found where parents are together
Datura stramonium	Thorn-apple	I	Casual; odd plants occasionally seen
Thymus pulegioides	Thyme, Large	N R	Very rare in good limestone grassland
Thymus polytrichus	Thyme, Wild	N	Rare; in limestone grassland
Linaria maroccana	Toadflax, Annual	I	Often planted; often establishes for short periods
Linaria vulgaris	Toadflax, Common	N	Grassland edges, railway ballast, road verges
Cymbalaria muralis			
ssp. muralis	Toadflax, Ivy-leaved	I	Walls
Linaria repens	Toadflax, Pale	N	A few places on the limestone; railway ballast
Linaria purpurea	Toadflax, Purple	I	Urban weed, wasteland, walls
Chaenorhinum minus	Toadflax, Small	N	Railway ballast, bare areas
Lycopersicon esculentum	Tomato	I	Garden origin; waste places
Potentilla erecta			
ssp. erecta	Tormentil	N	Rare; woods, grassland on less alkaline soils
Potentilla anglica	Tormentil, Trailing	N R	Grassland, by paths on less alkaline soils
Clematis vitalba	Traveller's-joy	N	Woods, hedgerows on calcareous soil
Lavatera thuringiaca	Tree-mallow, Garden	I	Rare; garden origin, frequently planted
Ailanthus altissima	Tree-of-heaven	I	Occasionally planted; saplings frequent close by
Trifolium campestre	Trefoil, Hop	N	Grassy places
Trifolium dubium	Trefoil, Lesser	N	Grassy places, open ground
Trifolium micranthum	Trefoil, Slender	N R	Rare; in acid grassland as at Woburn Sands
Brassica rapa			
ssp. campestris	Turnip, Wild	(I)	Occasional by riversides; wasteland
ssp. oleifera	Turnip-rape	I	Casual; birdseed alien
Hypericum androsaemum	Tutsan	N	Of garden, and other planting, origin
Valeriana officinalis			
ssp. sambucifolia	Valerian, Common	N	Damp woodland rides
Centranthus ruber	Valerian, Red	I R	Garden origin; naturalises freely on walls
Legousia hybrida	Venus's Looking-glass	N R	Decreasing; arable weed
Verbena officinalis	Vervain	N	CMK Bus Station car-park
Vicia sepium	Vetch, Bush	N	Hedges and wood margins
Vicia sativa			
ssp. segetalis	Vetch, Common	I	Grassy places, rough ground
Vicia villosa	Vetch, Fodder	I	Very rare; by Willen Lake-side
Vicia sativa			
ssp. nigra	Vetch, Narrow-leaved	N	Grassy places, rough ground
Vicia cracca	Vetch, Tufted	N	Grassy and bushy places, hedgerows
Lathyrus nissolia	Vetchling, Grass	N	Decreasing; grassy places, base of hedges
Lathyrus pratensis	Vetchling, Meadow	N	Grassy places, rough ground
Viburnum rhytidophyllum	Viburnum, Wrinkled	I	Planted in gardens and shrubberies
Hesperis matronalis	Violet, Dame's	I	Roadsides etc. close to habitation
Viola hirta	Violet, Hairy	N	Chalky grassland, scrub, railway banks
Viola odorata	Violet, Sweet	N	Woodlands, scrub, hedgebanks, gardens
Parthenocissus quinquefolia	Virginia-creeper	I	Garden origin; on walls; commoner than next
Parthenocissus inserta	Virginia-creeper, False	I	Garden origin; on walls
Erysimum cheiri	Wallflower	I	Naturalised on walls and in waste places

Erysimum x *marshallii*	Wallflower, Siberian	I	Garden origin
Diplotaxis muralis	Wall-rocket, Annual	N **R**	Rare; walls, waste places
Juglans regia	Walnut	I	Specimen trees in villages
Rorippa nasturtium-aquaticum	Water-cress	N	By canal, streams, in ditches
Rorippa microphylla	Water-cress, Narrow-fruited	N **R**	Rare; wet places; may be under-recorded
Apium nodiflorum	Water-cress, Fool's	N	Ditches, streams, river and canalsides
Ranunculus aquatilis	Water-crowfoot, Common	N **R**	Rare; ponds
Ranunculus peltatus	Water-crowfoot, Pond	N **R**	Ponds
Ranunculus fluitans	Water-crowfoot, River	N **R**	Rivers
Ranunculus penicillatus ssp. *pseudofluitans*	Water-crowfoot, Stream	N	In clear, running water
Oenanthe fluviatilis	Water-dropwort, River	N **R**	Rare; river
Oenanthes fistulosa	Water-dropwort, Tubular	N **R**	Rare; ditches, marshy grassland
Nymphoides peltata	Water-lily, Fringed	(N) **R**	Planted in lakes
Nymphaea alba ssp. *alba*	Water-lily, White	N **R**	Rare; river, (planted in lakes)
Nuphar lutea	Water-lily, Yellow	N	Rivers, canal, lakes
Myriophyllum spicatum	Water-milfoil, Spiked	N **R**	Canal, river, ponds
Berula erecta	Water-parsnip, Lesser	N **R**	Streams, rivers, ponds
Persicaria hydropiper	Water-pepper	N	Wet places including woodland rides
Veronica anagallis-aquatica	Water-speedwell, Blue	N	Rivers, streams, ponds
Veronica catenata	Water-speedwell, Pink	N	By ponds or rivers in the mud
Callitriche stagnalis	Water-starwort, Common	N	Ponds, streams, wet woodland rides, on mud
Callitriche obtusangula	Water-starwort, Blunt-fruited	N	In one man-made lake
Callitriche platycarpa	Water-starwort, Various-leaved	NR	Ponds, streams, on mud
Lagarosiphon major	Waterweed, Curly	I **VR**	Ponds, lakes
Viburnum lantana	Wayfaring-tree	N	Hedgerows, wood edges
Reseda luteola	Weld	N	Open ground, railway ballast
Sorbus aria	Whitebeam, Common	N	Uncommon; hedges and woods on limestone
Sorbus intermedia	Whitebeam, Swedish	I **VR**	Rare in the wild; often planted
Erophila verna	Whitlow-grass, Common	N	Dry places - walls, open grass, paths
Erophila glabrescens	Whitlow-grass, Glabrous	N	
Erophila majuscula	Whitlow-grass, Hairy	N (U)	Very rare or under-recorded; gravel paths
Salix triandra	Willow, Almond	N **R**	Rare; damp places; may be planted
Salix pentandra	Willow, Bay	N	Always planted in MK; a northern species
Salix fragilis	Willow, Crack	N	By rivers and ponds, hedgerows
Salix x *ehrhartiana*	Willow, Ehrhart's	(I)	Emberton Park
Salix caprea ssp. *caprea*	Willow, Goat	N	Hedges, woods, scrub, rough ground
Salix cinerea ssp. *oleifera*	Willow, Grey	N	Hedges, woods, scrub, damp places
Salix elaeagnos	Willow, Olive	I	Planted; rarely seeding
Salix purpurea	Willow, Purple	N	By waterways; probably planted in MK
Salix x *mollissima*	Willow, Sharp-stipuled	N	Only known from Joan's Piece
Salix x *meyeriana*	Willow, Shiny-leaved	N	Rare; planted: Bletchley and Bradwell
Salix x *sepulcralis*	Willow, Weeping	I	Ornamental planting (by water)
Salix alba	Willow, White	N	By rivers, canal, ponds
Salix x *reichardtii*	Willow, a Hybrid	N	Rare; damp places
Epilobium ciliatum	Willowherb, American	I	Common urban weed, still spreading
Epilobium montanum	Willowherb, Broad-leaved	N	Shady places; hedges, gardens, churchyards
Epilobium hirsutum	Willowherb, Great	N	Damp grass, watersides, woodland rides, gdns
Epilobium parviflorum	Willowherb, Hoary	N	Damp grassy places, garden weed
Epilobium brunnescens	Willowherb, New Zealand	I	Rare; garden weed; one record from Heelands
Chamerion angustifolium	Willowherb, Rosebay	N	Hedgerows, roadsides, waste places
Epilobium obscurum	Willowherb, Short-fruited	N **R**	Damp grassy places, garden weed
Epilobium lanceolatum	Willowherb, Spear-leaved	N **R**	North Bucks Way
Epilobium tetragonum	Willowherb, Square-stalked	N	Damp grassy places, garden weed
Epilobium ciliatum x *montanum*	Willowherb, a Hybrid	(N)	Churchyards; waste places
Barbarea vulgaris	Winter-cress	N	Roadsides, waterway margins
Galium odoratum	Woodruff	N	Planted in gardens; (escape at Woolstone)
Artemisia absinthum	Wormwood	N	Rare; waste places
Stachys sylvatica	Woundwort, Hedge	N	Woods, hedges, rough ground, churchyards
Stachys x *ambigua*	Woundwort, Hybrid	N	Very rare; hedgerow

Stachys palustris	Woundwort, Marsh	N	By rivers, canal, ponds
Achillea millefolium	Yarrow	N	Common in a wide range of grassy places
Rorippa sylvestris	Yellow-cress, Creeping	N R	Damp places, disturbed ground, gardens
Rorippa amphibia	Yellow-cress, Great	N	River margins
Rorippa palustris	Yellow-cress, Marsh	N	Damp open ground
Oxalis exilis	Yellow-sorrel, Least	I	Rare; garden weed or in short grass
Oxalis corniculata	Yellow-sorrel, Procumbent	I	Common garden weed; walls, churchyards
Oxalis stricta	Yellow-sorrel, Upright	I	Garden weed
Blackstonia perfoliata	Yellow-wort	N	Uncommon; open calcareous turf
Stachys annua	Yellow-woundwort, Annual	I	One garden record once; introduced with seeds
Euonymus fortunei		I	Garden origin; seedlings rare

Monocotyledons

Sagittaria sagittifolia	Arrowhead	N	Rivers, canal
Crocosmia paniculata	Aunt-Eliza	I	Garden origin; may survive as a throwout
Hyacinthoides non-scripta	Bluebell	N	Woods, old hedgerows; not on very alkaline soils
Hyacinthoides x variabilis	Bluebell, Hybrid	I	Garden origin; churchyards; may naturalise
Hyacinthoides hispanica	Bluebell, Spanish	I	May persist from spinney/copse plantings
Sparganium erectum	Bur-reed, Branched	N	Rivers, canal, ponds
Sparganium emersum	Bur-reed, Unbranched	N R	Rivers; not as common as above
Ruscus hypoglossum	Butcher's-broom, Spineless	I	One plant seen once at Bow Brickhill
Platanthera chlorantha	Butterfly-orchid, Greater	N R	Rare; woods
Schoenoplectus lacustris	Club-rush, Common	N	In rivers, canal, lakes
Schoenoplectus tabernaemontani	Club-rush, Grey	N	Very rare; planted by Campbell Park ponds
Bolboschoenus maritimus	Club-rush, Sea	N VR	Well established round some old gravel pits
Crocus tommasinianus	Crocus, Early	I	Garden origin
Crocus chrysanthus	Crocus, Golden	I	Garden origin
Crocus vernus	Crocus, Spring	I	Garden origin
Crocus x stellaris	Crocus, Yellow	I	Garden origin
Cyclamen hederifolium	Cyclamen	I	Garden origin; naturalises
Narcissus nobilis	Daffodil, Large-flowered	I	Garden origin; roadsides
Narcissus x incomparabilis	Daffodil, Nonesuch	I	Garden origin; Joan's Piece, waste places
Narcissus poeticus ssp. *poeticus*	Daffodil, Pheasant's-eye	I	Garden origin; roadsides
Narcissus pseudonarcissus ssp. *major*	Daffodil, Spanish	I	Garden origin; roadsides
ssp. *obvallaris*	Daffodil, Tenby	I	Planted in parks
Narcissus bicolor	Daffodil, Two-coloured	I	Garden origin; roadsides
Narcissus x boutigyanus	Daffodil, White & Orange	I	Garden origin; Railway Walk, Bradville
Narcissus pseudonarcissus ssp. *pseudonarcissus*	Daffodil, Wild	N VR	Bow Brickhill churchyard; often garden origin
Lemna minor	Duckweed, Common	N	On water - still or slowly moving
Lemna gibba	Duckweed, Fat	N R	Canal, river, ponds
Spirodela polyrhiza	Duckweed, Greater	N VR	Canal, rivers, ponds
Lemna trisulca	Duckweed, Ivy-leaved	N	In ponds, canal, backwaters of river
Lemna minuta	Duckweed, Least	I VR	Recent introduction to ponds, lakes; increasing
Carex otrubae	Fox-sedge, False	N	Ponds, ditches, streams, rivers, canals
Cyperus longus	Galingale	I	Planted around pond margins
Allium sativum	Garlic	I	Garden origin
Chionodoxa forbesii	Glory-of-the-snow	I	Garden origin
Muscari neglectum	Grape-hyacinth	N	Garden origin; roadsides, churchyards
Muscari armeniacum	Grape-hyacinth, Garden	I	Garden origin; occasional roadsides
Epipactis helleborine	Helleborine, Broad-leaved	N	Woods
Paris quadrifolia	Herb-Paris	N R	Rare; woods

Hyacinthus orientalis	Hyacinth	I	May occur as a garden throwout
Iris germanica	Iris, Bearded	I	Garden origin; may persist
Iris versicolor	Iris, Purple	I	Rare; by Caldecotte Lake
Iris sibirica	Iris, Siberian	I	Rare; by one track in New Bradwell
Iris foetidissima	Iris, Stinking	N R	Woods, hedges, churchyards
Iris pseudacorus	Iris, Yellow	N	Watersides
Allium paradoxum	Leek, Few-flowered	I R	Very rare; opposite Brown's Wood
Lilium x hollandicum	Lily, Orange	I	Very rare; garden origin
Arum maculatum	Lords-and-Ladies	N	Common; woods and hedge bottoms
Crocosmia x crocosmiiflora	Montbretia	I	Very rare; garden origin
Allium vineale	Onion, Wild	N R	Field margins, roadside verges
Ophrys apifera	Orchid, Bee	N R	Short open grassland or on bare clay
Neottia nidus-avis	Orchid, Bird's-nest	N R	Very rare; Salcey Forest
Orchis mascula	Orchid, Early-purple	N R	Woods, disused railway
Anacamptis pyramidalis	Orchid, Pyramidal	N	One plant unexpectedly, in planted woodland
Carex riparia	Pond-sedge, Greater	N	River and canal banks
Carex acutiformis	Pond-sedge, Lesser	N	Woods, watersides, wet grassland
Potamogeton natans	Pondweed, Broad-leaved	N	Ponds
Potamogeton crispus	Pondweed, Curled	N	Canal, ponds, lakes
Potamogeton pectinatus	Pondweed, Fennel	N	Canal, rivers, lakes, ponds
Potamogeton friesii	Pondweed, Flat-stalked	N R	Canal, rivers, lakes
Potamogeton trichoides	Pondweed, Hair-like	N R	Very rare; pond
Zannichellia palustris	Pondweed, Horned	N	Rare; lakes, ponds and brooks
Potamogeton pusillus	Pondweed, Lesser	N R	Canal, lakes, ponds
Potamogeton perfoliatus	Pondweed, Perfoliate	N R	Uncommon; canal
Potamogeton lucens	Pondweed, Shining	N VR	Canal, rivers, lakes
Potamogeton berchtoldii	Pondweed, Small	N VR	Canal, ponds, lakes
Narcissus x medioluteus	Primrose-peerless	I	Garden origin
Allium ursinum	Ramsons	N R	Woods
Typha latifolia	Reedmace, Common	N	Rivers, canal, ditches, ponds, lakes
Typha x glauca	Reedmace, Hybrid	N	Rare; lakes; Newfoundout
Typha angustifolia	Reedmace, Lesser	N VR	Lakes and ponds; sometimes planted
Juncus subnodulosus	Rush, Blunt-flowered	N R	A fen species; a single record
Juncus bulbosus	Rush, Bulbous	N R	Very rare; in wet, acid places on the Brickhills
Juncus conglomertus	Rush, Compact	N	Wet places on less alkaline soils
Butomus umbellatus	Rush, Flowering	N R	Rivers, canal
Juncus inflexus	Rush, Hard	N	Damp grassland and open places
Juncus squarrosus	Rush, Heath	N VR	Very rare on the Brickhills
Juncus articulatus	Rush, Jointed	N	Wet places
Juncus compressus	Rush, Round-fruited	N VR	Castlethorpe grassland; Stony and Linford Pits
Juncus acutiflorus	Rush, Sharp-flowered	N	Very rare; marshy grassland
Juncus tenuis	Rush, Slender	I	Rare; Stony Stratford reserve
Juncus effusus	Rush, Soft	N	Grassland, woodland, ditches; damp places
Juncus bufonius	Rush, Toad	N	Pathways, cart ruts, gardens; often damp places
Carex rostrata	Sedge, Bottle	N VR	One record only; from the Brickhills
Carex disticha	Sedge, Brown	N R	Fens, flushes
Carex panicea	Sedge, Carnation	N R	Very rare; only seen in one fen
Carex nigra	Sedge, Common	N R	Anything but common; one fen record only
Carex pseudocyperus	Sedge, Cyperus	N R	Canal banks; decreasing
Carex distans	Sedge, Distant	N VR	A fen species; a single record
Carex flacca	Sedge, Glaucous	N	Short grassland, often calcareous
Carex divulsa ssp. *divulsa*	Sedge, Grey	N	Rare; in a few grassy places
Carex hirta	Sedge, Hairy	N	Grassland, often damp
Carex x pseudoaxillaris	Sedge, a Hybrid	N VR	Very rare; pondside
Carex ovalis	Sedge, Oval	N R	Rare; woods

Carex pallescens	Sedge, Pale	N R	Rare; woods
Carex pendula	Sedge, Pendulous	N	Woods, occasionally planted in gardens
Carex pilulifera	Sedge, Pill	N R	A rare plant on the acid soils of the Brickhills
Carex remota	Sedge, Remote	N	Woods
Carex spicata	Sedge, Spiked	N	Roadsides, hedgerows, woodland margins
Galanthus nivalis	Snowdrop	(N)	Churchyards, woodland, grassy places
Galanthus elwesii	Snowdrop, Greater	I	Rare; garden origin; Bradwell Common
Galanthus ikariae	Snowdrop, Green	I	Rare; garden origin; Bradwell Common
Leucojum aestivum ssp. aestivum	Snowflake, Summer	N	Garden origin; well north of its native range
Polygonatum x hybridum	Solomon's-seal, Garden	I	Garden origin; may escape to pathsides
Eleocharis palustris	Spike-rush, Common	N	Ponds, lakes, streamsides
Dactylorhiza fuchsii	Spotted-orchid, Common	N	Woods, old meadows
Carex caryophyllea	Spring-sedge	N R	One record only, from limestone grassland
Ornithogalum angustifolium	Star-of-Bethlehem, Common	N R	Occasional in grassy places
Ornithogalum nutans	Star-of-Bethlehem, Drooping	I	Broughton churchyard
Ornithogalum pyrenaicum	Star-of-Bethlehem, Spiked	N (U)	Very rare; only record from by Loughton Brook
Acorus calamus	Sweet-flag	I R	Canal, riversides; decreasing
Carex acuta	Tufted-sedge, Slender	N R	Rare; riversides, lakesides
Tulipa gesneriana	Tulip, Garden	I	Garden origin; roadsides
Carex paniculata	Tussock-sedge, Greater	N R	Canal banks
Listera ovata	Twayblade, Common	N	Rare; woods
Alisma plantago-aquatica	Water-plantain	N	Rivers, canal, ponds
Alisma lanceolatum	Water-plantain, Narrow-leaved	N R	Rare; canalside
Stratiotes aloides	Water-soldier	N VR	Very rare; introduced into one pond
Elodea canadensis	Waterweed, Canadian	I	In ponds, lakes or streams
Elodea nuttallii	Waterweed, Nuttall's	I VR	Increasing; in lakes and ponds
Luzula campestris	Woodrush, Field	N	Short grassland
Luzula multiflora	Woodrush, Heath	N R	Rare; woods
Luzula pilosa	Woodrush, Hairy	N	Rare; woods
Luzula sylvatica	Woodrush, Great	N VR	Very rare; Brickhill Woods
Carex sylvatica	Wood-sedge	N	Woods
Carex strigosa	Wood-sedge, Thin-spiked	N VR	Rare; Salcey Forest (in abundance!)
Sisyrinchium striatum	Yellow-eyed-grass, Pale	I	Garden origin; Bradwell

Grasses

Hordeum jubatum	Barley, Foxtail	I	Uncommon; casual from bird-seed or gardens
Hordeum secalinum	Barley, Meadow	N	Old meadows and pastures
Hordeum vulgare	Barley, Six-rowed	I	An uncommon casual from cultivation
Hordeum distichon	Barley, Two-rowed	I	Arable crop; casuals common
Hordeum murinum ssp. murinum	Barley, Wall	N	Weed on wasteland, open areas of rough grass
Agrostis gigantea	Bent, Black	N	Arable weed; waste places, not uncommon
Agrostis capillaris	Bent, Common	N	Uncommon; light, usually acid soils
Agrostis stolonifera	Bent, Creeping	N	Widespread; grassy places, pond edges
Alopecurus myosuroides	Black-grass	N	Arable weed
Setaria viridis	Bristle-grass, Green	I	Casual; bird-seed origin
Setaria pumila	Bristle-grass, Yellow	I	Very rare; casual
Anisantha sterilis	Brome, Barren	N	Arable and garden weed, rough places
Brachypodium sylvaticum	Brome, False	N	Woods, hedgerows, churchyards; common
Bromopsis inermis	Brome, Hungarian	I VR	Rare; Wolverton Mill, roadside at Bletchley
Bromus commutatus	Brome, Meadow	N R	Old meadows
Bromus racemosus	Brome, Smooth	N VR	Rare; only record from a field near Bletchley
Bromopsis erecta	Brome, Upright	N	Railway banks, calcareous grassland
Phalaris canariensis	Canary-grass	I	Bird-seed alien; casual
Phalaris arundinacea	Canary-grass, Reed	N	Common; damp or wet places
Phleum bertolonii	Cat's-tail, Smaller	N	Common; grassland
Dactylis glomerata	Cock's-foot	N	Very common in a wide variety of grassy places
Echinochloa crus-galli	Cockspur	I	Very rare; waste ground

Species	Common Name	Status	Habitat
Elymus caninus	Couch, Bearded	N	Woods
Elytrigia repens			
ssp. *repens*	Couch, Common	N	Widespread weed; gardens, hedgerows
Cynosurus cristatus	Dog's-tail, Crested	N	Unimproved grassland
Catapodium rigidum	Fern-grass	N **R**	Walls, pavement cracks, churchyards
Vulpia ciliata			
spp. *ciliata*	Fescue, Bearded	N **VR**	One wall in Olney
Festuca rubra			
ssp. *commutata*	Fescue, Chewing's	N	A common component of grassland planting
Festuca gigantea	Fescue, Giant	N	Common; woods, hedges
Festuca brevipila	Fescue, Hard	I	Amenity area planting; found on a few roadsides
x *Festulolium loliaceum*	Fescue, Hybrid	N	Occasional; grassland
Festuca pratensis	Fescue, Meadow	N	Old grassland, meadows
Vulpia myuros	Fescue, Rat's-tail	(N) **R**	Bare, open areas, walls
Festuca rubra			
ssp. *rubra*	Fescue, Red	N	Very common; many types of grassland
Festuca ovina	Fescue, Sheep's	N	Short grassland
Vulpia bromoides	Fescue, Squirreltail	N	Rare; open areas, urban sites *e.g.* pavements
Festuca arundinacea	Fescue, Tall	N	Common; rank grassland, roadsides
Alopecurus geniculatus	Foxtail, Marsh	N	Damp/wet grassy places, pond margins
Alopecurus pratensis	Foxtail, Meadow	N	Widespread; in many grassy areas
Koeleria macrantha	Hair-grass, Crested	N **R**	Very rare; limestone grassland
Aira caryophyllea	Hair-grass, Silvery	N **VR**	Rare; on bare railway ballast; the Brickhills
Deschampsia cespitosa			
ssp. *cespitosa*	Hair-grass, Tufted	N	Common; damp or wet grassland
ssp. *parviflora*	Hair-grass, Tufted	N	More common in woodlands
Deschampsia flexuosa	Hair-grass, Wavy	N	Only on the greensand; woods, paths
Bromopsis ramosa	Hairy-brome	N	Common; woods, hedgerows, gardens
Zea mays	Maize	I	Casual from cereal crop or fishing bait
Poa annua	Meadow-grass, Annual	N	Abundant weed; open areas
Poa compressa	Meadow-grass, Flattened	N **R**	Walls, open gravel or pavements
Poa angustifolia	Meadow-grass, Narrow-leaved	N	Under-recorded; grasslands, walls
Poa trivialis	Meadow-grass, Rough	N	All grassy places, rough ground
Poa pratensis	Meadow-grass, Smooth	N	All grassy places, rough ground
Poa humilis	Meadow-grass, Spreading	N	In a water meadow by the R. Ouse; (elsewhere)
Poa nemoralis	Meadow-grass, Wood	N	Common; woods
Melica uniflora	Melick, Wood	N	Woods
Panicum miliaceum	Millet	I	Bird-seed origin; waste places, gardens
Milium effusum	Millet, Wood	N	Woods
Avena sativa	Oat	I	Escape from cultivation; roadsides
Helictotrichon pubescens	Oat-grass, Downy	N	In old, well-established grassland
Arrhenatherum elatius	Oat-grass, False	N	Very common; rank grassland, waste places
Trisetum flavescens	Oat-grass, Yellow	N	Meadows and other grass esp. on alkaline soil
Briza media	Quaking-grass	N	Uncommon; open calcareous grassland
Secale cereale	Rye	I	Rare casual from cultivation
Lolium multiflorum	Rye-grass, Italian	I	Fodder crop, escapes often persist
Lolium perenne	Rye-grass, Perennial	N	All types of grassland, frequently planted
Calamagrostis epigejos	Small-reed, Wood	N	Woods; occasionally by roadsides
Bromus hordeaceus			
ssp. *hordeaceus*	Soft-brome	N	Rough ground, old, open meadows
Bromus x *pseudothominei*	Soft-brome, Lesser	(N)	Rough ground, grassland; uncommon
Holcus mollis	Soft-grass, Creeping	N	Woods on acid soils
Glyceria fluitans	Sweet-grass, Floating	N	By ponds and rivers, muddy ditches
Glyceria x *pedicellata*	Sweet-grass, Hybrid	N	Rare; pondsides
Glyceria notata	Sweet-grass, Plicate	N	By ponds and rivers, muddy ditches
Glyceria maxima	Sweet-grass, Reed	N	Common; rivers, canals, ditches

Glyceria declinata	Sweet-grass, Small	N **R**	By ponds and rivers, muddy ditches
Phleum pratense	Timothy	N	Common; grassland, rough places
Brachypodium pinnatum	Tor-grass	N **R**	Rare; Linford Wood, roadside near Olney
Anthoxanthum odoratum	Vernal-grass, Sweet	N	Old grassland
Triticum aestivum	Wheat, Bread	I	Casual from cultivation
Avena fatua	Wild-oat	I	Arable weed
Avena sterilis ssp. *ludoviciana*	Wild-oat, Winter	I	Arable weed
Holcus lanatus	Yorkshire-fog	N	Very common; grassland, woods

Bryophytes

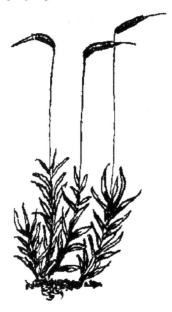

Moss with capsules

Bryophytes are relatively simple plants that generally require shade and humidity in which to grow. Some need wet conditions, others thrive totally submerged and a few veer to the other extreme in their toleration of more arid situations. Mosses are the more complex of the two types of bryophyte, having a stem with leaves arranged around it, and very fine rhizoids for anchorage. Groups of plants are usually found very close together forming 'mats' or 'cushions' - but there is a lot of variation. Liverworts are of two more or less distinct types - either flat 'plates' of cells anchored by rhizoids or those with stems and leaves which appear to be arranged in two distinct ranks.

Porella platyphylla, the liverwort which grows so well on part of the churchyard wall at Olney, has an unusually high tolerance of exposure - quite different from most other liverworts where constant humidity and shade are essential.

Mosses seem to grow almost anywhere. Walls, cracks between paving slabs, tops of churchyard memorial stones and tarmac offer very exposed habitats, but many such areas have a good moss cover. In dry weather, the plants can appear to be quite desiccated but, on the return of moisture, they have a remarkable ability to recover their normal form.

Stable habitats affording humidity and shade are prime places for bryophytes, so woods, churchyards, gardens, parks, banks, ditches and margins of water are good places to search. Areas of disturbed soil which remain bare for a year or so (as at Hazeley Wood) are likely to give rise to interesting species.

Winter and spring are the most rewarding seasons in which to look for mosses and liverworts as they are easier to see when the surrounding, larger, herbaceous plants are dormant (or dead!). They will be in their growing season and are more likely to be bearing the reproductive spores capsules. These are often essential when trying to identify the various species.

In the lists which follow, nomenclature follows that of Smith (1970 and 1990) and the notes refer to the situations in which the plants occur in Milton Keynes.

References and Further Reading

Higgs, F. (1998). An Introduction to the Bryophyte Flora of Milton Keynes in Journal of the Milton Keynes Natural History Society - Vol. 6, 1992-1998. This paper gives very useful distribution maps for most species listed here.

Paton, J.A. (1999). The Liverwort Flora of the British Isles. Harley Books

Smith, A.J.E. (1978). The Moss Flora of Britain & Ireland. Cambridge University Press

Smith, A.J.E. (1990). The Liverworts of Britain and Ireland. Cambridge University Press

Watson, E.V. (1981) British Mosses and Liverworts (3rd edition). Cambridge University Press

Liverworts

Conocephalum conicum	Large mats on damp, shaded stream banks
Lepidozia reptans	Found growing through mosses on acid woodland soil
Lophocolea bidentata	Damp habitats in churchyards and woods
Lophocolea heterophylla	Mainly in woods on stones, tree boles and rotting wood
Lunularia cruciata	Under-recorded; records from plant pot soil and shaded paths
Marchantia polymorpha	Under-recorded; flower pots; damp, shaded paths in gardens

Metzgeria furcata	Good growth visible on trees in Little Linford Wood
Pellia endiviifolia	One record only from wet lakeside soil
Pellia epiphylla	Records from damp soil in two woods
Plagiochila porelloides	Grows almost concealed in damp, shaded habitats
Porella platyphylla	Forms patches on shaded limestone walls and memorials
Ptilidium pulcherrimum	One record from a dead branch in Little Linford Wood
Radula complanata	A few small patches on tree trunks in one wood

Mosses

Amblystegium serpens	Moist shaded places on soil, stone, living and dead wood
Amblystegium riparium	Grows on various substrates in wet places
Amblystegium varium	The only record is from stones in a woodland stream
Atrichum undulatum	Noticeable patches on woodland floors and ditch sides
Aulacomnium androgynum	Found on wet, rotting wood in shady places
Barbula convoluta	
var. *commutata*	From bare soil and crevices in buildings and walls
var. *convoluta*	Found in similar habitats to the above
Barbula cylindrica	Favours soil-filled crevices in walls
Barbula fallax	One record on damp soil from a disused railway track
Barbula revoluta	On old mortar, stones and soil-filled crevices
Barbula rigidula	Found on limestone walls in several churchyards
Barbula tophacea	Forms tufts on damp, calcareous clay
Barbula trifaria	Two churchyard records on limestone and tarmac
Barbula unguiculata	A common colonist of soil patches
Barbula vinealis	Frequent on stones and walls in churchyards
Brachythecium albicans	Sandy or gravely places in several scattered localities
Brachythecium populeum	Found in one wood growing tightly pressed to a branch
Brachythecium rivulare	Found only in one wood in a permanently wet area
Brachythecium rutabulum	Commonly found in various habitats on many different substrates
Brachythecium velutinum	On living or dead wood, stones and bare soil
Bryum argenteum	Common; recognised by its silvery sheen on walls and in paving
Bryum bicolor	On soil in various situations
Bryum caespiticium	On old walls and hard, stony ground
Bryum capillare	Common on soil, stones, concrete, walls and wood
Bryum flaccidum	Forms patches on wood in moist, shaded situations
Bryum rubens	Frequent on damp soil in gardens, arable land & churchyards
Bryum ruderale	Colonist of bare soil patches
Calliergon cuspidatum	Common in lawns, other land habitats and may grow submerged
Campylopus introflexus	On peaty material in woods and some churchyards
Campylopus paradoxus	Growing on peaty ground in Wavendon Wood
Ceratodon purpureus	Common in churchyards on rotting wood, bare soil & wall tops
Cirriphyllum crassinervium	Grows over limestone in two churchyards
Cirriphyllum piliferum	Found in shaded habitats on soil and in turf
Cratoneuron filicinum	A plant of wet, calcareous habitats
Dicranella heteromalla	Grows on woodland humus and acid soil
Dicranella schreberana	A few patches on damp soil in Hazeley Wood
Dicranella staphylina	On soil patches amongst grass in Hazeley Wood
Dicranoweisia cirrata	On bark and stone in woodlands, hedgerows and churchyards
Dicranum majus	On acid woodland soil
Dicranum scoparium	Woodland and churchyard sites where the soil is acid
Dicranum tauricum	Found on living and dead wood in two woodlands
Drepanocladus aduncus	In marshy, semi-aquatic places at Great Linford Lakes
Encalyptera streptocarpa	One record from calcareous rock
Ephemerum serratum	
var. *serratum*	A microscopic moss growing among other mosses in damp places
Eurhynchium praelongum	Commonly found in shade on various substrates
Eurhynchium pumilum	This very slender species grows on shaded clay
Eurhynchium striatum	Widespread on soil in woods and churchyards
Eurhynchium speciosum	Recorded from wet soil by water at Willen Lake
Eurhynchium swartzii	Grows on damp soil in various habitats
Fissidens bryoides	One record only, from damp, shaded soil in Howe Park Wood
Fissidens exilis	Seen on clay in Shenley Wood when capsules made it visible
Fissidens incurvus	On damp, shaded soil in one wood and Tyringham churchyard

Fissidens taxifolius	On clay soil in woods, ditches, churchyards and gardens
Fontinalis antipyretica	An aquatic moss of still and running water
Funaria hygrometrica	Colonises bare soil in several habitats, especially bonfire sites
Grimmia pulvinata	Very common on walls, concrete and stones
Homalia trichomanoides	On shaded tree boles beside water in two woods
Homalothecium sericeum	Covers large areas of limestone walls and memorials
Hygrohypnum luridum	On concrete by the Grand Union Canal
Hypnum cupressiforme	
var. cupressiforme	Commonly found in various habitats
var. lacunosum	A robust form recorded from stone and gravel
var. resupinatum	A slender form growing on bark and stones
Hypnum jutlandicum	Pale, open patches in Wavendon Wood
Isopterygium elegans	Forms glossy patches on the sandy banks at Bow Brickhill
Isothecium myosuroides	A woodland species found on trees
Isothecium myurum	Found on tree boles in three woods
Leptobryum pyriforme	Colonises damp soil in a variety of habitats
Leucodon sciuroides	A new record for Bucks when discovered on limestone memorials
Mnium hornum	Frequent on slightly acid woodland humus
Mnium stellare	Recently discovered in one Milton Keynes wood
Neckera complanata	An uncommon, filmy, delicate moss requiring humidity and shade
Orthodontium lineare	In woodlands, hedgerows and on rotting woodwork
Orthotrichum affine	Epiphytic on shaded branches in humid situations
Orthotrichium anomalum	Frequent on stone and walls
Orthotrichium diaphanum	Widely recorded from walls, memorial stones and trees
Oxystegus sinuosus	On shaded stones in churchyards, gardens and woods
Phascum cuspidatum	
var. cuspidatum	Colonises bare soil often amongst other bryophytes
var. schreberanum	Hazeley Wood is the first known Bucks site
Physcomitrium pyriforme	Scattered plants were found on wet soil by a lake
Plagiomnium affine	Patches on shaded turf and in woods
Plagiomnium rostratum	Found in damp shade in only two locations
Plagiomnium undulatum	Common in woods and shaded churchyard grass
Plagiothecium curvifolium	Found on woodland leaf mould and on soil in a churchyard
Plagiothecium denticulatum	Recorded from stones, soil and decaying wood in woodlands
Plagiothecium nemorale	Records from damp, shaded soil in a few woods
Plagiothecium undulatum	A pale moss forming distinctive patches in Wavendon Wood
Pleurozium schreberi	Grows on acid soil in Bow and Little Brickhill churchyards
Pohlia carnea	Recorded from damp clay soil near water
Pohlia nutans	Found on a sandy bank at Bow Brickhill
Pohlia wahlenbergii	In damp places on a disused railway track
Polytrichum formosum	Churchyard and woodland sites where the soil is acid
Polytrichum juniperinum	On well-drained acid soil at Bow Brickhill and Blue Lagoon
Pottia starkeana	
ssp. minutula	A few scattered plants from Hazeley Wood with the following
Pottia truncata	In the tree rows at Hazeley Wood and other localities
Pseudoscleropodium purum	Grows in turf and various shaded places
Rhizomnium punctatum	Usually in damp, shaded woodland conditions
Rhynchiostegiella tenella	Several records from stones and bark in churchyards
Rhynchostegium confertum	Widely distributed in damp, shady situations
Rhynchostegium megapolitanum	Found on chippings in one churchyard
Rhynchstegium murale	Grows on limestone in several churchyards
Rhynchostegium riparioides	Grows by the Grand Union Canal and by woodland streams
Rhytidiadelphus squarrosus	A common plant of grassland and turf
Rhytidiadelphus triquetrus	Recorded from a grassy bank and soil in open woodland
Schistidium apocarpum	Frequently found on stonework, concrete or tarmac
Tetraphis pellucida	On shaded peaty debris in one churchyard
Thamnobryum alopecurum	A robust species of shaded stone, soil and tree boles
Thuidium tamariscinum	Beautiful fronds in woodland on soil, stones and tree boles
Tortula intermedia	On limestone walls and memorials in churchyards
Tortula laevipila	Usually an epiphyte but both M K records are from limestone
Tortula latifolia	On concrete by the River Tove
Tortula muralis	Common on stone, mortar, concrete and compact soil
Tortula marginata	On Olney church in damp shade

Tortula ruralis	From stony ground roofs and wall tops
Tortula subulata	A few plants were found from amongst other mosses at Broughton
Trichostomum brachydontium	Scattered patches on soil in Hazeley Wood
Ulota crispa	One record from woodland elder
Weissia longifolia	
var. *angustifolia*	At Hazeley Wood, on more calcareous soil
var. *longifolia*	Found on soil patches at Hazeley Wood; a new Bucks record
Weissia microstoma	
var. *brachycarpa*	Found on soil patches in the grass at Hazeley Wood
Weissia squarrosa	Found on soil patches in the grass at Hazeley Wood
Wiessia sterilis	Found on mildly calcareous clay at Hazeley Wood
Zygodon viridissimus	Epiphytic on elder and damp shaded stones

Fungi

Ink Caps

The fungi occupy a large and diverse biological kingdom, separate and distinct from both animals and plants. This group includes not just the familiar gilled mushrooms of the woodland floor and open fields and the brackets growing on old logs, but also many other species such as the moulds, yeasts, cup fungi, puffballs, stinkhorns and the rusts and smuts that infect plants. Slime moulds are usually included with the fungi too. It is estimated that there are some 1.5 million species world-wide, but less than a tenth have been identified!

In Britain, something like 20,000 species have been described or found. The fungi are always an important component of any study of the biodiversity of an area. They are found in virtually every habitat in large numbers and play a vital ecological role. Fungi are well known decomposers of vegetation - rotting logs, leaf litter or piles of dung are all home to hundreds of fungal species, decaying material and returning it to the soil. Another vital role is through an intimate relationship between fungi and the roots of flowering plants, the majority of which depend upon this 'mycorrhizal' link to obtain vital nutrients from the soil.

In recording fungi, what is seen is the fruiting body which the organism produces in order to distribute its spores. The organism itself remains in the ground, in the wood or whatever the substrate. It is often necessary to collect specimens of these fruiting bodies in order to determine correctly which species it is. Autumn is the time of year when many of the larger fungi produce their fruiting bodies, although some appear in the spring or at other times and some can be found throughout the year. Since it is not possible to predict exactly when a fungus will fruit and, as most of them are not visible unless they do, many years of observation are needed before a full picture of the fungal biodiversity of a site can be obtained.

The recently formed Buckinghamshire Fungus Group organises fungus forays, including some in Milton Keynes. The records listed below are an unusual mix of species. This reflects the limited amount of recording of larger fungi so far and the limited range of habitats for these. Combined, however, are some very interesting records provided by specialists at the Open University. The list includes some common names, but it is not possible to provide a common name for every species, since there are so many species and most have not been given common names in the past (many of the 'common' names used in popular guides have been simply invented by authors and are not understood by other specialists).

Technically, fungi are mainly classified by using their methods of spore production and the structure of their hyphae. The main groups identified here are:

Agaricales	Gill Fungi and Boleti
Aphyllophorales	Bracket Fungi *etc.*
Ascomycetes	Cup Fungi *etc.*
Gasteromyces	Puff-balls, Earth Stars *etc.*
Heterobasidiomycetes	Jelly Fungi *etc.*
Hyphomycetes, Phycomycetes *etc.*	
Myxomycetes	Slime Moulds
Teleomycetes	Rusts and Smuts

In the list the following should be noted:

> Sp = spring
> Su = summer
> A = autumn
> W = winter
> 1 = January
> 2 *etc.* = other months of the year
> 1-12 = all year
> Specimen = the organism(s) associated specifically for a Milton Keynes record

References and Further Reading

'Field Mycology' - a quarterly magazine published by the British Mycological Society and devoted to the mushroom enthusiast. Published by Cambridge University Press.

Courtecuisse, R. & Duhem, B. (1995) Mushrooms & Toadstools of Britain & Europe. Collins Field Guides

Courtecuisse, R., (1999). Mushrooms of Britain & Europe. Collins Wildlife Trust Guides, HarperCollins

Laessoe, T., (1998). Mushrooms. Eyewitness Handbooks (Dorling Kindersley)

Phillips, R., (1981) Mushrooms and Other Fungi of Great Britain & Europe. Pan Books

Gill Fungi

Agaricus arvensis	Horse Mushroom	A	Pasture grassland or thickets; may form rings
Agaricus campestris	Field Mushroom	S-A	Pastures; may be associated with horses
Agaricus silvicola	Wood Mushroom	A	Coniferous and deciduous woods
Agrocybe praecox	Spring Field-cap	Sp-A	Woods, parks, gardens in grass; woodchip
Amanita citrina	False Death Cap	Su-A	Coniferous or deciduous (esp. with Beech) woods
var. *alba*	White False Death Cap		Completely white form of the above
Amanita muscaria	Fly Agaric	Su-A	Found with Birch (or Spruce) trees
Amanita rubescens	The Blusher	Su-A	Coniferous and deciduous woods
Armillaria mellea s.l.	Honey Fungus	Su-W	Dangerous parasite of trees
Bolbitius vitellinus	Yellow Cow-pat Toadstool	Su-A	Manure, manured soil, rotting straw/wood chip
Calocybe gambosa	St George's Mushroom	Sp	Grass at roadsides, pastures; wood edges
Clitocybe flaccida	Tawny Funnel-cup	Su-W	Clustered groups in woodland leaf litter
Clitocybe geotropa	Rickstone Funnel-cup	A	Mainly deciduous woods
Clitocybe nebularis	Clouded Agaric	Su-A	Mainly woods; form rings or in groups
Clitocybe phyllophila	a Funnel-cup	A	Leaf litter in woods
Clitocybe rivulosa	Lawn Funnel-cap	Su-A	Grassy areas
Collybia butyracea	Butter Cap	Su-W	Leaf litter or rich soil in woods
Collybia confluens	Clustered Tough-shank	Su-A	Leaf letter or rich soil in woods
Collybia dryophila	Russet Tough-shank	Sp-A	Leaf litter or rich soil; mostly woods
Collybia fusipes	Spindle-shank	Su-A	Clustered at base of deciduous trees
Collybia maculata	Cocoa-spot	Su-A	Woodland and heathland
Collybia peronata	Wood Woolly-foot	Su-A	Leaf litter in woods
Conocybe subovalis		A	In pastures and on grassy paths
Coprinus atramentarius	Common Ink-cap	Sp-A	Tufts formed, associated with buried wood
Coprinus comatus	Shaggy Ink-cap	Su-A	Recently disturbed soil; lawns; rubbish heaps
Coprinus cortinatus	an Ink-cap	Sp-A	Soil
Coprinus disseminatus	Fairies' Bonnets	Sp-A	Groups on tree stumps or buried wood
Coprinus galericuliformis	an Ink-cap	Su-A	Soil
Coprinus hiascens	an Ink-cap	Sp-A	Soil, grass, paths
Coprinus lagopus	an Ink-cap	Su-A	Soil or leaf litter
Coprinus leiocephalus	an Ink-cap	Sp-A	Soil, grass, paths
Coprinus micaceus	Glistening Ink-cap	Sp-W	On wood - tree stumps or buried logs
Coprinus niveus	Snow-white Ink-cap	Su-A	On cow or horse dung
Coprinus picaceus	Magpie Ink-cap	Su-A	Soil or leaf litter, especially with beech
Coprinus plicatilis	Little Jap Umbrella	Sp-A	Grass of lawns or other grassy places
Coprinus subimpatiens	an Ink-cap		Soil or humus
Cortinarius hemitrichus		A	Woodland
Cortinarius saturninus		A	Willow

Crepidotus cesatii		A-W	On woody or herbaceous debris
Crepidotus mollis	Soft Slipper Toadstool	Sp-A	On wood; has a gelatinous cap
Crepidotus pubescens		A-W	On woody or herbaceous debris
Entoloma clypeatum		Sp-Su	Under Rose, Hawthorn bushes or Cherry
Entoloma hirtipes		Sp-A	Soil
Entoloma sericeum		Su-A	Grassland, roadsides. woodland
Galerina autumnalis		A-W	On deciduous wood
Galerina mutabilis		Sp-W	Dense clusters on deciduous tree stumps
Galerina triscopa			Specimen on rotten wood
Gymnopilus penetrans		A	On wood, usually Pine or Birch *etc.*
Hebeloma crustuliniforme	Poison Pie	Su-A	Soil
Hebeloma leucosarx		A	Often with Willow
Hemimycena tortuosa		1-12	Undersides of damp, rotten, deciduous logs
Hygrophoropsis aurantiaca	False Chanterelle	A	Coniferous woods; on wood or in litter
Hypholoma fasciculare	Sulphur Tuft	1-12	Clusters on tree stumps
Hypholoma sublateritium	Brick Caps	A	Stumps of deciduous trees
Inocybe geophylla		Su-A	Paths in woodland
var. *lilacina*		Su-A	Paths in woodland
Inocybe langei	Hawthorn hedges		
Laccaria amethystina	Amethyst Deceiver	Su-W	Beech & other deciduous or coniferous woods
Laccaria laccata	Deceiver	Su-W	Woods and heaths
Laccaria tortilis		A	Bare soil in damp wooded areas
Lacrymaria velutina	Weeping Widow	Sp-A	Grass on woodland paths; roadsides
Lactarius cimicarius	Watery Milk-cap	Su-A	Under Oak and Beech
Lactarius mitissimus		A	Deciduous and coniferous woods
Lactarius pyrogalus		A	Under Hazel
Lactarius quietus	Oak Milk-cap	A	Under Oak
Lactarius rufus	Rufous Milk-cap	Sp-A	Under Pine
Lactarius subdulcis		Su-A	Deciduous woods, especially Beech
Lactarius tabidus		Su-A	Damp places under Birch & other decid. trees
Lactarius turpis	Ugly Milk-cap	Su-A	Damp places under Birch & other decid. trees
Leccinum versipelle	Orange Birch Bolete	Su-A	With Birch
Lepiota cristata		Su-A	Woods, roadsides, gardens
Lepista nuda	Wood Blewit	A-W	Woods, hedges and gardens
Lepista saeva	Field Blewit	A-W	Pastureland
Leucoagaricus holosericeus		Su-A	Specimen under Butterfly-bush
Leucocoprinus birnbaumii		Sp-A	With indoor or greenhouse potted plants
Leucopaxillus giganteus	Giant Funnel-cup	Su-A	In grass of pastures, hedgerows and roadsides
Macrolepiota rhacodes	Shaggy Parasol	Su-A	Coniferous woods especially or with shrubs
var. *hortensis*			In grass, woodlands, gardens, greenhouses
Marasmiellus ramealis		Su-A	Dead stems, roots and other woody debris
Marasmius epiphyllus		A	On twigs and leaf stalks
Marasmius oreades	Fairy-ring Champignon	Sp-A	Forms rings in lawns and pastures
Marasmius rotula	Pin-wheel Marasmius	Su-W	Dead twigs and roots
Megacollybia platyphylla		Su-A	Attached to buried wood by white mycelia
Melanoleuca melaleuca		Su-A	Woodland and pasture
Melanoleuca polioleuca		Su-A	Woodland and pasture
Mycena adscendens		1-12	On deciduous wood
Mycena arcangeliana		A	On deciduous wood
Mycena flavoalba		Su-A	In grass, lawns
Mycena galericulata	Bonnet Mycena	1-12	Clustered on deciduous wood
Mycena galopus		Su-A	On soil, leaf litter; bleeds white juice
Mycena galopus			
var. *candida*		Su-A	As above, but pure white
Mycena haematopus		A	On wood; bleeds red juice
Mycena hiemalis		Sp-A	
Mycena inclinata		Su-A	Dense tufts on Oak stumps
Mycena polyadelpha		1-12	On fallen Oak leaves
Mycena sanguinolenta		Su-A	Woodland debris; bleeds red juice
Mycena stylobates		Sp-A	On twigs, leaves and herbaceous stems
Mycena vitilis		A	Woodland soil, leaf litter
Panaeolus rickenii		Su-A	In grass; damp pastures
Panaeolus semiovatus		Sp-W	On dung

Paxillus involutus	Brown Roll-rim	Su-A	Woods with Birch
Pholiota squarrosa	Shaggy Pholiota	A	Dense clusters at the base of deciduous trees
Pleurotellus graminicola		1-12	Grass stems and other herbaceous debris
Pleurotus cornucopiae		Sp-A	Clustered on deciduous tree stumps
Pleurotus dryinus		A	On wood
Pluteus cervinus	Deer Toadstool	1-12	On deciduous tree wood
Pluteus salicinus		Sp-A	On deciduous tree wood
Pluteus luteovirens		A	On deciduous tree wood
Pluteus thomsonii		A	On deciduous tree wood
Pluteus umbrosus		A	On stumps or buried wood
Psathyrella candolleana		Sp-A	On stumps or buried wood
Psathyrella hydrophila	Watery Psathyrella	A	Clustered on deciduous tree wood
Psathyrella prona			
f. *cana*		A	In grass, pastures, pathsides
Pseudoclitocybe cyathiformis	The Goblet	A-W	In grass or woodland debris
Psilocybe semilanceata	Liberty Cap	Su-A	Lawns, pastures, roadsides
Russula betularum		Su-A	Under Birch trees in damp places
Russula cyanoxantha		Su-A	Under deciduous trees
var. *peltereaui*		Su-A	Under deciduous trees
Russula emetica	The Sickener	Su-A	Under Pine trees
Russula fragilis	Fragile Russula	Su-A	Under broad-leaved or coniferous trees
Russula mairei	Beechwood Sickener	A	Under Beech
Russula ochroleuca	Common Yellow Russula	Su-A	Under broad-leaved or coniferous trees
Schizopora paradoxa		Sp-W	White/cream patches on dead wood
Stropharia aeruginosa	Verdigris Agaric	Sp-A	In grass in woods, hedges, parks and gardens
Stropharia aurantiaca		A	Woodchip
Stropharia caerulea		Sp-A	Waste places, wood edges, paths, under Nettles
Tricholmopsis rutilans	Plums and Custard	Su-A	On and around coniferous tree stumps
Tubaria autochthona		Su-A	On buried Hawthorn berries
Tubaria conspersa		A-W	Woody debris
Tubaria furfuracea		1-12	Woody debris
Volvariella speciosa		Su-A	Compost heaps; rotting straw; manure
Xerocomus badius	Bay Bolete	A	Woodland
Xerocomus chrysenteron	Red-cracked Bolete	A	With deciduous trees
Xerula radicata	Rooting Shank	Su-A	Attached to roots, buried wood, some stumps

Bracket Fungi *etc.*

Abortiporus biennis		A	On the ground on roots or buried decid. wood
Bjerkandera adusta		1-12	On wood of deciduous trees
Byssomerulius corium		1-12	Branches and twigs of dead deciduous trees
Chondrostereum purpureum	Silver-leaf Fungus	1-12	Parasite on trees esp. of Rose family *e.g. Prunus* spp.
Clavulina cristata	White Coral Fungus	Su-A	On the soil in broad-leaved or coniferous woods
Clavulina rugosa	Wrinkled Club	Su-A	On the ground in woodland
Coniophora puteana	Wet Rot Fungus	1-12	Tree trunks, decaying wood or timbers
Coriolus (=Trametes) versicolor	Turkey Tail	Sp-W	Small, 'zoned' brackets on deciduous trees
Daedaleopsis confragosa	Blushing Bracket	1-12	Deciduous trees
Fistulina hepatica	Beefsteak Fungus	Su-A	Parasitic on Sweet Chestnut and Oak
Ganoderma adspersum		1-12	Large brackets, on trunks of deciduous trees
Ganoderma applanatum	Artist's Fungus	1-12	Trunks of deciduous trees
Gloiothele lactescens		A	Logs and branches of deciduous trees
Grifola frondosa	Hen of the Woods	A	At the base of Oak and Beech tree trunks
Hapalopilus rutilans		Su-A	On wood of deciduous trees
Hyphodontia sambuci	(Crust Fungus)	1-12	On elder, less often other deciduous trees
Inonotus cuticularis		1-12	On deciduous wood, especially Oak and Beech
Inonotus dryadeus		1-12	Parasitic; at the base of Oaks
Laetiporus sulphureus	Chicken of the Woods	Sp-A	On deciduous trees
Merulius tremellosus		A-Sp	On stumps & branches of, usually decid. wood
Peniophora polygonia		1-12	Often on Poplar. Specimen on Ash
Phlebia merismoides		1-12	On bark of dead deciduous trees esp. Beech
Piptoporus betulinus	Birch Polypore	1-12	Brackets on Birch logs or standing trees
Polyporus brumalis	Winter Polypore	A-Sp	On wood of deciduous trees
Polyporus squamosus	Dryad's Saddle	Sp-Su	Scaly brackets on deciduous trees
Polyporus varius		Sp-A	On dead or dying wood of deciduous trees

Pseudotrametes gibbosa		1-12	On wood of deciduous trees esp. Beech
Rigidoporus ulmarius		1-12	Base of Elm and other deciduous tree trunks
Schizopora paradoxa		1-12	On dead wood, usually of deciduous trees
Serpula lacrymans	Dry Rot Fungus	1-12	A danger to wet wood in buildings; spreads
Skeletocutis nivea		Sp-W	On dead wood of deciduous trees
Stereum gausapatum		1-12	Usually on Oak; bleeds red
Stereum hirsutum	Hairy Stereum	1-12	Stumps and fallen branches of deciduous trees
Stereum rugosum		1-12	On wood of deciduous trees; bleeds red
Trametes versicolor	Turkey Tail	1-12	Small, 'zoned' brackets on deciduous trees
Typhula quisquiliaris		A	Dead stems of Bracken
Tyromyces stipticus		Su-W	On dead (or living) coniferous trees

Cup Fungi *etc.*

Aleuria aurantia	Orange-peel Fungus	A-W	In grass, lawns, roadsides, bare soil
Apiospora montagnei		1-12	Imperfect state on dead grass stems
Ascocoryne cylichnium		Su-W	On dead wood, especially Beech
Ascocoryne sarcoides		Su-W	On dead wood, especially Beech
Belonidium sulphureum		1-12	On dead Nettle stems
Bisporella citrina		A	Gregarious on dead deciduous wood
Botryosphaeria festucae		6-8	On dead grass leaves and stems
Bulgaria inquinans	Black Bulgar	A	Gregarious on dead Oak and Beech
Burenia inundata		7-10	On Fool's Water-cress
Calloria neglecta		Sp	On dead Nettle stems
Ceratocystis ulmi		6-	On Elms; causes Dutch Elm disease
Chlorociboria aeruginescens	Green Wood-cup	Sp-A	Fallen branches of trees, especially Oak
Claviceps purpurea	Ergot	Su-A	Black 'spindles' in grass flowers
Crocicreas cyathoideum		Sp	On dead plant stems
Cryptodiaporthe salicella		1-6	On dead Willow
Cudoniella acicularis		A-W	Gregarious on rotten wood, especially Oak
Cymadothea trifolii	Black Blotch		Black blotch or sooty blotch on Clover
Daldinia concentrica	King Alfred's Cakes	1-12	Black 'balls' on dead or decaying Ash
Epichloe typhina	Choke Disease	esp.8	On grasses
Erysiphe aquilegiae var. ranunculi			Powdery mildew on Creeping Buttercup
Erysiphe cichoracearum			Downy mildew on Aster and other plants
Erysiphe circaeae		9-10	Powdery mildew on Enchanter's-nightshade
Erysiphe cruciferarum			Powdery mildew of Swede and Turnip
Erysiphe depressa			Powdery mildew of Burdock
Erysiphe galeopsidis			Powdery mildew of Hemp-nettle & Ground Ivy
Erysiphe heraclei		7-10	Common on Hogweed and Ground-elder
Erysiphe polygoni			Powdery mildew on Knotgrass
Erysiphe sordida			Powdery mildew on Plantains
Gibberella avenacea			On rotted Barley straw
Helminthosphaeria clavariarum			On fruit bodies of *Clavulina cristata*
Hormotheca robertiana		5-9	On upper surface of overwintered Crane's-bill
Hyalinia dilutella		9-10	On dead stems of Willowherb
Hymenoscyphus repandus		5-10	On various dead stems
Hypomyces aurantius		Sp-A	On fruit body of Polypore fungus
Hypomyces chrysospermus		Su-A	On fruit body of Bolete fungi
Hypospilina pustula		3-8	On dead Oak leaves
Hypoxylon fuscum		1-12	On dead branches and sticks of Hazel
Hypoxylon multiforme		1-12	On bark of Beech and Birch
Lasiosphaeria ovina		9-4	On wood, esp. when decayed by Honey Fungus
Lasiosphaeria spermoides		11-4	On wood, esp. when decayed by Honey Fungus
Leptosphaeria acuta		2-5	On dead Nettle stems
Leptosphaeria doliolum		1-12	On dead stems of *e.g.* Nettles and Umbellifers
Leptotrochila ranunculi		10-7	On living leaves of Buttercups
Lidophia graminis		7	Imperfect state on grasses
Melanomma pulvis-pyrius		9-5	On decorticated deciduous branches
Microsphaera alphitoides		10-11	Powdery mildew on (new) Oak leaves
Microsphaera hedwigii			Powdery mildew on Wayfaring Tree
Microsphaera hypericacearum			Powdery mildew on St John's-wort
Microsphaera lonicerae			Powdery mildew on leaves of Honeysuckle

Microsphaera tortilis			Powdery mildew on Dogwood
Microsphaera trifolii			Powdery mildew on Clover
Mollisia cinerea		1-12	On dead wood and branches of deciduous trees
Mollisia hydrophila		7-8	On dead stem of Reeds
Mycosphaerella isariophora		4-5	On dead leaves of Chickweeds
Nectria cinnabarina	Coral Spot	1-12	Red flasks or pink pustules on dead wood
Nectria lugdunensis		1-12	Aquatic; in foam or scum in running water
Peziza domiciliana		1-12	In sand, plaster, buildings
Peziza micropus		9-11	On rotten wood of deciduous trees
Peziza repanda		Sp-A	In leaves around stumps; sawdust
Peziza varia		1-12	Specimen on brickwork/mortar. Also sawdust
Pezizella alniella		10-4	On old female catkins of Alder
Phaeosphaeria fuckelii			Dead grass stems esp. Reed Canary-grass
Phomatospora berkeleyi		2-9	On dead grass stems
Phomatospora dinemasporium		1-12	Dead stems etc. of grasses, sedges and rushes
Phyllachora graminis			On living and dead leaves of some grasses
Phyllactinia guttata		10-12	On new leaves of Hazel and a few other trees
Podosphaera clandestina		10-11	Powdery mildew on Hawthorn
Podosphaera tridactyla		7-10	Powdery mildew on leaves & twigs of Prunus
Protomyces macrosporus		3-10	Living stems and leaves of Ground-elder etc.
Pseudopeziza trifolii			On living leaves of Clover
Rhytisma acerinum	Tar Spot	1-12	On leaves of Sycamore
Rutstroemia firma		A-W	On fallen branches of Oak
Sarea resinae		Sp-A	On resin of coniferous trees
Sawadaea bicornis		10	Powdery mildew under leaves of Maples
Scutellinia scutellata	Eyelash Fungus	Sp-A	On damp humus-rich soil or rotten wood
Sphaerotheca dipsacearum			Powdery mildew on Teasel
Sphaerotheca epilobii			Powdery mildew on Willowherbs
Sphaerotheca ferruginea			Powdery mildew on Great Burnet
Sphaerotheca fugax			Powdery mildew on Crane's-bills
Tapesia fusca		1-12	On fallen branches of deciduous trees esp. Alder
Taphrina betulina	Witch's Broomstick		On Silver Birch
Taphrina deformans	Peach Curl		On Prunus spp.
Taphrina populina	Yellow Leaf Blister	7-9	On living leaves of Poplar
Taphrina pruni	Pocket Plum		On Blackthorn
Xylaria hypoxylon	Candle-snuff	1-12	Short, antler-like white candles on dead wood
Xylaria polymorpha	Dead Man's Fingers	1-12	Stubby black 'fingers' on tree stumps

Puff-balls, Earth Stars etc.

Calvatia gigantea	Giant Puff-ball	Su-A	Up to football-sized balls in grassland
Lycoperdon perlatum	Common Puff-ball	Su-A	Woodland
Lycoperdon pyriforme	Stump Puff-ball	Su-A	On rotting stumps or buried wood
Mutinus caninus	Dog Stinkhorn	Su-A	Leaf litter in woods
Phallus impudicus	Stinkhorn	Su-A	Shape & foul smell characteristic; leaf litter
Scleroderma citrinum	Common Earth-ball	Su-W	On mossy ground or woods on sandy soil

Jelly Fungi etc.

Auricularia auricula-judae	Jew's-ear Fungus	1-12	On Elder and other trees
Auricularia mesenterica	Tripe Fungus	1-12	Stumps and fallen logs of deciduous trees
Calocera cornea		1-12	Twigs and braanches of deciduous trees
Calocera viscosa	Jelly Antler	A	Stumps and roots of coniferous trees
Dacrymyces stillatus		1-12	On damp, decaying wood; fences and posts
Exidia glandulosa	Witches' Butter	1-12	On wood of deciduous trees
Exidia truncata		1-12	On wood of deciduous trees
Myxarium nucleatum		1-12	On twigs and branches of deciduous trees
Tremella foliacea		1-12	On wood of deciduous trees
Tremella mesenterica	Yellow Brain Fungus	1-12	On dead branches of deciduous trees

Hyphomycetes, Phycomycetes etc.

Alatospora acuminata			Aquatic; in foam and scum of running water
Albugo candida	Crucifer White Blister		Specimen on Shepherd's-purse
Albugo tragopogonis			Specimen on Goat's-beard

Anguillospora longissima	Aquatic; in foam or scum of running water
Botrytis cinerea	Specimens on Sweet Chestnut & Buttercup
Camposporium pellucidum	Aquatic; in foam or scum of running water
Cladosporium cladosporioides	Specimen on False Brome
Cladosporium herbarum	Specimen on dead stem of Bluebell
Clavatospora stellata	Aquatic; in foam and scum of running water
Dendryphion comosum	Specimen on dead stem of Nettle
Endophragmiella boothii	Specimen on stem of Bramble
Fusarium culmorum	Specimen on submerged dead leaf of Bur-reed
Fusarium sporotrichoides	Specimen on rotted Barley
Graphium ulmi	
Mastigosporium album	Specimen on Meadow Foxtail
Mycocentrospora acerina	Aquatic; in foam and scum of running water
Periconia atra	Specimen on dead Lesser Pond-sedge
Periconia cookei	Specimen on dead Thistle
Peronospora niessleana	Specimen on living Garlic Mustard
Peronospora parasitica	Specimen on Swine-cress
Peronospora ranunculi	Specimen on Creeping Buttercup
Plasmopara crustosa	Specimens on Wild Angelica & Cow Parsley
Pythium salpingophorum	Specimen on dead root of Willow
Ramularia didyma	Specimen on live leaf of Creeping Buttercup
Ramularia picridis	On Bristly Ox-tongue
Ramularia rubella	Specimens on living leaves of docks
Saprolegnia parasitica	Aquatic; in foam/scum of running water
Sesquicillium microsporum	Specimen on *Stemonitopsis typhina* (slime m.)
Spinellus fusiger	On fruit bodies of *Collybia* spp. & *Mycena* spp.
Tetracladium marchalianum	Aquatic; in foam/scum of running water
Tetracladium setigerum	Aquatic; in foam/scum of running water
Torula herbarum	Specimens on dead stems of Cow Parsley *etc.*
Tricladium angulatum	Aquatic; in foam/scum of running water
Verticillium rexianum	Specimen on *Metatrichia floriformis* (slime m.)

Slime Moulds

Badhamia foliicola	Specimen on woodchip
Comatricha tenerrima	Specimen on Common Reed
Cribraria argillacea	Specimen on fallen branch of Hazel
Enerthenema papillatum	Specimen on bark of Pedunculate Oak
Enteridium lycoperdon	Specimen on standing Birch
Fuligo septica	
var. *flava*	Specimen on fallen branch of Birch
Leocarpus fragilis	Specimen on stem of Bracken
Lycogala epidendrum	On wood of various deciduous trees
Lycogala terrestre	On wood of various deciduous trees
Metatrichia floriformis	Specimen on fallen branch of Birch
Paradiacheopsis solitaria	Specimen on bark of Pedunculate Oak
Stemonitopsis typhina	Specimen on fallen branch of Birch

Rusts and Smuts

Coleosporium tussilaginis	On Colt's-foot and Sow-thistle
Entyloma microsporum	Smut on Buttercup
Melampsora allii-populina	Rust on leaves and bud scales of Poplar
Melampsora capreum	Rust on leaves of Willow
Melampsora epitea	Rust on Willow
Melampsora hypericorum	Rust on St John's-wort
Melampsora populnea	Rust on Dog's-mercury
Melampsoridium betulinum	Rust on leaves of Birch
Miyagia pseudosphaeria	On Sow-thistle
Phragmidium bulbosum	Rust on Bramble
Phragmidium mucronatum	Rust on roses
Phragmidium violaceum	Rust on Bramble
Puccinia calcitrapae	Rust on knapweeds and some thistles
Puccinia caricina	Rust on sedges and nettles

Puccinia caricina var. *ribesii-pendulae*		Rust on Pendulous Sedge
Puccinia caricina var. *urticae-acutiformis*		Rust on Lesser Pond-sedge and Cyperus Sedge
Puccinia circeae		Rust on Enchanter's-nightshade
Puccinia cnici		Rust on some thistles
Puccinia coronata		Rust on grasses
Puccinia glechomatis		Rust on Ground Ivy
Puccinia hieracii		Rust on hawk-weeds, dandelions & knapweeds
Puccinia lapsanae		Rust on Nipplewort
Puccinia malvacearum		Rust on mallows
Puccinia menthae	Mint Rust	Rust on wild and garden mints
Puccinia obscura		Rust on Daisy and woodrush
Puccinia poarum		Rust on meadow-grasses and Colt's-foot
Puccinia punctata		Rust on bedstraws
Puccinia punctiformis		Rust on some thistles
Puccinia sessilis		Rust on Lords-and-Ladies & Reed Canary-grass
Puccinia veronicae		Rust on speedwells
Pucciniastrum circaeae		Rust on Enchanter's-nightshade
Urocystis anemones		Specimen (smut) on Creeping Buttercup
Urocystis eranthidis		Smut on winter Aconite
Uromyces polygoni-aviculariae		Smut on Knotgrass
Ustilago avenae	Loose Smut	Smut on oats and False-oat
Ustilago longissima		Smut on sweet-grasses
Ustilago violacea	Carnation-anther Smut	Smut on pinks and campions
Xenodochus carbonarius		On Great Burnet

Lichens

Lichens are strange (and often beautiful) organisms in that they consist of an intimate (symbiotic) relationship between two different components - an alga and a fungus. The relationship is so specific that separate lichen species are recognised.

They frequently grow in apparently inhospitable situations like walls, roofs, tree trunks and among other plants, such as mosses, but the larger ones are often quite conspicuous. The wide range of colours is produced as a result of their peculiar lifestyle and chemistry. This also means that many of them are sensitive to anything which can upset the delicate symbiotic balance *e.g.* changes in their environment, and their presence (or absence) is often used as an indicator of pollution.

There has not (yet!) been an extensive survey of lichens in Milton Keynes. The list which follows has been drawn up almost exclusively from surveys carried out by Tom Chester in six churchyards, but it does show the wide range of species to be expected in such sites. This range is due, at least in part, to the wide variety of habitats suitable for lichen growth in a churchyard. For example, there is a good variety of solid surfaces with walls and tombs - made of acid (*e.g.* granite) or alkaline (*e.g.* limestone, marble) rocks arranged horizontally, vertically or sloping and facing north, south, east or west. Nutrient enrichment on these surfaces is often brought about by droppings produced by perching birds! Any trees or shrubs may also have lichens growing on them and some may even be intermingled with mosses. Even the chippings within graves may have their own lichen flora.

Key to Churchyards visited:

A	=	Astwood
C	=	Calverton
E	=	Emberton
L	=	Great Linford
H	=	Hardmead
O	=	Olney

References and Further Reading

Barron, G. (1999). Understanding Lichens. Richmond

Chester, T.W. (1997). And Some Fell on Stony Ground: The Saxicolous Churchyard Lichens of Lowland England in British Wildlife Vol.8, No.3

Gilbert, O.L. (2000). Lichens. HarperCollins (New Naturalist series)

Purvis, O.W., Coppins, B.J. & James, P.W. (1994). Checklist of Lichens of Great Britain and Ireland. Natural History Museum.

Acarospora fuscata	E,O	Common on nutrient-rich acid stone
Acarospora rufescens	E	Occasional on tops of recent sandstone headstones
Agonimia tristicula	A,H,O	Frequent among shaded mosses
Amandinea punctata	A,H	Common on nutrient-enriched bark; occ. on acid stone
Arthonia lapidicola	C,E	Occasional on iron-stained, limestone window sills
Aspicilia calcarea	A,C,E,L,H,O	Common on limestone, especially horizontal surfaces
Aspicilia contorta	A,E,H, O	Frequent on limestone, especially horizontal surfaces
Aspicilia subcircinata	O	Occasional on limestone, especially horizontal surfaces
Bacidia rubella	H	Occ. on ironstone. Nationally rare on stone. On trees
Bacidia sabuletorum	E,L,O	Common over shaded mosses
Belonia nidarosiensis	A	Occasional on shaded, vertical limestone
Buellia aethalea	E,O	Common on acid stone rock
Buellia ocellata	O	Occasional on acid stone
Caloplaca aurantia	A,L,E,H,O	Frequent on limestone
Caloplaca chlorina	A,E,O	Frequent on horizontal ironstone
Caloplaca citrina	A,C,E,H,O	Common, especially on rather damp limestone
Caloplaca decipiens	A,C	Occasional on nutrient-enriched limestone
Caloplaca flavescens	A,C,E,L,H,O	Common on limestone

Caloplaca holocarpa	A,C,E,O	Common on limestone marble
Caloplaca lactea	A,O	Occasional on old limestone
Caloplaca saxicola	A,E,H,O	Common on limestone, mortar & concrete.
Caloplaca teicholyta	A,C,E,O	Common on limestone
Caloplaca variabilis	A,E,O	Occasional on horizontal limestone
Candelariella aurella	A,E,O	Common on limestone and marble
Candelariella medians	A,C,E,L,H,O	Common on nutrient-enriched limestone and marble
Candelariella vitellina	A,E,L,O	Common on nutrient-enriched acid stone
Catillaria lenticularis	A,E,H,O	Common, but overlooked, on limestone
Cladonia chlorophaea	A,H,O	Occasional on mossy tops of headstones and walls
Cladonia fimbriata	E,L	Occasional among mosses and over acid chippings
Cliostomum griffithii	H	Frequent on trees
Collema auriforme	L,O	Occasional among damp, shaded mosses
Collema crispum	A,C	Frequent among mosses in wall crevices
Diploicia canescens	A,C,E,H,O	Common on limestone and ironstone
Diploschistes scruposus	L	Occasional on ironstone
Diplotomma alboatrum	A,E,H,O	Common on limestone and mortar
Dirina massiliensis f. *sorediata*	A,C,E,H	Frequent on limestone & mortar on north-facing walls
Haematomma ochroleucum var. *porphyrium*	A,L,H,O	Frequent on vertical shaded stonework & headstone sides
Lecania erysibe	A,C,E,H,O	Frequent, especially on damp, low horizontal ironstone
Lecania turicensis	O	Frequent on south-facing mortar courses of church walls
Lecanora albescens	A,C,E,O	Common on limestone
Lecanora campestris	A,C,E,H,O	Common on limestone and sandstone
Lecanora conizaeoides	A,C,E,L,H,O	Common on wood, bark & acid stone. Pollution tolerant
Lecanora crenulata	A,E,H,O	Common, but overlooked, on limestone
Lecanora dispersa	A,C,E,L,H,O	Common on basic stone; occasional on acid stone
Lecanora expallens	A,E,H,O	Occasional on acid stone; frequent on trees
Lecanora muralis	A,C,E,L,O	Common, especially on horizontal stone and paths
Lecanora pannonica	A	Locally common on vertical, acid stone. Nationally not so
Lecanora orosthea	O	Occasional on vertical acid stone
Lecanora polytropa	A,E,L,O	Common on acid stone, especially granite
Lecanora soralifera	A	Infrequent on horizontal acid stone. An upland species
Lecanora sulphurea	E,L,H,O	Frequent on acid stone. Often with Tephromela atra
Lecidea fuscoatra	L,O	Frequent on horizontal and sloping acid stone
Lecidella carpathica	O	Occasional on ironstone and brick
Lecidella scabra	A,E,H,O	Common, but overlooked, on horizontal, acid stone
Lecidella stigmatea	A,C,E,H,O	Frequent on limestone, plaster and ironstone
Lepraria incana	A,C,E,L,H,O	Common on shaded acid stone and the bases of trees
Lepraria lesdainii	O	Occasional on walls in deep crevices between stones
Leproloma vouauxii	A,E,H,O	Frequent on shaded limestone and over mosses
Leptogium gelatinosum	O	Occasional among mosses over chippings or on wall tops
Leptogium plicatile	O	Infrequent among mosses on boundary walls
Leptogium schraderi	O	Infrequent among mosses on boundary walls
Micarea denigrata	A,L	Frequent, but overlooked, on worked wood
Micrarea erratica	A	Occasional on sandstone
Parmelia glabratula ssp. *fuliginosa*	O	Not infrequent on horizontal acid stone, especially granite
Parmelia mougeotii	E,O	Frequent on acid stone, especially granite chippings
Parmelia subrudecta	E,O	Rare on nutrient-enriched acid stone; commoner on trees
Parmelia sulcata	L,H,O	Common on trees; less so on nutrient-enriched acid stone
Perusaria amara	L,H	Occasional on vertical acid stone
Phaeophyscia nigricans	O	On nutrient-enriched limestone, marble and concrete
Phaeophyscia orbicularis	A,C,E,L,H,O	Common on nutrient-enriched, basic stone. And on trees
Phlyctis argena	A,E	Occasional on fairly shaded, vertical stone and tree trunks
Physcia adscendens	A,C,E,H,O	Common on nutrient-enriched, basic stone. And on trees
Physcia caesia	C,E,L,H,O	Frequent on nutrient-enriched basic and acid stone
Physcia dubia	E,L,H	Occasional on nutrient-enriched acid stone
Physconia grisea	A,C,E,L,H,O	Common on nutrient-enriched, basic stone. And on trees
Placynthiella icmalea	H	Frequent on rotting wood
Polysporina simplex	E	Frequent, but overlooked, on acid stone especially granite
Porpidia tuberculosa	A,E,L,O	Frequent on acid stone

Species	Sites	Notes
Protoblastenia rupestris	A,C,E,H,O	Common; on hard, horizontal and sloping limestone
Psilolechia leprosa	E,O	Occasional on copper-stained mortar and limestone. First national record on wood of a wooden peg next to the lightning conductor at Olney
Psilopechia lucida	A,C,E,L,H,O	Common on east- and north-facing acid stone and brick
Ramalina farinacea	C	Infrequent on acid stone and trees
Ramalina fastigiata	C	Extremely rare on churchyard stone. Infrequent on trees
Rhizocarpon reductum	A,O	Frequent on horizontal acid stone, especially granite
Rinodina gennarii	C,L,O	Frequent on limestone & mortar, esp. south-facing walls
Rinodina teichophila	A,C,L,O	Frequent on ironstone, esp. window sills & headstone tops
Sarcopyrenia gibba	A,E,H,O	Fruits frequent in 'bare' patches on horizontal limestone
Sarcogyne regularis	E	Frequent, but overlooked, on cemented wall tops
Scoliciosporum chlorococcum		Frequent, but overlooked, on twigs
Scoliciosporum umbrinum	A,E,O	On acid stone, including run-off from lead flashing
Tephromela atra	A,C,E,L,O	Frequent on acid stone; more occasional on limestone
Toninia aromatica	E,H	Frequent in mortar crevices and the tops of chest tombs
Trapelia involuta	E	Infrequent on damp, horizontal sandstone and brick
Trapelia placodioides	A	Occasional on damp, horizontal sandstone and brick
Trapeliopsis granulosa	H	Frequent on rotting wood
Verrucaria baldensis	A,E,L	Common on sloping and horizontal limestone
Verrucaria glaucina	E,H,O	Frequent on limestone, especially boundary walls
Verrucaria hochstetteri	E,H	Common on hard, sloping and horizontal limestone
Verrucaria macrostoma	E,H	On limestone
Verrucaria macrostoma f. *furfuracea*	E,H	Common on limestone walls
Verrucaria muralis	A,E,L,H,O	Common, especially on mortar
Verrucaria nigrescens	A,C,E,O	Common especially on rather damp limestone
Verrucaria viridula	A,C,E,H,L,O	On limestone
Xanthoria calcicola	A,C,E,L,O	Common on nutrient-enriched limestone
Xanthoria candelaria	A,H,O	Frequent on nutrient-enriched sandstone and some trees
Xanthoria elegans	E	Infrequent on recent limestone, concrete and tiling
Xanthoria parietina	C,E,O	Common on nutrient-enriched limestone and some trees
Xanthoria polycarpa		Common on twigs in nutrient-enriched situations

Mammals

Badger

Cats, dogs, horses, goats, sheep, cows and pigs are all mammals, but do not feature in the list which follows as they are not part of the wildlife of the Borough. They are so well-known as they are closely associated with man, either as pets or are domesticated as a source of food, either directly as for meat, or for milk and its products. The production of milk is one of the characteristics which separate the mammals from all other animals. The other main, observable characteristic is the possession of hair.

Few of the mammals which appear in the list are regularly seen, but those which are include Rabbits (introduced by the Romans), Grey Squirrels (introduced from North America), Brown Hare (native) and Fox (native). Deer of various sorts may be glimpsed occasionally and bats (the only flying mammals) may be seen overhead.

So - how do we know that all the other mammals are present in Milton Keynes? Without seeing the animals you have to rely on a variety of signs. Footprints (tracks) in the ground are all diagnostic, droppings (*e.g.* spraints) of various shapes and sizes, size and shape of pathways through vegetation and holes made, bits of fur or hair on twigs or barbed wire fences are all used by experts to piece together the whereabouts of the various mammals. For small mammals, the way they break into nuts or leave moth wings behind after feeding can also be useful. Foxes are unusual in that they produce a characteristic smell which may persist where they have been for some time; they also bark. Another method available to the trained and licensed mammalologist is that of trapping small mammals, identifying them and then releasing them.

Bats pose special problems: most are tiny, most fly at night, but none is blind, none will fly into your hair nor yet do they live in belfries (though the odd male may live inside the church itself and be seen flying at dusk). In recent years, identity has been confirmed by the use of 'bat detectors'. These are sophisticated pieces of electronic apparatus which can pick up the high frequency sounds produced by the bats and transform them into lower, audible-to-us frequency patterns. Each is so characteristic that the species may be identified. The identification of the Soprano Pipistrelle is a recent discovery made possible by this means. Bats do not make nests, but do roost in holes in trees, barns, ice-houses, church porches, old and new houses (behind hanging tiles and boarding or in roof spaces). The different species have different roost preferences, but some may share the same roost.

The order in which the mammals appear in the following list is that used to show relationships.

References and Further Reading

Corbet, G.B. and Southern, H.N. (eds.) (1977 2nd ed.) The Handbook of British Mammals. Blackwell Scientific. Publication for The Mammal Society

Corbet, G.B. (1969) The Identification of British Mammals. British Museum (Natural History)

Lawrence, M.J. and Brown, R.W. (1967) Mammals of Britain their Tracks, Trails and Signs. Blandford Press

Matthews, L.H. (1968). (2nd ed.) British Mammals. Collins (New Naturalist series)

Richardson, P. (1985). Bats. Whittet Books

Erinaceus europaeus	Hedgehog	N	Urban; woods and hedges in 'city' area
Talpa europaea	Mole	N	Woods, fields, hedges, parkland, churchyards
Sorex araneus	Shrew, Common	N	Woods, hedges, fields, parkland
Sorex minutus	Shrew, Pygmy	N	Woods, hedges, long grass
Sorex fodiens	Shrew, Water	N	Infrequent; ditches, streams
Myotis daubentoni	Bat, Daubenton's	N	Over lakes and canal
Plecotus auritus	Bat, Brown Long-eared	N	Secretive; deciduous woods, parkland
*Myotis mystacinus	Bat, Whiskered	N	Fly near water or in woodland
*Myotis brandtii	Bat, Brandt's	N	As above; difficult to separate the two spp.
Myotis nattereri	Bat, Natterer's	N	Around trees and water

Nyctalus noctula	Bat, Noctule	N	Hunt high over woods, hedgerows and water
Pipistrellus pipistrellus	Pipistrelle, Common	N	Gardens, hedgerows, around water
Pipistrellus pygmaeus	Pipistrelle, Soprano	N	Gardens, hedgerows, around water
Vulpes vulpes	Fox	N	Common. Urban or open countryside
Mustela erminea	Stoat	N	Woods, hedges, open fields; crossing roads
Mustela nivalis	Weasel	N	Woods, hedges, open fields; crossing roads
Mustela putorius ssp. *furo*	Ferret	I	May escape from captivity; feral
Mustela vison	Mink	I	Rivers, canals and adjacent land, lakes
Meles meles	Badger	N	Woods, hedges, open fields; many road deaths
Lutra lutra	Otter	N	Rare; rivers and banks
Dama dama	Deer, Fallow	I	Little Linford Wood
Capreolus capreolus	Roe-deer	N	Recently returned to Salcey Forest
Muntiacus reevesi	Muntjac, Chinese	I	Woods, hedges, gardens; road deaths
Hydropotes inermis	Water-deer, Chinese	I	One road death reported at Lathbury
Lepus capensis	Hare, Brown	N	Not common; open grassy places
Oryctolagus cuniculus	Rabbit	I	Woods, hedges, fields; wide road verges
Sciurus carolinensis	Squirrel, Grey	I	Woods, tall trees, hedgerows, parks, gardens
Sciurus vulgaris	Squirrel, Red	N	One confirmed escapee in 1997
Muscardinus avellanarius	Dormouse	N	Recently reintroduced to one wood
Micromys minutus	Harvest-mouse	N	Long grass adjacent to hedges
Apodemus sylvaticus	Wood-mouse	N	Dense woods; fields and hedges in autumn
Mus musculus	Mouse, House	I	Urban
Rattus norvegicus	Rat, Brown	I	Urban gardens, farmyards, adjacent to water
Clethrionomys glareolus	Bank-vole	N	Dense woods
Arvicola terrestris	Water-vole	N	Rivers, streams, canals; much decreased recently
Microtus agrestis	Field-vole	N	Open grass

* Because of the difficulties in separating these two species they are usually grouped together when recording. However, there are definite records for whiskered Bat whilst others may be for either species.

Birds

Lapwing

Birdwatching is probably the most popular aspect of natural history. People of all ages can indulge and can start at home, simply by looking out of the window. Nowadays, it might be the magpies which draw most attention to themselves; they certainly seem to be more common than they were. When members of the Natural History Society started to write articles for *The Bucks Standard* early in the 1970s, an easily recognisable logo in black and white was required - so the magpie became our emblem and, later, the title of our Newsletter. Blackbirds probably come next in awareness, closely followed by Sparrows and Starlings, though their numbers are not as great as they were a few years ago.

Making observations beyond the window and garden soon catch on once the habit of birdwatching has begun. A wide variety of features capture the imagination - the red breast of the Robin, the hovering of the Kestrel, the screeching of Swifts or the welcoming of better weather by listening for the first cuckoo in spring, and even the mess left by the vast numbers of Canada Geese. Once the identification of common species has been mastered, there comes the need to learn more - to be able to see more species, to find out where they live, to find out how many there are, to discover if they are around for the whole year or only part of it. If only part, which part? Where are they for the rest of the year, and why?

Not surprisingly, one of the earliest activities of the Natural History Society was the spawning of a monthly bird bulletin which developed into the North Bucks Bird Report in 1977. This still flourishes, with many of our members still contributing records. Like so many aspects of natural history, the more one knows about a particular subject, the more one wants to know. With birds, it can be the acquisition of a long list of birds seen ('twitching'); it can be the finding out of a lot of detail about species of one habitat (a wood or participating in the winter wildfowl counts) or becoming an expert in one or a few species (*e.g.* owls, the swift).

The following list contains over 230 species (plus 28 escapes) arranged (where possible) in the order (Voous order) now generally accepted by ornithologists. Some of them are well-known to most people, some well-known to a few and a few known only to a few people. These last ones are those which help to make birdwatching so popular: the hope that one day you will see something very rare and special.

The development of the urban environment of Milton Keynes has meant that there are far more people looking for birds, so our knowledge is increasing. The most outstanding environmental change for birds has undoubtedly been the construction of the balancing lakes with their changing water levels, large areas of open water *etc.* as at Caldecotte, Lodge Lake, Tongwell, Walton and Willen. They have attracted far more species of bird to the area than was ever imagined possible. The other lakes, developed from mineral extraction sites (as at Bletchley brick pits (with and without water), Cosgrove, Emberton, Linford, Newport Pagnell and Stony Stratford), are also still very attractive to birds. Certainly the birds associated with water are the best recorded within Milton Keynes.

In the list which follows the status of the birds refers to Milton Keynes only.

References and Further Reading

Flegg, J. (1993). Green Guide Birds of Britain and Europe. Aura Books

Jonson, L. (1992). Birds of Europe with North Africa and the Middle East. Helm

Lack, P. & Ferguson, D. (1993). The Birds of Buckinghamshire. Buckinghamshire Bird Club.

Mullarney, K., Svensson, L., Zetterstrom, D., Grant, P. J. (1999). Bird Guide. HarperCollins.

1987 to 1999 Buckinghamshire Bird Reports. Buckinghamshire Bird Club.

Gavia stellata	Red-throated Diver	Very rare vagrant, 1 record: Willen 1989
Gavia arctica	Black-throated Diver	Very rare vagrant, 1 record: New Bradwell 1996
Gavia immer	Great Northern Diver	Very rare vagrant, 2 records: Willen 1994, Caldecotte 1997-98
Tachybaptus ruficollis	Little Grebe	Fairly common resident & winter visitor
Podiceps cristatus	Great Crested Grebe	Common resident & winter visitor
Podiceps grisegena	Red-necked Grebe	Uncommon migrant & winter visitor
Podiceps auritus	Slavonian Grebe	Annual migrant & winter visitor
Podiceps nigricollis	Black-necked Grebe	Annual migrant
Fulmaris glacialis	Fulmar	Rare vagrant 3 records:1989, 1990, 1992
Puffinus gravis	Great Shearwater	Very rare vagrant, 1 record: Willen 1999
Puffinus puffinus	Manx Shearwater	Very rare vagrant, 1 record: found dead 1996
Oceanodroma leucorhoa	Leach's Petrel	Very rare vagrant, 2 record: 1987 & 1989
Morus bassana	Gannet	Very rare vagrant, 1 record: Caldecotte 1994
Phalacrocorax carbo	Cormorant	Common migrant & winter visitor
Phalacrocorax aristotelis	Shag	Uncommon migrant
Botaurus stellaris	Bittern	Irregular migrant & winter visitor
Nycticorax nycticorax	Night Heron	Very rare vagrant, 1 record: Willen 1987
Egretta garzetta	Little Egret	Rare vagrant & escaped
Ardea alba	Great White Egret	Very rare vagrant, 1 record: Linford 1994
Ardea cinerea	Grey Heron	Common resident
Platalea leucorodia	Spoonbill	Very rare vagrant, 1 record: Willen 1995
Cygnus olor	Mute Swan	Common resident
Cygnus columbianus	Bewick's Swan	Annual passage migrant
Cygnus cygnus	Whooper Swan	Annual passage migrant
Anser fabalis	[Bean Goose]	Presumed escaped
Anser brachyrhynchus	Pink-footed Goose	Scarce vagrant & escaped
Anser albifrons	White-fronted Goose	Scarce vagrant
Anser anser	Greylag Goose	Introduced resident
Anser caerulescens	[Snow Goose]	Escaped/released
Branta canadensis	Canada Goose	Common introduced resident
Branta leucopsis	[Barnacle Goose]	Escaped/released
Branta bernicla	Brent Goose	Uncommon migrant
Alopochen aegyptiacus	[Egyptian Goose]	Escaped/released
Tadorna tadorna	Shelduck	Fairly common migrant
Aix galericulata	Mandarin	Uncommon resident
Anas penelope	Wigeon	Common migrant & winter visitor
Anas strepera	Gadwall	Scarce resident & common winter visitor
Anas crecca	Teal	Scarce resident & common winter visitor
Anas platyrhynchos	Mallard	Abundant resident & common winter visitor
Anas acuta	Pintail	Scarce migrant & winter visitor
Anas querquedula	Garganey	Regular passage migrant
Anas clypeata	Shoveler	Scarce resident & common winter visitor
Netta rufina	Red-crested Pochard	Scarce migrant, origin uncertain
Aythya ferina	Pochard	Scarce resident & common winter visitor
Aythya collaris	Ring-necked Duck	Rare vagrant, 3 records: 1991, 1994, 1996
Aythya fuligula	Tufted Duck	Common resident & winter visitor
Aythya marila	Scaup	Uncommon winter migrant
Somateria mollissima	Eider	Very rare vagrant, 2 records: Linford 1993
Clangula hyemalis	Long-tailed Duck	Rare vagrant, 3 records: 1991, 1996, 1999
Menalitta negra	Common Scoter	Uncommon passage migrant
Bucephela clangula	Goldeneye	Fairly common migrant & winter visitor
Mergus albellus	Smew	Uncommon winter visitor
Mergus serrator	Red-breasted Merganser	Scarce winter migrant
Mergus merganser	Goosander	Common winter visitor
Oxyura jamaicensis	Ruddy Duck	Fairly common migrant
Pernis apivorus	Honey Buzzard	Rare vagrant, 5 records
Milvus milvus	Red Kite	Rare vagrant,
Circus aeruginosus	Marsh Harrier	Uncommon passage migrant
Circus cyaneus	Hen Harrier	Very rare vagrant, 1 record: Shenley Brook End 1987
Accipiter gentilis	Goshawk	Scarce resident
Accipiter nisus	Sparrowhawk	Common resident
Buteo buteo	Buzzard	Scarce resident & uncommon migrant

Pandion haliaetus	Osprey	Uncommon passage migrant
Falco tinnunculus	Kestrel	Common resident
Falco columbarius	Merlin	Uncommon winter migrant
Falco subbuteo	Hobby	Fairly common passage migrant
Falco peregrinus	Peregrine	Scarce winter visitor
Alectoris rufa	Red-legged Partridge	Fairly common introduced resident
Perdix perdix	Grey Partridge	Scarce resident, declining
Coturnix coturnix	Quail	Scarce passage migrant
Phasianus colchicus	Pheasant	Common introduced resident
Chrysolophus pictus	Golden Pheasant	Scarce released resident
Chrysolophus amherstiae	Lady Amherst's Pheasant	Uncommon released resident
Rallus aquaticus	Water Rail	Fairly common passage migrant & winter visitor
Porzana porzana	Spotted Crake	Very rare vagrant, 2 records: Willen 1995
Gallinula chloropus	Moorhen	Abundant resident
Fulica atra	Coot	Abundant resident, declining
Grus grus	Crane	Very rare vagrant, 1 record: Fenny Stratford 1993
Haematopus ostralegus	Oystercatcher	Fairly common passage migrant
Himantopus himantopus	Black-winged Stilt	Very rare vagrant, 1 record: Willen 1988
Recurvirostra avosetta	Avocet	Scarce vagrant
Burhinus oedicnemus	Stone Curlew	Very rare vagrant, 1 record: Linford 1999
Charadrius dubins	Little Ringed Plover	Annual summer visitor & passage migrant, rare breeder
Charadrius hiaticula	Ringed Plover	Common summer visitor & passage migrant, fairly common breeder
Pluvialis dominica	American Golden Plover	Very rare vagrant, 1 record: Broughton 1991
Pluvialis apricaria	Golden Plover	Abundant winter visitor
Pluvialis squatarola	Grey Plover	Uncommon passage migrant
Vanellus vanellus	Lapwing	Common winter visitor & fairly common resident, declining
Calidris canutus	Knot	Scarce vagrant
Calidris alba	Sanderling	Fairly common passage migrant
Calidris minuta	Little Stint	Fairly common passage migrant
Calidris temminckii	Temminck's Stint	Scarce passage migrant
Calidris melanotos	Pectoral Sandpiper	Very rare vagrant, 2 records: Linford 1989, Willen 1995
Calidris ferruginea	Curlew Sandpiper	Scarce passage migrant
Calidris alpina	Dunlin	Common passage migrant
Philomachus pugnax	Ruff	Common passage migrant
Lymnocryptes minimus	Jack Snipe	Uncommon winter visitor
Gallinago gallinago	Snipe	Common winter visitor & scarce resident
Scolopax rusticola	Woodcock	Scarce resident & passage migrant
Limosa limosa	Black-tailed Godwit	Common passage migrant
Limosa lapponica	Bar-tailed Godwit	Fairly common passage migrant
Numenius phaeopus	Whimbrel	Common passage migrant
Numenius arquata	Curlew	Common passage migrant
Tringa erythropus	Spotted Redshank	Fairly common passage migrant
Tringa totanus	Redshank	Common passage migrant & scarce breeder
Tringa nebularia	Greenshank	Fairly common passage migrant
Tringa ochropus	Green Sandpiper	Common passage migrant & scarce winter visitor
Tringa glareola	Wood Sandpiper	Scarce passage migrant
Actitis hypoleucos	Common Sandpiper	Common passage migrant & scarce winter visitor
Arenaria interpres	Turnstone	Fairly common passage migrant
Phalaropus lobatus	Red-necked Phalarope	Rare vagrant, 3 records: 1989, 1992, 1995
Phalaropus fulicarius	Grey Phalarope	Very rare vagrant, 2 records: Willen 1987, Linford 1998
Stercorarius pomarinus	Pomarine Skua	Very rare vagrant, 1 record: Campbell Park 1994
Stercorarius skua	Great Skua	Very rare vagrant, 1 record: Willen 1987
Larus melanocephalus	Mediterranean Gull	Uncommon passage migrant & winter visitor
Larus pipixcan	Franklin's Gull	Very rare vagrant, 1 record: Willen 1999
Larus minutus	Little Gull	Fairly common passage migrant
Larus ridibundus	Black-headed Gull	Abundant passage migrant & winter visitor
Larus delawarensis	Ring-billed Gull	Very rare vagrant, 1 record: Willen 1994
Larus carnus	Common Gull	Common passage migrant & winter visitor
Larus fuscus	Lesser Black-backed Gull	Common passage migrant & winter visitor
Larus argentatus	Herring Gull	Fairly common passage migrant & winter visitor
Larus glaucoides	Iceland Gull	Uncommon winter visitor
Larus hyperboreus	Glaucous Gull	Scarce winter visitor
Larus marinus	Great Black-backed Gull	Fairly common passage migrant & winter visitor

Rissa tridactyla	Kittiwake	Uncommon passage migrant
Sterna caspia	Caspian Tern	Very rare vagrant, 2 records: Willen 1992, Caldecotte 1996
Sterna sandvicensis	Sandwich Tern	Scarce passage migrant
Sterna dougallii	Roseate Tern	Very rare vagrant, 1 record: Willen 1994
Sterna hirundo	Common Tern	Common passage migrant & breeder
Sterna paradisaea	Arctic Tern	Irregular passage migrant
Sterna albifrons	Little Tern	Scarce passage migrant
Chlidonius hybridus	Whiskered Tern	Very rare vagrant, 1 record: Willen 1994
Chlidonius niger	Black Tern	Fairly common passage migrant
Alca torda	Razorbill	Very rare vagrant, 1 record: Caldecotte 1996
Alle alle	Little Auk	Very rare vagrant, 2 records: Willen 1988 & 1993
Columbia livia	Rock Dove/Feral Pigeon	Common resident
Columbia oenas	Stock Dove	Uncommon resident
Columbia palumbus	Woodpigeon	Abundant resident
Streptopelia decaocto	Collared Dove	Common resident
Streptopelia turtur	Turtle Dove	Scarce summer visitor & breeder, declining
Cuculus canorus	Cuckoo	Fairly common passage migrant & breeder
Tyto alba	Barn Owl	Uncommon resident & released
Athene noctua	Little Owl	Uncommon introduced resident
Strix aluco	Tawny Owl	Fairly common resident
Asio otus	Long-eared Owl	Uncommon winter migrant
Asio flammeus	Short-eared Owl	Scarce passage migrant
Apus apus	Swift	Common summer visitor & breeder
Alcedo atthis	Kingfisher	Fairly common resident
Upupa epops	Hoopoe	Very rare vagrant, 1 record: North Crawley 1996
Jynx torquilla	Wryneck	Very rare vagrant, 2 records: Newport Pagnell & Wolverton 1997
Picus viridis	Green Woodpecker	Common resident
Dendrocopos major	Great Spotted Woodpecker	Common resident
Dendrocopos minor	Lesser Spotted Woodpecker	Scarce resident
Alauda arvensis	Skylark	Uncommon resident, migrant & winter visitor
Riparia riparia	Sand Martin	Common summer visitor & scarce breeder
Hirundo rustica	Swallow	Common summer visitor & fairly common breeder, declining
Delichon urbica	House Martin	Common summer visitor & breeder
Anthus novaeseelandiae	Richard's Pipit	Very rare vagrant, 1 record: Blue Lagoon 1990
Anthus trivialis	Tree Pipit	Scarce passage migrant
Anthus pratensis	Meadow Pipit	Common passage migrant & winter visitor, scarce breeder
Anthus petrosus	Rock Pipit	Scarce passage migrant
Anthus spinoletta	Water Pipit	Very rare vagrant, 2 records: Willen 1990 & 1991
Motacilla flava	Yellow Wagtail	Fairly common passage migrant
Motacilla cinerea	Grey Wagtail	Fairly common passage & winter migrant, scarce breeder
Motacilla alba	Pied Wagtail	Common resident & passage migrant
Bombycilla garrulus	Waxwing	Irruptive rare vagrant, 10 records covering 1991, 1996 & 1997
Troglodytes troglodytes	Wren	Abundant resident
Prunella modularis	Dunnock	Common resident
Erithacus rubecula	Robin	Common resident & passage migrant
Luscinia megarhynchos	Nightingale	Scarce summer migrant & breeder
Phoenicurus ochruros	Black Redstart	Scarce passage migrant
Phoenicurus phoenicurus	Redstart	Fairly common passage migrant & scarce breeder
Saxicola rubetra	Whinchat	Fairly common passage migrant
Saxicola torquata	Stonechat	Fairly common passage migrant & scarce winter visitor
Oenanthe oenanthe	Wheatear	Common passage migrant
Turdus torquatus	Ring Ouzel	Scarce passage migrant
Turdus merula	Blackbird	Abundant resident & winter migrant
Turdus pilaris	Fieldfare	Abundant winter visitor
Turdus philomelos	Song Thrush	Fairly common resident & winter migrant
Turdus iliacus	Redwing	Abundant winter visitor
Turdus viscivorus	Mistle Thrush	Fairly common resident
Cettia cetti	Cetti's Warbler	Rare vagrant, 5 records
Locustella naevia	Grasshopper Warbler	Regular passage migrant & scarce breeder
Locustella fluviatilis	River Warbler	Very rare vagrant, 1 record: Linford 1997
Acrocephalus paludicola	Aquatic Warbler	Very rare vagrant, 1 record: Blue Lagoon 1990
Acrocephalus schoenobaenus	Sedge Warbler	Common summer visitor & breeder
Acrocephalus scirpaceus	Reed Warbler	Common summer visitor & breeder

Sylvia curruca	Lesser Whitethroat	Uncommon summer visitor & breeder
Sylvia communis	Whitethroat	Fairly common summer visitor & breeder
Sylvia borin	Garden Warbler	Common summer visitor & breeder
Sylvia atricapilla	Blackcap	Common summer visitor & breeder, scarce winter visitor
Phylloscopus sibilatrix	Wood Warbler	Scarce passage migrant
Phylloscopus collybita	Chiffchaff	Common passage migrant & summer visitor, scarce winter visitor
Phylloscopus trochilus	Willow Warbler	Abundant summer visitor, passage migrant & breeder
Regulus regulus	Goldcrest	Common resident & passage migrant
Regulus ignicapillus	Firecrest	Scarce passage migrant
Muscicapa striata	Spotted Flycatcher	Uncommon summer visitor & passage migrant
Ficedula hypoleuca	Pied Flycatcher	Scarce passage migrant
Panurus biarmicus	Bearded Tit	Rare vagrant, 3 records: 1988, 1992, 1994
Aegithalos caudatus	Long-tailed Tit	Abundant resident
Parus palustris	Marsh Tit	Uncommon resident, declining
Parus montanus	Willow Tit	Scarce resident, declining
Parus ater	Coal Tit	Common resident
Parus caeruleus	Blue Tit	Abundant resident
Parus major	Great Tit	Abundant resident
Sitta europaea	Nuthatch	Fairly common resident
Certhia familiaris	Treecreeper	Fairly common resident
Oriolus oriolus	Golden Oriole	Very rare vagrant, 1 record: Willen 1997
Lanius excubitor	Great Grey Shrike	Very rare vagrant, 2 records: Linford 1987, Woughton Park 1994
Garrulus glandarius	Jay	Fairly common resident
Pica pica	Magpie	Abundant resident
Corvus monedula	Jackdaw	Abundant resident
Corvus frugilegus	Rook	Abundant resident
Corvus corone	Carrion Crow	Abundant resident
Corvus corax	Raven	Very rare vagrant, 1 record: Stoke Goldington 1999
Sturnus vulgaris	Starling	Abundant resident & winter visitor, declining
Passer domesticus	House Sparrow	Common resident, declining
Passer montanus	Tree Sparrow	Scarce resident, declining
Fringilla coelebs	Chaffinch	Abundant resident & common passage migrant
Fringilla montifringilla	Brambling	Fairly common passage migrant & winter visitor
Carduelis chloris	Greenfinch	Common resident & winter migrant
Carduelis carduelis	Goldfinch	Common resident & winter migrant
Carduelis spinus	Siskin	Common winter visitor
Carduelis cannabina	Linnet	Uncommon resident & passage migrant, declining
Carduelis flammea	Redpoll	Fairly common winter visitor & scarce breeder
Loxia curvirostra	Crossbill	Irruptive migrant & scarce breeder
Pyrrhula pyrrhula	Bullfinch	Uncommon resident
Coccothraustes coccothraustes	Hawfinch	Rare vagrant, 3 records: 1988, 1989, 1995
Plectrophenax nivalis	Snow Bunting	Rare vagrant, 4 records
Emberiza citrinella	Yellowhammer	Uncommon resident, declining
Emberiza schoeniclus	Reed Bunting	Fairly common resident & winter migrant, declining
Miliaria miliaria	Corn Bunting	Uncommon resident, declining

The following have been recorded, but are known to have been escapes from captivity:

Black Swan; Lesser White-fronted Goose; Bar-headed Goose; Ruddy Shelduck; Wood Duck; Cockatiel; Canary; Magellan Goose; Cape Shelduck; Chiloe Wigeon; Sacred Ibis; Fulvous Whistling Duck; Ross's Goose; White-cheeked Pintail (aka Bahama Pintail); African Grey Parrot; Zebra Finch; Budgerigar; Reeve's Pheasant; Chukar; Cape Teal; Sulphur-crested Cockatoo; Golden-backed Weaver; Yellow-billed Stork; Yellow-fronted Canary; Sudan Golden Sparrow; Grey Teal; Black-necked Swan; Muscovy Duck.

Reptiles

Anguis fragilis	Slow Worm	N	Undisturbed grassland; old orchards
Emys orbicularis	European Pond Terrapin	I	Very rare; cast out from aquaria
Lacerta vivipara	Viviparous/Common Lizard	N	Rare; suns itself on rocks
Natrix natrix	Grass Snake	N	Rough grass

Amphibians

Bufo bufo	Common Toad	N	In and around ponds;. gardens
Rana temporaria	Common Frog	N	As above, but more aquatic
Triturus helveticus	Palmate Newt	N	Common; ponds
Titurus cristatus	Crested Newt	N	Nationally rare but in several ponds locally
Triturus vulgaris	Smooth Newt	N	Ponds

Fish

Abramis brama	Common Bream	N	Ouse, Ouzel, Canal, stillwaters
Acipenser ruthenus	Sterlet	I	Introduced into 1 or 2 stillwaters
Alburnus alburnus	Bleak	N	Ouse, Ouzel, Canal
Anguilla anguilla	Eel	N	Ouse, Ouzel, Canal, Loughton Brook, stillwaters
Barbus barbus	Barbel	N	Reintroduced into Ouse only
Blicca bjoerkna	Silver Bream	N	Ouse, Ouzel, Canal, stillwaters
Carassius auratus	Goldfish	I	Introduced into some ponds
Carassius carassius	Crucian Carp	I	Introduced into a few stillwaters
Cobitus taenia	Spined Loach	N	Ouse, Ouzel, Loughton Bk., some stillwaters (Schedule 1)
Cottus gobio	Bullhead	N	Ouse, Ouzel, Canal, Loughton Brook
Ctenopharyngodon idella	Grass Carp	I	Introduced into a very few stillwaters
Cyprinus carpio	Common Carp	I	Canal, stillwaters
Cyprinus carpio	Leather & Mirror Carp	I	Canal, stillwaters
Cyprinus carpio	Ghost Carp	I	Albino form introduced to Linford Lakes
Cyprinus carpio var.	Koi Carp	I	Introduced into a very few stillwaters
Esox lucius	Pike	N	Ouse, Ouzel, Canal, Loughton Brook, stillwaters
Gasterosteus aculeatus	3-spined Stickleback	N	Ouzel, Loughton Brook, stillwaters
Gobio gobio	Gudgeon	N	Ouse, Ouzel, Canal, Loughton Brook, stillwaters
Gymnocephalus cernus	Ruffe	N	Ouse, Ouzel, Canal, Loughton Brook, stillwaters
Leuciscus cephalus	Chub	N	Ouse, Ouzel, Loughton Brook
Leuciscus idus	Golden Orfe or Ide	I	Introduced into a very few stillwaters
Leuciscus leuciscus	Dace	N	Ouse, Ouzel, Canal, Loughton Brook
Noemacheilus barbatus	Stone Loach	N	Ouse, Ouzel, Canal
Perca fluviatilis	Perch	N	Ouse, Ouzel, Canal, Loughton Brook, stillwaters
Phoxinus phoxinus	Minnow	N	Ouse, Ouzel, Loughton Brook
Rutilus rutilis	Roach	N	Ouse, Ouzel, Canal, Loughton Brook, stillwaters
	Roach/Bream hybrids	N	Ouse, Ouzel, Canal, stillwaters
Salmo gairdneri	Rainbow Trout	I	Stocked (put and take) in a few stillwater fisheries
Salmo trutta	Brown Trout	N	Upper Ouse, Upper Ouzel
Scardinus erythrophthalmus	Rudd	N	Ouzel, Canal, stillwaters
Silurus glanis	Wels	N	Introduced into Canal and a very few stillwaters
Tinca tinca	Tench	N	Ouse, Ouzel, Canal, Loughton Brook, stillwaters
Tinca tinca var.	Golden Tench	I	Introduced into the Ouzel

Key

N = Native, *i.e.* indigenous to the British Isles
I = Introduced

Invertebrates

There are many forms of invertebrate (animals without backbones) with numerous examples to be found in Milton Keynes. However, not all of the known groups have been recorded, so in order to clarify those that appear in this document, the following list shows their classification within the animal kingdom. Each group in the right-hand column below is subsequently dealt with separately.

PHYLUM	**MOLLUSCA**	**Slugs, Snails and Bivalves**
PHYLUM	**ARTHROPODA**	**Arthropods**
Class	**CRUSTACEA**	**Crustaceans: Waterfleas, Woodlice and Fresh-water Shrimps**
Class	**DIPLOPODA**	**Millipedes**
Class	**CHILOPODA**	**Centipedes**
Class	**ARACHNIDA**	**Spiders, Harvestmen, Ticks and Mites**
Order	**Araneae**	**Spiders**
	Opiliones	**Harvestmen**
	Acari	**Ticks and Mites**
Class	**INSECTA**	**Insects**
Sub-Class	**Apterygota**	Primitive Wingless insects
Order	**Thysanura**	**Bristletails**
	Diplura	**Two-tailed Bristletails**
	Collembola	**Springtails**
Sub-Class	**Exopterygota**	Winged insects with incomplete metamorphosis
Order	**Ephemeroptera**	**Mayflies**
	Odonata	**Dragonflies and Damselflies**
	Orthoptera	**Grasshoppers and Bush-crickets**
	Dermaptera	**Earwigs**
	Dictyoptera	**Cockroaches**
	Psocoptera	**Booklice**
	Anoplura	**Sucking Lice**
	Hemiptera	**True Bugs**
Sub-Class	**Endopterygota**	Winged insects with complete metamorphosis
Order	**Neuroptera**	**Lacewings and Alder Flies**
	Mecoptera	**Scorpion Flies**
	Lepidoptera	**Butterflies and Moths**
	Diptera	**True Flies**
	Siphonaptera	**Fleas**
	Hymenoptera	**Sawflies, Ants, Bees and Wasps**
	Coleoptera	**Beetles**
PHYLUM	**ANNELIDA**	**Earthworms and Leeches**
Class	**OLIGOCHAETA**	**Earthworms**
	HIRUDINEA	**Leeches**
PHYLUM	**ASCHELMINTHES**	
Class	**ROTIFERA**	**Rotifers**

Slugs and Snails

Two groups of Mollusc are found in Milton Keynes: Gastropods (snails and slugs) and Lamellibranchs or Bivalves (cockles and mussels). All are characterised by having a soft body which may be surrounded by a single shell, two shells hinged along one edge or have no shell at all. They are found in a wide range of habitats including grassland, woods, gardens and many aquatic habitats, always being more abundant in neutral or calcareous habitats. Those living on land (particularly slugs) are very dependent on moisture and so are most active at night or in rainy weather. In daylight or dry weather they will take shelter under various objects like logs or stones or bury into soil or leaf litter.

Many of the species are herbivorous, feeding on plants and fungi, whilst others feed on dead organisms or even actively hunt down other invertebrates such as earthworms. Several species are particularly associated with gardens, some being major horticultural pests *e.g.* Garden Snail and Budapest Slug. This has, probably unfairly, led to a general dislike of all species by many people.

Identification of molluscs can, up to a point, be done with the naked eye and the use of a hand lens, but some species are particularly difficult to separate from closely related ones. The Garden Snail is one of the most familiar species and is a good example of one which can be readily identified, despite showing extreme variation. A familiar slug (in gardens and elsewhere) is the Great Black Slug. This can extend up to 15cm in length and shows considerable colour variation from black through brown to grey-white and red. (But care - as more than one true species may be involved!)

The list which follows includes the most up-to-date names (both scientific and common) but, unfortunately, the distribution of some of the species within the Borough is not known.

References and Further Reading

Kerney, M. (1999) Atlas of the Land and Freshwater Molluscs of Britain and Ireland. Harley Books

Kerney, M & Cameron, R.A.D. (1979) A Field Guide to the Land Snails of Britain and North-west Europe. Collins

Macan, T.T. (1994) (4th ed.) British Fresh- and Brackish-Water Gastropods. Freshwater Biological Association

Slugs

Arion ater	Large Black Slug	Abundant in grassland, gardens, woods *etc.*
Arion circumscriptus	Dotted Slug	Frequent in gardens and woods
Arion distinctus	Common Garden Slug	Common in gardens (as a pest)
Arion fasciatus	Bourguignat's Slug	Gardens
Arion hortensis	Southern Garden Slug	Gardens. Probably rare
Arion intermedius	Hedgehog Slug	
Arion silvaticus	Silver Slug	
Arion subfuscus	Dusky Slug	Woods and gardens
Deroceras panormitanum	Caruana's Slug	Increasing in gardens and possibly elsewhere
Deroceras reticulatum	Field Slug	Abundant in a wide variety of habitats (pest)
Lehmannia marginata	Tree Slug	Characteristically in old woodlands
Limax maximus	Great Grey Slug	Woods and gardens
Tadonia budapestensis	Budapest Slug	Common in gardens (as a pest)
Tadonia sowerbyi	Keeled Slug	Uncommon, a garden species
Testacella haliotidea	Shelled Slug	Rare; gardens
Testacella scutulum	Shield Slug	Rare; gardens

Snails

Acroloxus lacustris	Lake Limpet	
Aegopinella nitidula	Smooth Glass Snail	
Ancylus fluviatilis	River Limpet	Rivers; probably overlooked
Anisus leucostoma	Button Ram's-horn	
Anisus vortex	Whirlpool Ram's-horn	Rivers, streams and ponds
Arianta arbustorum	Copse Snail	Rare; woods and watersides
Ashfordia granulata	Silky Snail	Uncommon; rough damp places

Species	Common Name	Notes
Bathyomphalus contortus	Twisted Ram's-horn	
Bithynia leachii	Leach's Bithynia	
Bithynia tentaculata	Common Bithynia	Common in ponds and rivers
Candidula intersecta	Wrinkled Snail	Dry grassland
Carychium minimum agg.	Herald Snail	
Cepaea hortensis	White-lipped Snail	Frequent in a wide variety of habitats
Cepaea nemoralis	Grove Snail	Frequent in a wide variety of habitats
Cernuella virgata	Striped Snail	Dry grassland and occasionally gardens
Clausilia bidentata	Common Door Snail	Woods
Cochlicopa lubrica	Slippery Moss Snail	
Cochlodina laminata	Plaited Door Snail	Rare; Salcey Forest
Discus rotundatus	Rounded Snail	
Ena obscura	Lesser Bulin	
Euconulus fulvus agg.	Tawny Snail	
Gyraulus albus	White Ram's-horn	Rivers, streams and ponds
Gyraulus crista	Nautilus Ram's-horn	
Gyraulus laevis	Smooth Ram's-horn	Uncommon; rivers
Helicigona lapicida	Lapidary Snail	Rare; found on a limestone wall
Helix aspersa	Garden Snail	Abundant everywhere
Hippeutis complanatus	Flat Ram's-horn	
Lauria cylindracea	Common Chrysalis Snail	Rare; found on a limestone wall
Lymnaea auricularia	Ear Pond Snail	Balancing lakes; possibly elsewhere
Lymnaea palustris	Marsh Pond Snail	Frequent in a variety of water bodies
Lymnaea peregra	Common Pond Snail	Common in all types of water body
Lymnaea stagnalis	Great Pond Snail	Common especially in ponds and rivers
Lymnaea truncatula	Dwarf Pond Snail	
Monacha cantiana	Kentish Snail	Abundant in a wide variety of habitats
Oxychilus alliarius	Garlic Snail	Woods
Oxychilus cellarius	Cellar Snail	Frequent in woods and gardens
Oxychilus drapernaldi	Drapernaud's Glass Snail	Common in gardens
Oxychilus helveticus	Glossy Glass Snail	Frequent in woods and gardens
Oxyloma pfeifferi	Pfeiffer's Amber Snail	Frequent by ponds and lakes
Phenacolimax major	Greater Pellucid Glass Snail	Very rare; Salcey Forest
Physa fontinalis	Common Bladder Snail	
Physa sp.	a Bladder Snail	An introduced species
Planorbarius corneus	Great Ram's-horn	Frequent in ponds and streams
Planorbis carinatus	Keeled Ram's-horn	Frequent in lakes and rivers
Planorbis planorbis	Margined Ram's-horn	Frequent ponds, rivers and streams
Potamopyrgus antipodarum	Jenkins's Spire Snail	Often in large numbers on water plants
Punctum pygmaeum	Dwarf Snail	
Pyramidula rupestris	Rock Snail	Rare; walls
Succinea putris	Large Amber Snail	Common by water; rarely in damp gardens
Trichia hispida	Hairy Snail	Frequent in damp places
Trichia striolata	Strawberry Snail	Abundant in a wide variety of habitats
Vallonia excentrica	Eccentric Grass Snail	Few records; probably overlooked
Vallonia pulchella	Smooth Grass Snail	Few records; probably overlooked
Valvata piscinalis	Common Valve Snail	Occasional in a variety of water bodies
Vitrea contracta	Milky Crystal Snail	
Vitrina pellucida	Pellucid Glass Snail	Few records; probably overlooked
Zonitoides excavatus	Hollowed Glass Snail	Rare; damp/wet areas on the Brickhills
Zonitoides nitidus	Shiny Glass Snail	By lakes and streams

Bivalves

Species	Common Name	Notes
Anodonta anatina	Duck Mussel	
Anodonta cygnea	Swan Mussel	Common in a variety of water bodies
Dreissena polymorpha	Zebra Mussel	Canal and lakes
Pisidium amnicum	River Pea Shell	Rivers
Sphaerium corneum	Horny Orb Mussel	Rivers
Unio pictorum	Painter's Mussel	Rivers

Arthropods

Arthropods are animals with a hard external skeleton and, as the name suggests, jointed legs. In terms of both numbers of species and of individuals, this is the largest grouping of animals and may be found in every habitat in the world. Amongst such a wealth, it may be noted that some of the lists of species given below may appear to be long, others are very short or indeed even absent. This imbalance reflects more the interests and distribution of the recorders rather than the true representation of the distribution of this major group of animals in Milton Keynes. Most arthropods are small, often obscure creatures although they have great ecological significance; most are readily identifiable with a hand lens or microscope. Our Society is always more than willing to help, advise and support the interested amateur who wishes to explore the still largely unknown world of invertebrates with whom we share our locality.

In general, each record list is in three columns: the first gives the Latin name (in alphabetical order); the second shows either the common English name or an indication of the type within the group; the third provides relevant comments about the species. In some groups this basic pattern is modified but the changes are always specified in the preamble.

In the groups listed below, only the Insects together with Spiders and their relatives have been further subdivided into their major types (Orders).

In all the listings below, great use has been made of the following general books and, in addition, the more specialised publications given with some of the lists. On a few occasions where it is difficult to identify down to species, the generic name only is given with the unknown species indicated by sp. (or spp. if likely to be more than one).

References & Further Reading
Arlott, N., Fitter, R., and Fitter, A. (1981). The Complete Guide to British Wildlife. Collins.

Chinery, M. (1993). Collins Pocket Guide; Insects of Britain and Western Europe. Collins.

Dipper, F. and Powell, A. (1996). Field Guide to the Waterlife of Britain. Readers Digest Association.

Fitter, R. and Manuel, R. (1995). Lakes, Rivers, Streams and Ponds of Britain & NW Europe. HarperCollins.

Wickham, J.C. et.al. (1994). Hazeley Wood Study Group. Annual Report for 1993. Milton Keynes Parks Trust.

Wickham, J.C. et.al. (1995). Hazeley Wood Study Group. Annual Report No. 2, 1994. Milton Keynes Parks Trust.

Waterfleas, Woodlice and Fresh-water Shrimps

Most of the members of this group are aquatic so that in Milton Keynes, where there are many bodies of water (lakes, streams, rivers, ponds and canal), there is plenty of scope to widen this list. However, woodlice are terrestrial.

References & Further Reading
Scourfield, D.J. and Harding, J.P. (1966). Key to British Species of Freshwater Cladocera Scientific Publication No. 5. Freshwater Biological Association, Windermere.

Oliver, P. G. (1993). Woodlice. Field Studies Council

Acroperus harpae	a Water flea	Common in still water
Armadillidium vulgare	Pill Woodlouse	Grassland on calcareous soils; common
Asellus aquaticus	Water Slater	Often abundant in stagnant water
Bosmina longirostris	a Water flea	Common in still water
Ceriodaphnia sp.	a Water flea	Common in still water
Chydorus spaericus	a Water flea	Common in still water
Cyclops spp.	Cyclopoids	Common in still water
Daphnia cucullata	a Water flea	Common still water; sig. part of fish diet in season

Gammarus pulex	Freshwater shrimp	Common; in well aerated waters within vegetation
Oniscus asellus	Common Woodlouse	Almost anywhere damp with shelter
Philoscia muscorum	a Woodlouse	Grassland, hedgerows and open woods
Platyarthrus hoffmannseggi	a Woodlouse	Only in ant nests; often on calcareous soils
Porcellio scaber	a Woodlouse	Common in a variety of habitats; gardens
Scapholeberis mucronata	a Water flea	Common in still water
Simocephalus vetulus	a Water flea	Common in still water
Trichoniscus pusillus	a Woodlouse	Common in leaf litter in woods or grassland
Trichoniscus pygmaeus	a Woodlouse	Common, lives in soil so often unobserved

Millipedes

Millipedes live in soil and leaf litter and are characterised by the body segments being nearly circular in cross-section and each having two pairs of legs. They are relatively slow moving and feed on plant material.

Cylindroiulus londiniensis	a Millipede	Common in hedges and leaf litter
Glomeris marginata	Pill-millipede	Common in hedges and leaf litter
Polydesmus angustus	a Millipede	Common in hedges and leaf litter

Centipedes

Centipedes have just one pair of legs per body segment and are rather more flattened. They can move quite quickly and readily burrow when disturbed. They are predatory and have a pair of claws near the head and the last pair of legs are long and sensory.

Lithobius forficatus	Common Centipede	Gardens, woods, grassland; under stones
Necrophloeophagus longicornis	a Centipede	Pale coloured; lives in soil; feeds on earthworms

Spiders, Harvestmen, Ticks and Mites

All members of these groups have eight legs as adults, although beware of larvae which sometimes have six and may initially be confused with insects! They are very abundant in our area. Spiders are the familiar eight-legged "creepy crawlies"; harvestmen are very long-legged voracious predators with a body which is rounded and undivided, whilst ticks and especially mites tend to be small in size with shortish legs.

References & Further Reading
Darlington, A. (1968). The Pocket Encyclopaedia of Plant Galls in Colour. Blandford.

Redfern, M. and Askew, R.R. (1992). Plant Galls. Naturalists' Handbook 17. Richmond Publishing Company.

Spiders

Alopecosa pulverulenta	a Wolf spider	Common in open places, grassland
Amaurobius fenestralis	a Lace-web spider	Common, makes scruffy lace-like web
Amaurobius similis	a Lace-web spider	Common in damp places, tree trunks
Araneus diadematus	Garden spider	Abundant in gardens, on fences, hedgerows
Araniella cucurbitina	an Orb-web spider	Abundant in trees ,bushes; bright green / red spot
Dysdera crocata	Woodlouse spider	Nocturnal hunter of woodlice, prefers compost heap
Enoplognatha ovata	a Comb-footed spider	Abundant among nettles, may have red markings
Linyphia triangularis	a Money spider	One of many v. small spiders, abundant in woods
Meta segmentata	an Orb-web spider	
Misumena vatia	Crab spider	Common in bushes, have crab-like movement
Nuctenea umbratica	a Spider	
Oedothorax apicatus	a Money spider	An early coloniser of rough bare ground
Pachygnatha degeeri	a Spider	
Pardosa amentata	a Wolf spider	Common, chases prey rather than trapping in web
Pardosa palustris	a Wolf spider	Common, chases prey rather than trapping in web
Pardosa pullata	a Wolf spider	Common, chases prey rather than trapping in web
Pholcus phalangioides	Daddy-long-legs spider	Common in houses, has long legs
Pisaura mirabilis	Nursery-web spider	Common in dense vegetation, male strong marked
Salticus scenicus	Zebra spider	Widespread small spider with black/white stripes

Tegenaria domestica	Common House spider	Common indoors, sheds, cellars; long-legged
Tegenaria duellica	a House spider	Common indoors, sheds, cellars; long-legged
Tegenaria parietina	Cardinal spider	Common indoors, sheds, cellars; long-legged
Tetragnatha extensa	an Orb-web spider	
Tetragnatha montana	an Orb-web spider	
Trochosa ruricola	a Wolf spider	Common, chases prey rather than trapping in web
Xysticus cristatus	a Crab spider	Common in low herbage, have crab-like movement
Zygiella x-notata	an Orb-web Spider	Common in sheds, bushes; abdomen edged pink

Harvestmen

Leiobunum rotundum	a Harvestman	Abundant on walls, in woods, grassland

Ticks and Mites

Aceria fraxinivora	a Mite	Gall on Ash flower stalks
Argas vespertillionis	a Tick	Occasional; parasitic on Daubenton's bat
Artacris macrorhynchus	a Mite	Gall on Sycamore and Field Maple leaves
Eriophyes axillare	a Mite	Gall on Alder leaves
Eriophyes campestricola	a Mite	Gall on Elm leaves
Eriophyes laevis		
ssp. *inangulis*	a Mite	Gall on Alder leaves
Eriophyes macrochelus	a Mite	Gall on Field Maple leaves
Eriophyes similis	a Mite	Gall on Blackthorn leaves
Eriophyes tiliae		
ssp. *tiliae*	a Mite	Bugle-gall on Lime leaves
ssp. *typicus*	a Mite	Nail-gall on Lime leaves
Eriophyes triradiatus	Willow Gall mite	Common on Willow leaves
Eriophyes viburni	a Mite	Gall on Wayfaring Tree leaves
Eutrombidium rostratus	Velvet mite	Common in gardens
Haemogamosus sp.	a Mite	Occasional; parasitic on Pipistrelle bat
Hydrachna globosus	Water mite	Common in ponds
Spinturnix sp.	a Mite	Occasional; parasitic on Daubenton's bat

Insects

Insects are most readily distinguished by the presence of three pairs of legs, although this is occasionally difficult to establish. They are by far the most numerous and diverse group of living creatures and in species total more than all other living organisms put together - so there is plenty of scope for new recorders in Milton Keynes. The large, spectacular groups of insects, such as the dragonflies, butterflies and large moths, have been well recorded in Milton Keynes, as nationally. Many of the less obvious organisms, though often no less interesting and important, have not received the attention they deserve and hence our records are sometimes very incomplete.

References & Further Reading
In addition to those noted under Arthropods (above) please also see
Chinery, M. (1973). A Field Guide to the Insects of Britain and Northern Europe. Collins.

Bristletails, Two-tailed Bristletails and Springtails

These are small wingless long-bodied insects, most often found among leaf litter and in soil. Springtails are readily recognised by the possession of a forked springing organ at the rear which enables them to hop in the air when disturbed.

Campodea spp.	Two-tailed Bristletails	Common in soil / under bark; identification difficult
Isotoma palustris	a Springtail	Common in damp leaf litter and mosses
Lepisma saccharina	Silverfish	A Bristletail; common in houses; nocturnal

Mayflies

Delicate weak-flying insects with two or three long 'tails' extending from the rear end. The nymphs are aquatic, hence the adults are found near water and provide food for some fish. Artificial 'flies' used by fishermen are attempts to mimic this group.

Baetis rhodani	a Mayfly	Common in or near fast-flowing streams
Caenis horaria	a Mayfly	Common in or near lakes and rivers
Cloeon dipterum	a Mayfly	Common in or near ponds and ditches
Ephemerella ignita	a Mayfly	Common in or near fast-flowing streams

Dragonflies and Damselflies

Banded Demoiselle

Eighteen breeding species of Odonata (dragonflies and damselflies) may be found in Milton Keynes. One vagrant species, the Yellow-winged Darter has also been recorded (1995). With the large number of water bodies, including the Rivers Ouse and Ouzel, the Grand Union Canal, balancing lakes, old gravel workings, ponds and streams, the area is well suited to observing these insects.

Odonata are dependent on water for their breeding cycle. The eggs are laid in water, or on plants in or near water. On hatching, the larva spends from a few weeks to 2 years feeding on other freshwater invertebrates (it is wholly carnivorous) before emerging to undergo a final moult into the winged adult stage. Generally speaking, damselflies are small, weak flyers keeping close to pond side vegetation and resting with their wings closed along the length of their body. Dragonflies are larger (up to 80 mm long), strong flyers often found well away from water and resting with their wings held out at right angles to the body.

Damselflies are on the wing from April through to late summer. On warm summer days a haze of Common Blue Damselflies may be seen over the surface of many of the lakes in Milton Keynes. The White-legged Damselfly is a speciality of the area and can be found in great numbers, in late June and July, in breeding pairs laying eggs on Water Crowfoot in rivers. The River Ouzel near the Open University is a good site to observe this species.

Dragonflies may be observed as adults during late spring to autumn. The earliest species likely to be seen in Milton Keynes is the Hairy Dragonfly, on the wing from early May. This species was only first proven to breed here in 1999. The height of the season is high summer when dragonflies can become very common in suitable habitats. You may be lucky enough to see large swarms of Migrant Hawkers hunting near hedgerows and woodland edges. In August 1991 a swarm of between 1000 and 2000 was seen near Shenley Wood. Other commonly observed dragonflies in Milton Keynes include the Brown Hawker, easily recognised because of its amber-brown wings, and the Common Darter, a small red dragonfly seen from high summer well into the autumn.

References & Further Reading

Askew, R. R., *The Dragonflies of Europe,* 1988 (Harley Books)

Brooks, S., ill. by Lewington, R., *Field Guide to the Dragonflies and Damselflies of Great Britain and Ireland,* 1997 (British Wildlife Publishing)

Corbet, P. S., *Dragonflies, Behaviour and Ecology of Odonata,* 1999 (Harley Books)

McGeeney, Andrew, *British Dragonflies,* 1986 (Jonathan Cape)

Damselflies - *Zygoptera*

Calopteryx splendens	Banded Demoiselle	6-8	Mostly on rivers
Lestes sponsa	Emerald Damselfly	7-9	Marshy land
Platycnemis pennipes	White-legged Damselfly	6-7	Rivers & canal (scarce in UK)
Pyrrhosoma nymphula	Large Red Damselfly	4-8	Earliest seen damselfly
Coenagrion puella	Azure Damselfly	5-8	Common on ponds
Enallagma cyathigerum	Common Blue Damselfly	5-9	Common throughout
Ischnura elegans	Blue-tailed Damselfly	6-8	Common, pollution tolerant
Erythromma najas	Red-eyed Damselfly	6-8	Patrols from water lilies

Dragonflies - *Anisoptera*

Brachytron pratense	Hairy Dragonfly	5-6	Earliest seen dragonfly
Aeshna mixta	Migrant Hawker	8-10	Sometimes in large swarms
Aeshna cyanea	Southern Hawker	7-9	Hunts woodland rides
Aeshna grandis	Brown Hawker	6-10	Often in gardens
Anax imperator	Emperor Dragonfly	6-8	Lakes and ponds
Libellula quadrimaculata	Four-spotted Chaser	6-8	Common on lakes
Libellula depressa	Broad-bodied Chaser	5-7	Less common – looks 'fat'
Orthetrum cancellatum	Black-tailed Skimmer	5-7	Basks on bare ground
Sympetrum striolatum	Common Darter	7-10	Often last on wing
Sympetrum sanguineum	Ruddy Darter	7-10	Similar to previous species
Sympetrum flaveolum	Yellow-winged Darter	vagrant	Infrequent visitor (Aug. 1995)

Grasshoppers and Crickets

Robust insects with hind legs enlarged for jumping. Males of many species stridulate ('sing') especially during sunny spells. Species may be herbivorous or omnivorous.

References & Further Reading

Brown, V. K. (1983). Grasshoppers. Cambridge University Press

Acheta domesticus	House Cricket	Occasional; needs artificial warmth
Chorthippus albomarginatus	Lesser Marsh Gr'hopper	Local; by water
Chorthippus brunneus	Common Field Gr'hopper	Widespread; flies well
Chorthippus parallelus	Meadow Grasshopper	Common and widespread
Leptophytes punctatissima	Speckled Bush-cricket	Common; flightless; stridulates ultrasonically
Meconema thalassinum	Oak Bush-cricket	Occasional; arboreal species
Metrioptera roeselii	Roesel's Bush-cricket	Occasional; spreading from south-east
Omacestus viridulus	Com. Green Grasshopper	Occasional; less common than *C. parallelus*
Pholidoptera griseoaptera	Dark Bush-cricket	Common in hedges and roadside verges
Tetrix undulata	Common Groundhopper	In open areas low in vegetation
Tettigonia viridissima	Great Green Bush Cricket	In shrubs and rough vegetation

Earwigs

These insects are elongate with familiar pincer-like organs (cerci) at the rear end.

Forficula auricularia	Common Earwig	Widespread; common in gardens, woods, *etc.*
Labia minor	Lesser Earwig	Rare; a small, often flying, earwig

Cockroaches

Many cockroaches are pests found in warm areas of buildings and are rather flat, fast-running insects with long antennae.

Blattella germanica	German Cockroach	Occasional pest in domestic and industrial kitchens

Booklice

Booklice are small winged or sometimes wingless insects, found in vegetation on bark, but some live indoors feeding on starchy materials and hence may cause damage to books, *etc.*

Liposcelis terricolis	Booklouse	Common in domestic premises, damages paper *etc.*

Sucking Lice

Soft-bodied insects with a small head and pear-shaped body, which suck mammalian blood.

Pediculus humanus var. *capitis*	Human Head Louse	Familiar as occasional parasites on children's heads

True Bugs

Insects in this large group show many different forms but all have piercing mouthparts, which are generally used to suck plant sap although a few species may feed on animals.

Although this is not done here, True Bugs may be divided into:-

Heteroptera   Plant, Ground and Water Bugs – forewing divided into two regions, a leathery basal area with a membranous tip. Wings folded flat at rest.

Homoptera   Aphids and Leaf Hoppers – forewings uniform in texture, either leathery or membranous, usually held roof-shaped over the body at rest.

Acanthosoma haemorrhoidale	Hawthorn Shield-bug	Feeds on leaves & fruit of Hawthorn
Aphis fabae	Bean Aphid / Black Fly	Common pest on a variety of garden plants
Arctocorisa germani	a Lesser Water-boatman	Swims right way up in ponds and slow water
Cercopis vulnerata	Red & Black Froghopper	Common among damp herbage in woods
Corixa dentipes	a Lesser Water-boatman	Swims right way up in ponds and slow water
Corixa panzeri	a Lesser Water-boatman	Swims right way up in ponds and slow water
Corixa punctata	Lesser Water-boatman	Common; swims right way up in ponds &slow water
Cymatia bonsdorffii	a Lesser Water-boatman	Common; in still water with vegetation; predaceous
Cymatia coleoptrata	a Lesser Water-boatman	Common; in still water with vegetation; predaceous
Deraeocoris ruber	a Capsid bug	Common among vegetation
Elasmucha grisea	Parent Bug	Female guards eggs; mostly on Birch
Erisoma lanigerum	Woolly Aphid	Often on damaged bark of Apple
Gerris lacustris	Common Pond Skater	Lives on pond surface; carnivorous
Gerris gibbifer	a Pond skater	Lives on pond surface; carnivorous
Hayhurstia atriplicis	a Gall aphid	Gall on Goosefoot & Orache leaves
Heterotoma merioptera	a Mirid bug	Common in nettles, dense vegetation and trees
Hydrometra stagnorum	Water Measurer	Margins of ponds and streams
Macrosiphum rosae	Rose Aphid / Greenfly	Common on a variety of garden plants
Micronecta scholtzii	a Water-boatman	Common in ponds
Nepa cinerea	Water Scorpion	On mud and plants in shallow water
Notonecta glauca	Common Backswimmer	Active predator in still water
Palomena prasina	Green Shield-bug	On trees and shrubs in autumn
Pemphigus spirothecae	a Gall Aphid	Causes spiral galls on Poplar leaf stalks
Philaenus spumarius	Common Froghopper	Forms the 'Cuckoo-spit' on many plants
Plea leachii	a Submerged Water-bug	Common in ponds
Pseudococcus longispinus	Greenhouse Mealybug	On a variety of greenhouse plants
Psylla buxi	Box Sucker	Nymphs in shoot tips of Box cause clustering

Ranatra linearis	Water Stick-insect	Common in deep ponds with vegetation
Sigara concinna	a Lesser Water-boatman	Common in still water
Sigara distincta	a Lesser Water-boatman	Common in still water
Sigara dorsalis	a Lesser Water-boatman	Common in still water
Sigara falleni	a Lesser Water-boatman	Common in still water
Sigara fossarum	a Lesser Water-boatman	Common in still water
Trialeuroides vaporariorum	Greenhouse Whitefly	Pest of tomatoes & cucumbers in greenhouses
Velia caprai	Water Cricket	Uncommon; surface of ponds & slow streams

Lacewings and Alder Flies

These free-flying insects have wings that are membranous usually with a dense network of cross-veins.

Chrysopa perla	a Green Lacewing	Common in MK woods
Chrysopa septempunctata	a Green Lacewing	Large; in woods, hedges and gardens
Chrysoperla carnea	Common Green Lacewing	Common in MK woods; well vegetated habitats
Coniopteryx tineiformis	a Lacewing	Occasional in MK woods; small white waxy
Conwentzia psociformis	a Lacewing	Common in MK woods; small white waxy
Cunctochrysa albolineata	a Green Lacewing	Common in MK woods
Dichochrysa flavifrons	a Lacewing	
Hemerobius humulinus	a Lacewing	Common in MK woods
Hemerobius lutescens	a Lacewing	Common in MK woods
Hemerobius micans	a Lacewing	Common in MK woods
Micromus paganus	a Lacewing	Common in MK woods
Micromus variegatus	a Lacewing	Common in MK woods
Nineta flava	a Lacewing	
Wesmaelius nervosa	a Lacewing	Common in MK woods
Wesmaelius subnebulosus	a Lacewing	Common in MK woods
Sialis lutaria	an Alder fly	Relatively common; flies near water; larva aquatic

Scorpion Flies

In these insects the head has a downward elongation resembling a beak and males of some species have an upturned tail like a scorpion's sting, hence the name, but they are harmless.

Panorpa communis	a Scorpion Fly	Common in MK woods; damp vegetated habitats
Panorpa germanica	a Scorpion Fly	Common in MK woods; damp vegetated habitats

Butterflies and Moths

Butterflies

Most of the records given here were gathered during the period 1995-1999 as a contribution to the Butterfly Atlas Millennium project. A dedicated team of enthusiasts periodically covered each of the 100 tetrads (*i.e.* 2 x 2 km squares) in Milton Keynes and the figures in the list show the number of tetrads from which each species was recorded. The letters represent the status of each species:

C Common
U Uncommon
L Local and uncommon
V Vagrant *i.e.* a species outside its normal range

Other symbols used in the list:

*1 As there are difficulties in identifying the Essex Skipper as opposed to the Small Skipper, it is likely that the former is under-recorded.

Meadow Brown

*2 The Purple Hairstreak frequents the upper levels of Oak and Ash trees and is usually identified using binoculars; consequently, it is regularly under-recorded.

*3 The Chalkhill Blue and Dark Green Fritillary are normally seen much further south in Buckinghamshire (*e.g.* on the Chiltern Hills). The records for Milton Keynes are most unusual.

The list also indicates the months (1 - 12 = January through December) when the adult butterflies are most likely to be seen on the wing.

The arrangement of species in the list is that used by lepidopterists and indicates the relationships of the various families.

References and Further Reading
Asher, J. (1994). The Butterflies of Berkshire, Buckinghamshire and Oxfordshire. Pices Publications for Butterfly Conservation.

Brooks, M. and Knight, C. (1982). A Complete Guide to British Butterflies. Jonathan Cape

Thomas, J.A. (1989). The Hamlyn Guide to Butterflies of the British Isles. Hamlyn with RSNC.

Thomas, J.A. and Lewington, R. (1991). The Butterflies of Britain & Ireland. Dorling Kindersley Limited, in association with the National Trust.

Thymelicus sylvestris	Small Skipper	6-8	C	61	Grassy places, verges
Thymelicus lineola	Essex Skipper	7-8	C*129		Hedges, verges, rank grass
Ochlodes venata	Large Skipper	6-8	C	43	Rough grassy places
Erynnis tages	Dingy Skipper	5-7	L	4	Short grass with Bird's-foot-trefoil
Pyrgus malvae	Grizzled Skipper	5-6	L	4	Woodland clearings, rides; open scrub
Leptidea sinapsis	Wood White	5-6	L	8	Clearings in woods or sunny open rides
Colias croceus	Clouded Yellow	5-6/7-11	U	10	Open places with clovers
Gonepteryx rhamni	Brimstone	1-12	C	41	Woods, hedges, scrub
Pieris brassicae	Large White	4-9	C	86	Gardens
Pieris napi	Green-veined White	4-9	C	88	Damp uncultivated places
Pieris rapae	Small White	4-10	C	87	Gardens
Anthocharis cardamines	Orange Tip	4-7	C	57	Grass, hedgerows, wasteland
Callophrys rubi	Green Hairstreak	4-7	L	4	Woods, rough scrub
Quercusia quercus	Purple Hairstreak	7-9	C*2 21		Woodlands; high in oak or ash
Strymonidia w-album	White-letter Hairstreak	7-8	U	8	High in wood edges
Strymonidia pruni	Black Hairstreak	6-7	U	4	Woods with blackthorn
Lycaena phlaeas	Small Copper	5-10	C	45	Rough open places
Cupidio minimus	Small Blue	5-6/8	L	1	Short, open grass with Kidney Vetch

Aricia agestis	Brown Argus	5-9	U	29	Open grass
Polyommatus icarus	Common Blue	5-10	C	67	Rough grass with Bird's-foot-trefoil
Lysandra coridon	Chalkhill Blue	7-9	V*3	1	Chalk or limestone grassland
Celastrina argiolus	Holly Blue	4-9	C	49	Woods, parks, gardens
Ladoga camilla	White Admiral	6-7	U	11	Shady woods
Vanessa atalanta	Red Admiral	3-10	C	61	Hedges, woods, gardens
Cynthia cardui	Painted Lady	4-10	C	48	Any flowery habitat
Aglais urticae	Small Tortoiseshell	1-12	C	86	Gardens; in houses in winter
Inachis io	Peacock	1-12	C	83	Commonest round woods; widespread
Polygonia c-album	Comma	1-12	C	57	Woods, hedges, scrub
Nymphalis antiopa	Camberwell Beauty			1	An extremely rare migrant; one record
Argynnis aglaja	Dark Green Fritillary	6-8	V*	31	Rough grassland
Pararge aegeria	Speckled Wood	4-10	C	78	Woods, hedges
Lasiommata megera	Wall Brown	5-10	U	16	Rough grass, bare ground
Melanargia galathea	Marbled White	6-8	U	26	Areas of tall unimproved grassland
Pyronia tithonis	Gatekeeper	7-9	C	68	Grassy places with shrubs
Maniola jurtina	Meadow Brown	6-9	C	81	Tall grass in sun
Aphantopus hypernatus	Ringlet	7-8	C	51	Glades, verges, rank grass
Coenonympha pamphilus	Small Heath	5-10	C	39	Verges, hedges, rides, grass

Moths

Humming-bird Hawkmoth

Thirty years ago there was little regular moth recording in North Buckinghamshire. Today, the picture has changed and there is a very enthusiastic group who regularly record from their gardens (as in Lavendon, Newport Pagnell, Stony Stratford, Two Mile Ash and Willen), and sometimes from other localities such as local woods. In 1999, the Parks Trust commissioned moth research over several months in six localities. This intensive study added several species to the local list.

Gradually, over the years an interesting list is being formed - the results of which are seen below. There are nationally common species, those which are frequently seen but never in great numbers, those that occur very locally in just one or two places and those which are rarely seen. Even in our central position in the country, immigrant and coastal species are sometimes seen. For example, the Silver Y (*Plusia gamma*) which is one such immigrant, is regularly recorded and sometimes reaches the area in great numbers.

Species which were recorded from Milton Keynes prior to 1987 are not included in the present list, but out of interest there were the Goat Moth (*Cossus cossus*), Grass Emerald (*Pseudoterpna pruinata* ssp. *atropunctaria*), Clouded Magpie (*Ennominae sylvata*), Lunar Thorn (*Selenia lunularia*), Hedge Rustic (*Tholera cespitis*), Striped Wainscot (*Mythimna pudorina*), Red Swordgrass (*Xylena vestuta*) and White-spotted Pinion (*Cosmia diffinis*). The decrease in the populations of the last species is due to the loss of the elms on which the caterpillars feed.

Most of the recording itself has been carried out using mercury vapour and actinic light traps. These lights attract moths (sometimes from quite long distances) and the containers below them hold the moths so that they can be examined, identified and then released. The methods of using a light over a large white sheet and 'sugaring' (*i.e.* smearing a sugar solution on to a suitable surface which attracts the moths) are also used occasionally. Day flying species are recorded by direct observation. Caterpillars and chrysalises may also provide a useful method of identification.

Most Micro moths are extremely small, as their name suggests, but some are larger than the smallest Macro moths. The collection of Micro moths can be done in much the same way as for the Macros and this is being done by some members of the moth group. However, their identification is much more difficult and specialised and the records here rely almost entirely on the work of Mr David V. Manning (Micro moth Recorder for Bedfordshire and Northamptonshire), to whom we are most grateful. The whole group is seriously under-recorded in Buckinghamshire, but now that a start has been made locally the situation is slowly being rectified.

Obviously, it is the more common and frequently occurring species that are mostly recorded. However, some of the rarer and unexpected moths have also been noted, a few of which are new to the county list.

Prefixing the Latin names in the lists that follow are the identification numbers used in 'The Checklist of Lepidoptera Recorded from the British Isles'. The list of Macros has the moths arranged in alphabetical order by English names, whilst the Micros are listed by Latin name as in 'The Checklist' mentioned above.

Other symbols used:
The figures 1-12 refer to months of the year (January through December) when the adult moths are most likely to be seen on the wing.

/ between months represents two flight periods, usually indicating two broods.

C = Common, the moths being widespread in Milton Keynes and occurring in large numbers.
F = Frequent, the moths being widespread in Milton Keynes but occurring in smaller numbers.
L = Local, with moths recorded from a few Milton Keynes localities only.
R = Rare, for moths where only one or two records have been made; locality names are often included here.

References and Further Reading
Arnold, V.W., Baker, C.R.B., Manning, D.V. and Woiwod, I.P. (1997) The Butterflies and Moths of Bedfordshire. Bedfordshire Natural History Society

Bradley, J.D. (1998) The Checklist of Lepidoptera Recorded from the British Isles. Bradley and Bradley

*Brooks, M. (1991) A Complete Guide to British Moths. Jonathan Cape

Goater, B. (1996) British Pyralid Moths - a Guide to their Identification. Harley Books

*Skinner, B. (1998 2nd ed.) Colour Identification Guide to Moths of the British Isles. Viking

* = books only dealing with Macro moths

Macromoths

2281	Acronicta alni	Alder Moth	5-6	L	Woods and commons
2306	Phlogophora meticulosa	Angle Shades	5-10	C	Rests on dead vegetation
2313	Enargia paleacea	Angle-striped Sallow	7-9	R	A northern species; seen at N. Pagnell
2176	Cerapteryx graminis	Antler Moth	7-9	L	Sometimes day flying
1849	Eupithecia fraxinata	Ash Pug	5-6	R	Woodlands and hedges; Willen only
1912	Ennomos quercinaria	August Thorn	8-9	L	Woodlands
1797	Epirrita autumnata	Autumnal Moth	9-10	C	Widespread
2117	Paradiarsia glareosa	Autumnal Rustic	8-9	L	- but quite rare
2121	Diarsia dahlii	Barred Chestnut	8-9	R	Newport Pagnell, but vagrant
1962	Hylaea fasciaria	Barred Red	6-8	L	Most frequent in conifer plantations
1804	Perizoma bufaciata	Barred Rivulet	7-8	F	Rough pastures
2272	Xanthia aurago	Barred Sallow	9-10	F	Woodlands and hedgerows
1758	Eulithis pyraliata	Barred Straw	6-8	C	Widespread
1765	Cidaria fulvata	Barred Yellow	6-7	C	Woods, hedgerows, gardens *etc.*
2267	Agrochola lychnidis	Beaded Chestnut	9-10	F	Very variable; many colour forms
2442	Autographa pulchrina	Beautiful Golden Y	6-7	F	Beautiful; comes to flowers at night
2473	Laspeyria flexula	Beautiful Hook-tip	6-8	F	Woodlands
1677	Cyclophora albipunctata	Birch Mocha	5-6/8	R	Willen only
2301	Dypterygia scabriuscula	Bird's Wing	8-9	R	Willen & Lavendon on sugar
2033	Lymantria monacha	Black Arches	7-8	L	Woodlands
2466	Lygephila pastinum	Blackneck, The	6-7	L	Very local
2232	Aporophyla nigra	Black Rustic	9-10	F	A recent new-comer to the area
2240	Lithophane leautieri	Blair's Shoulder-knot	6-11	F	1st Brit. record 1951; now seen here
1833	Eupithecia expallidata	Bleached Pug	7-8	R	Willen records only
1682	Timandra griseata	Blood-vein	5-7/8-9	C	Frequently comes to light
1667	Comibaena bajularia	Blotched Emerald	6-7	L	Comes readily to moth traps
1766	Plemyria rubiginata	Blue-bordered Carpet	6-8	F	Flies frequently at dusk
1907	Epione repandaria	Bordered Beauty	7-9	F	Damp woodlands and marshy areas
1839	Eupithecia succenturiata	Bordered Pug	7-8	L	Waste places and roadside verges

2399	*Pyrrhia umbra*	Bordered Sallow	6-7	R Few records; Willen & N. Pagnell
2403	*Heliothis peltigera*	Bordered Straw	6-8	R Immigrant; several local records
1954	*Bupalus piniaria*	Bordered White	5-6	L Most often in coniferous woods
2160	*Lacanobia oleracea*	Bright-line Brown-eye	5-7	F Larva often damages tomatoes
1906	*Opisthograptis luteolata*	Brimstone Moth	4-10	C Widespread
1927	*Lycia hirtaria*	Brindled Beauty	3-4	F Males frequent at light
1852	*Eupithecia abbreviata*	Brindled Pug	4-5	F Often seen locally
2164	*Hecatera bicolorata*	Broad-barred White	6-8	L Trees & posts by day; flowers later
1773	*Electrophaes corylata*	Broken-barred Carpet	5-6	F Woodlands and bushy places
2110	*Noctua fimbriata*	Broad-bordered Yellow Underwing	7-9	C Widespread
2302	*Rusina ferruginea*	Brown Rustic	6-7	C Comes regularly to light
1791	*Philereme vetulata*	Brown Scallop	7	L Not often seen
2029	*Euproctis chrysorrhoea*	Brown-tail	7-8	L Larvae may be pests; generally scarce
2262	*Agrochola circellaris*	Brick, The	8-10	F At light, even on cold nights
2248	*Dryobotodes eremita*	Brindled Green	8-9	F Oak woodland; over-ripe brambles
2163	*Ceramica pisi*	Broom Moth	5-7	F Very attractive and variable
2192	*Mythimna conigera*	Brown-line Bright Eye	6-8	L Seems to prefer damp areas
1902	*Petrophora chlorosata*	Brown Silver-line	5-6	L Bracken feeder so few records
2266	*Agrochola litura*	Brown-spot Pinion	9-10	L Seems to be decreasing
2371	*Archanara dissoluta*	Brown-veined Wainscot	7-9	R Reedbeds; one at Walton Lake
1653	*Habrosyne pyritoides*	Buff Arches	6-8	C Attractive; comes readily to light
2061	*Spilosoma luteum*	Buff Ermine	5-7	F Often with variable markings
2049	*Eilema deplana*	Buff Footman	7-8	L Woodlands and bushy places
1994	*Phalera bucephala*	Buff-tip	5-6	F Resembles a broken Birch twig
2369	*Nonagria typhae*	Bulrush Wainscot	7-9	F Near reed beds, river banks *etc.*
2463	*Euclidia glyphica*	Burnet Companion	5-6	L Day flying; over meadows, waste
2434	*Diachrysia chrysitis*	Burnished Brass	6-7/8-9	C Late specimens smaller than earlier
2154	*Mamestra brassicae*	Cabbage Moth	5-7	F A pest of Brassica crops
2166	*Hadena rivularis*	Campion, The	5-6/7-8	L Attracted to many flowers
1913	*Ennomos alniaria*	Canary-shouldered Thorn	7-10	C Widely distributed
2269	*Atethemia centrago*	Centre-barred Sallow	8-9	F Commonly in woods; elsewhere too
2214	*Cucullia chamomillae*	Chamomile Shark	4-6	L Colourful larva on mayweeds
2258	*Conistra vaccinii*	Chestnut, The	9-5	F Adult overwinters; mostly in woods
1755	*Eulithis testata*	Chevron	5-6	L Variable; in various habitats
1870	*Odezia atrata*	Chimney Sweeper	6-7	L Day flying over grass
1651	*Cilix glaucata*	Chinese Character	5-6/7-8	C Woods, hedgerows and bushy places
2019	*Clostera curtula*	Chocolate-tip	4-5	F Mostly with sallows
2069	*Tyria jacobaeae*	Cinnabar, The	5-7	F In rough pastures *etc.*
2193	*Mythimna ferrago*	Clay, The	7-8	C Widespread and fairly common
1681	*Cyclophora linearia*	Clay Triple-lines	5-7/8-10	L Usually in Beech woods
2341	*Mesoligia furuncula*	Cloaked Minor	6-7	F Very variable
1887	*Lomaspilis marginata*	Clouded Border	6-7	C Damp woodlands and marshy areas
2326	*Apamea crenata*	Clouded-bordered Brindle	5-7	L Various forms; difficult to identify
2327	*Apamea epomidion*	Clouded Brindle	6-7	F Woods and gardens
2188	*Orthosia incerta*	Clouded Drab	3-5	C Varies greatly in colour
1958	*Lomographa temerata*	Clouded Silver	5-6	F Woodlands
1738	*Epirrhoe alternata*	Common Carpet	6-7	C Widespread
1669	*Hemithea aestivaria*	Common Emerald	6-7	C Widespread
2050	*Eilema lurideola*	Common Footman	7-8	C On wild flowers; comes to light
1657	*Ochropacha duplaris*	Common Lutestring	6-8	L Oak woodland
1764	*Chloroclysta truncata*	Common Marbled Carpet	5-6	C Has various colour forms
1834	*Eupithecia vulgata*	Common Pug	5-6/8	C Widespread; variable
2187	*Orthosia stabilis*	Common Quaker	3-4	C In all habitats
2343	*Mesapamea secalis*	Common Rustic	7-8	C Widespread
17	*Hepialus lupulinus*	Common Swift	5-7	C Large numbers often come to light
2199	*Mythimna pallens*	Common Wainscot	6-10	C - very
1956	*Cabera exanthemata*	Common Wave	5-7/7-8	C Woods, hedgerows and bushy areas
1955	*Cabera pusaria*	Common White Wave	5-6/7-8	C Widespread; easily disturbed by day
2297	*Amphipyra pyramidea*	Copper Underwing	8-10	F In woods, parks and hedgerows
2008	*Ptilodon capucina*	Coxcomb Prominent	5-6/8-9	F Widespread
2418	*Earias clorana*	Cream-bordered Green Pea	5-7	L Usually close to sallow bushes
2368	*Celaena leucostigma*	Crescent, The	7-9	L Mainly in damp situations
2090	*Agrotis trux*	Crescent Dart	7-8	R Coastal; one seen in Newport Pagnell

373	Synanthedon tipuliformis	Currant Clearwing	6-7	R	One site only; Stony Stratford
1832	Eupitheica assimilata	Currant Pug	5-6/8	F	Frequently comes to light
2321	Apamea monoglypha	Dark Arches	6-8	C	Normal and melanic forms frequent
1725	Xanthorhoe ferrugata	Dark-barred Twin-spot Carpet	5-6/7-8	F	Widespread
2250	Blepharita adusta	Dark Brocade	6-7	R	Drab; not often seen; Willen
2259	Conistra ligula	Dark Chestnut	10-11	L	Mostly a woodland species
(2284	Acronicta tridens	(Dark Dagger	6-8	)	Two frequent species almost
(2283	Acronicta psi	(Grey Dagger	6-8	)	impossible to separate in the field
1762	Chloroclysta citrata	Dark Marbled Carpet	7-8	L	Woodlands
1749	Pelurga comitata	Dark Spinach	7-8	L	- but rarely seen
2091	Agrotis ipsilon	Dark Sword-grass			Immigrant; few seen most years
1792	Philereme transversata	Dark Umber	7	L	Widespread, but not often seen
1631	Poecilocampa populi	December Moth	10-12	L	Comes readily to light
2231	Aporophyla lutulenta	Deep-brown Dart	9-10	L	Comes to light; very darkly coloured
2195	Mythymna vitellina	Delicate, The	5-11	R	Immigrant; rare inland. Willen
2044	Eilema griseola	Dingy Footman	7-8	F	Damp woodlands; larva on lichens
2314	Parastichtis ypsillon	Dingy Shears	6-8	F	Damp woodlands and marshy places
2874	Euchoeca nebulata	Dingy Shell	6-7	R	Stony Stratford only
2155	Melanchra persicariae	Dot Moth	7-8	C	Commonly visits moth traps
1934	Agriopis marginaria	Dotted Border	2-4	F	Males on trunks; females wingless
2105	Rhyacia simulans	Dotted Rustic	6-7/8-10	L	Once common; now much decreased
2114	Graphiphora augur	Double Dart	6-7	L	Comes to light & sugar; not plentiful
2311	Ipimorpha retusa	Double Kidney	7-9	R	Willen; requires damp situations
2336	Apamea ophiogramma	Double Lobed	6-8	L	Found in damp areas
2128	Xestia triangulum	Double Square-spot	6-7	C	Gardens, woodlands etc.
1862	Gymnoscelis rufifasciata	Double-striped Pug	4-5	C	Very frequent in moth traps
1640	Philudoria potatoria	Drinker, The	7-8	C	Males very frequently come to light
2318	Cosmia trapezina	Dun-bar, The	7-9	C	Larva cannibalistic! Adult variable
2330	Apamea remissa	Dusky Brocade	6-7	L	Care! Easy to confuse with other spp
2275	Xanthia gilvago	Dusky-lemon Sallow	8-10	L	Woodlands
2352	Eremobia ochroleuca	Dusky Sallow	7-8	L	During day rests on knapweeds etc.
1914	Ennomos fuscantaria	Dusky Thorn	7-10	L	Frequent visitor to light
1705	Idaea fuscovenosa	Dwarf Cream Wave	6-7	F	Various habitats; flies from dusk on
1857	Eupithecia tantillaria	Dwarf Pug	5-6	L	Larva feeds on conifers
2360	Amphipoea oculea	Ear Moth	7-9	R	Visits flowers by day
2243	Xylocampa areola	Early Grey	3-5	F	Woodlands and gardens
1960	Theria primaria	Early Moth	1-2	F	Light attracts males; females wingless
1917	Selenia dentaria	Early Thorn	4-5/8-9	C	The two broods are very different
1991	Deilephila elpenor	Elephant Hawk-moth	5-7	F	Comes frequently to light
1643	Pavonia pavonia	Emperor Moth	4-5	L	Males fly by day; females at night
1947	Ectropis bistortata	Engrailed, The	3-4/6-8	C	Woodlands
1980	Smerinthus ocellata	Eyed Hawk-moth	5-7	F	Occasionally comes to light
2489	Herminia tarsipennalis	Fan-foot, The	6-7	F	Gardens, hedgerows and bushy areas
2178	Tholera decimalis	Feathered Gothic	8-9	L	Widespread and locally common
2255	Eumichtis lichenea	Feathered Ranunculus	8-10	R	Normally coastal; seen at Lavendon
1923	Colotois pennaria	Feathered Thorn	9-11	C	Comes to light in the autumn
2377	Arenostola phragmitidis	Fen Wainscot	7-8	R	Reedbeds; Lavendon & Howe Park
1782	Horisme tersata	Fern, The	6-8	L	Larva on Traveller's-joy; scarce
2020	Diloba caeruleocephala	Figure of Eight	5-6	F	Males at light; white females rarely
1654	Tethea ocularis	Figure of Eighty	5-7	F	Often comes to light
2098	Axylia putris	Flame, The	6-7/8	C	In most locations
1722	Xanthorhoe designata	Flame Carpet	5-6/8	L	Damp woodlands
2102	Ochropleura plecta	Flame Shoulder	4-6/8-9	C	- very
2353	Luperina testacea	Flounced Rustic	8-9	C	Frequently attracted to light
2465	Tyta luctuosa	Four-spotted, The	5-8	R	Very rare at Willen & Lavendon
1638	Macrothylacia rubi	Fox Moth	5-6	R	Day flying males
1817	Eupithecia pulchellata	Foxglove Pug	5-6	R	Beautiful; Lavendon only
1827	Eupithecia intricata	Freyer's Pug	5-6	F	Flies from dusk onwards
1660	Polyploca ridens	Frosted Green	4-5	L	Woodlands. Variable in colour
2364	Gortyna flavago	Frosted Orange	8-10	F	Attractive; larva in some plant stems
1740	Epirrhoe galiata	Galium Carpet	5-7/8	R	Willen only; very rare
1728	Xanthorhoe fluctuata	Garden Carpet	4-10	C	Variable
2082	Euxoa nigricans	Garden Dart	7-8	L	Drab; waste places, gardens etc.

2057	Arctia caja	Garden Tiger	7-8	F	Not nearly as common as it was
1720	Orthonama obstipata	Gem, The			Immigrant; several records
14	Hepialus humuli	Ghost Moth	6-7	F	White males fly over grass at dusk
2439	Plusia festucae	Gold Spot	6-7/8-9	R	Few records; Willen
16	Hepialus hecta	Gold Swift	6	L	Woodlands; flies at dusk
2437	Polychrysia moneta	Golden Plusia	6-8/9	L	Larva on Delphinium & Monkshood
1851	Eupithecia virgaureata	Golden-rod Pug	5-6/8	R	Stony Stratford record only
2137	Eurois occulata	Great Brocade	7-8	R	Immigrant; Lavendon & S. Stratford
2136	Naenia typica	Gothic, The	6-7	F	Few regularly attracted to light
2138	Anaplectoides prasina	Green Arches	6-7	L	Beautiful; woods, rarely to light
2245	Allophyes oxyacanthae	Green-brindled Crescent	9-11	F	Normal and melanic forms found
1776	Colostygia pectinataria	Green Carpet	5-7	C	Beautiful, but colour soon fades
1860	Chloroclystis rectangulata	Green Pug	6-7	C	Widespread
2422	Pseudoips fagana	Green Silver-lines	6-7	L	Oak woodland
2150	Polia nebulosa	Grey Arches	6-7	L	More common in woodlands
2254	Antitype chi	Grey Chi	8-9	R	N. Pagnell & Lavendon records only
1951	Aethalura punctulata	Grey Birch	5-6	R	Records from Willen & Lavendon
1768	Thera obeliscata	Grey Pine Carpet	5-7/9-10	F	Woodlands and gardens
1837	Eupithecia subfuscata	Grey Pug	5-6	C	Widespread
2237	Lithophane ornitopus	Grey Shoulder-knot	9-10/2-4	L	Adult overwinters. On tree trunks *etc.*
1813	Eupithecia haworthiata	Haworth's Pug	6-7	L	Comes readily to light
2315	Dicycla oo	Heart Moth	6-7	R	From Lavendon only
2088	Agrotis clavis	Heart and Club	6-7	L	Comes to light; very uncommon here
2089	Agrotis exclamationis	Heart and Dart	5-7	C	Extremely common esp. in traps
2190	Orthosia gothica	Hebrew Character	3-4	C	- very common at light
2469	Scoliopteryx libatrix	Herald, The	7-11/3-6	F	Overwinters in sheds and the like
370	Sesia apiformis	Hornet Moth	6-7	L	Larva wood boring. On Poplar
1984	Macroglossum stellatarum	Humming-bird Hawk-moth			Has been seen in most months
2120	Diarsia mendica	Ingrailed Clay	6-8	L	Woodlands; variable
2000	Notodonta dromedarius	Iron Prominent	5-6/8	F	Widespread locally
1734	Scotopteryx luridata	July Belle	6-8	R	Few records from Newport Pagnell
1777	Hydriomena furcata	July Highflyer	7-8	F	Woodlands and along hedgerows
1771	Thera juniperata	Juniper Carpet	9-10	R	In gardens at Willen and N. Pagnell
1854	Eupithecia pusillata	Juniper Pug	7-9	R	Mainly in gardens & conifer cvs.
2289	Acronicta rumicis	Knot Grass	5-7	L	Once common, now less so
1634	Malacosoma neustria	Lackey, The	7-8	C	Larval webs easily found
1642	Gastropacha quercifolia	Lappet, The	6-8	R	Large; Willen & Lavendon only
1856	Eupithecia lariciata	Larch Pug	5-6	R	Willen and Shenley Wood only
1666	Geometra papilionaria	Large Emerald	6-8	L	Beautiful; woodlands
2333	Apamea anceps	Large Nutmeg	6-7	F	Comes to light; drab looking
2252	Polymixis flavicinca	Large Ranunculus	9-10	L	Rests by day on lichens on walls
1726	Xanthorhoe quadrifasciata	Large Twin-spot Carpet	6-7	F	Mainly woodlands
2375	Rhizedra lutosa	Large Wainscot	8-10	L	Reed beds and damp areas
2107	Noctua pronuba	Large Yellow Underwing	7-9	C	Fore wings rather variable
1894	Semiothisa clathrata	Latticed Heath	5-6/7-9	L	Flies by day over grassland *etc.*
2185	Orthosia populeti	Lead-coloured Drab	3-4	L	Most often near Poplar or Aspen
2078	Nola confusalis	Least Black Arches	5-6	L	Tiny; woodlands
1699	Idaea vulpinaria	Least Carpet	7-8	R	Few Willen records; may spread
2112	Noctua interjecta	Least Yellow Underwing	7-8	C	Widespread
161	Zeuzera pyrina	Leopard Moth	6-8	F	Larva bores wood of various trees
2111	Noctua janthe	Lesser Broad-bordered Yellow Underwing	7-9	C	Widespread
2316	Cosmia affinis	Lesser-spotted Pinion	7-8	R	Lavendon; was more common
2006	Pheosia gnoma	Lesser Swallow Prominent	5-6/8	L	Few records
1868	Aplocera efformata	Lesser Treble-bar	5-6/8-9	R	Only seen at Willen
2109	Noctua comes	Lesser Yellow Underwing	7-9	C	- very; at light and sugar
2322	Apamea lithoxylaea	Light Arches	6-8	F	Comes to light and various flowers
2157	Lacanobia w-latinum	Light Brocade	5-7	L	Rarely seen here
1961	Campaea margaritata	Light Emerald	7-8	C	Comes frequently to light
1662	Archiearis notha	Light Orange Underwing	3-4	L	Day flying; around tops of Aspen
1910	Apeira syringaria	Lilac Beauty	6-7	F	Beautiful; wings peculiarly held
1979	Mimas tiliae	Lime Hawk-moth	5-6	F	Locally comes readily to light
1825	Eupithecia centaureata	Lime-speck Pug	4-9	C	Frequently comes to light

1674	Jodis lactearia	Little Emerald	5-6	L Woodlands and hedgerows
371	Sesia bembeciformis	Lunar Hornet Moth	7-8	L Larva wood boring. On sallows
2015	Drymonia ruficornis	Lunar Marbled Brown	4-5	L Oak woodland; comes to light
2319	Cosmia pyralina	Lunar-spotted Pinion	7-8	F Woodland, parkland and hedgerows
2270	Omphaloscelis lunosa	Lunar Underwing	8-10	C Widespread
2173	Hadena bicruris	Lychnis, The	5-7/8-9	F Quite widespread
1884	Abraxas grossulariata	Magpie, The	7-8	C Most frequent in gardens
1680	Cyclophora punctaria	Maiden's Blush	5-6/8	L Woodlands
1745	Larentia clavaria	Mallow, The	9-10	L Most frequent records from gardens
2009	Ptilodontella cucullina	Maple Prominent	5-7	L A few small 'pockets' of distribution
1812	Eupithecia inturbata	Maple Pug	7-8	F Can be in good numbers when seen
2293	Cryphia domestica	Marbled Beauty	7-8	F More common in towns & villages
2014	Drymonia dodonaea	Marbled Brown	5-6	L Little Linford Wood, with Oak
2171	Hadena confusa	Marbled Coronet	5-7	L Rare locally
2337	Oligia strigilis	Marbled Minor	5-7	F Frequently taken at light
2410	Protodeltote pygarga	Marbled White-spot	5-7	L Rarely recorded
1663	Alsophila aescularia	March Moth	3-4	F Males to light; females wingless
1778	Hydriomena impluviata	May Highflyer	5-7	L Mainly in woodlands
2349	Photedes fluxa	Mere Wainscot	7-8	F Damp woodlands
2247	Dichonia aprilina	Merveille du Jour	9-10	L More frequent in Oak woods
2340	Oligia fasciuncula	Middle-barred Minor	6-7	F Tiny and variable in colour
2280	Acronicta leporina	Miller, The	6-8	L Larva unusual; feeds on Birch
2225	Brachylomia viminalis	Minor Shoulder-knot	7-8	L Woodlands
2462	Callistege mi	Mother Shipton	5-6	L Day flying, especially in the sun
1941	Alcis repandata	Mottled Beauty	6-7	C Easily seen at rest on tree trunks
1819	Eupithecia exiguata	Mottled Pug	5-6	C Widespread
2387	Caradrina morpheus	Mottled Rustic	6-8	C - extremely so
1935	Erannis defoliaria	Mottled Umber	10-12	F Males very variable; females wingless
2299	Amphipyra tragopoginis	Mouse Moth	7-9	F Mouse-coloured; adult runs
2221	Cucullia verbasci	Mullein, The	4-5	L Obvious larva on Mullein
1689	Scopula marginepunctata	Mullein Wave	5-6/8-9	R A few records from Willen
2038	Nudaria mundana	Muslin Footman	6-8	R Rarely seen locally; Lavendon
2063	Diaphora mendica	Muslin Moth	5-6	F Males at light; white females rarely
171	Zygaena lonicerae	Narrow-bordered Five-spot Burnet	6-7	L Day flying
1846	Eupithecea nanata	Narrow-winged Pug	4-6/8	L Larva on Heather so adults rare
1823	Eupithecia venosata	Netted Pug	5-6	R Variable; Lavendon only
1800	Operophtera fagata	Northern Winter Moth	10-12	R Woodlands; Stony Stratford
1795	Epirrita dilutata	November Moth	10-11	C Widespread
2145	Discestra trifolii	Nutmeg, The	5-6/8-9	F May be on flowers in hot sunshine
2425	Colocasia coryli	Nut-tree Tussock	4-6/7-9	R Only Chilterns melanic form seen
1930	Biston strataria	Oak Beauty	3-4	L Woodlands
1637	Lasiocampa quercus	Oak Eggar	7-8	R Weston Underwood & Lavendon
1646	Drepana binaria	Oak Hook-tip	5-6/7-8	F Woodlands
1853	Eupithecia dodoneata	Oak-tree Pug	5-6	L In Oak woodland
1658	Cymatophorima diluta	Oak Lutestring	8-9	L Woodlands
2423	Nycteola revayana	Oak Nycteoline	9-11	L Woodlands
2300	Mormo maura	Old Lady	7-8	L Attracted to sugar rather than light
2312	Ipimorpha subtusa	Olive, The	7-9	L Requires damp situations
2271	Xanthia citrago	Orange Sallow	8-9	L Near Lime trees
15	Hepialus sylvina	Orange Swift	6-9	F Waste land and gardens
1926	Apocheima pilosaria	Pale Brindled Beauty	1-3	L Males on trunks; females wingless
1632	Trichiura crataegi	Pale Eggar	8-9	L Both sexes come to light
2276	Xanthia ocellaris	Pale-lemon Sallow	9-10	R Vagrant; Newport Pagnell
2389	Caradrina clavipalpis	Pale Mottled Willow	2-11	F Frequent visitor to moth traps
1796	Epirrita christyi	Pale November Moth	9-11	F Mainly in woodlands
1944	Serraca punctinalis	Pale Oak Beauty	5-7	L Woodlands
2236	Lithophane hepatica	Pale Pinion	10-5	R Shenley Wood; visits Ivy flowers
2011	Pterostoma palpini	Pale Prominent	5-6/8	F Frequently comes to light
2148	Polia bombycina	Pale Shining Brown	6-7	R Once common, now rare; Lavendon
2158	Lacanobia thalassina	Pale-shouldered Brocade	5-7	L Mostly woodlands
2028	Calliteara pudibunda	Pale Tussock	5-6	F One of the first to light after dusk
1652	Thyatira batis	Peach Blossom	8-9	L Mostly woodlands
1889	Semiothisa notata	Peacock Moth	5-6	Woodlands; Hazeley Wood

2119	Peridroma saucia	Pearly Underwing	9-10		Immigrant; does not breed here
1648	Drepana falcataria	Pebble Hook-tip	5-6/8	F	Woodlands
2003	Eligmodonta ziczac	Pebble Prominent	5-6/8	F	Mostly woodlands; comes to light
1931	Biston betularia	Peppered Moth	5-8	F	Normal common; melanic form few
1754	Eulithis prunata	Phoenix, The	7-8	L	In gardens, esp. with currants
2273	Xanthia togata	Pink-barred Sallow	9-10	F	Damp situations
2179	Panolis flammea	Pine Beauty	3-5	L	Most common in coniferous woods
1767	Thera firmata	Pine Carpet	7-11	L	Coniferous woodlands
1978	Hyloicus pinastri	Pine Hawk-moth	5-6	L	Most frequent in conifer plantations
1820	Eupithecia insigniata	Pinion-spotted Pug	5	R	Old orchards and hedges; Lavendon
2484	Schrankia costaestrigalis	Pinion-streaked Snout	6-8	L	Tiny; probably overlooked
2443	Autographa jota	Plain Golden Y	6-8	L	May be getting less common
1842	Eupithecia simpliciata	Plain Pug	6-8	L	Comes readily to light when in area
1715	Idaea straminata	Plain Wave	7	L	Woodlands; similar to Riband Wave
2278	Acronicta megacephala	Poplar Grey	5-5	F	Fairly widespread; comes to light
1981	Laothoe populi	Poplar Hawk-moth	5-7	C	Frequently comes to light
1998	Furcula bifida	Poplar Kitten	5-7	L	Seldom recorded locally
1655	Tethea or	Poplar Lutestring	5-8	L	Woodlands with Aspen
2186	Orthosia gracilis	Powdered Quaker	4-5	F	Woodlands, gardens *etc.*
1784	Melanthia procellata	Pretty Chalk Carpet	6-8	L	On limestone so few records
1976	Sphinx ligustri	Privet Hawk-moth	6-7	R	Was common; now rarely seen
1752	Cosmorhoe ocellata	Purple Bar	5-7	F	Lots of habitats; easily disturbed
2122	Diarsia brunnea	Purple Clay	6-8	L	Deciduous woodland
1919	Selenia tetralunaria	Purple Thorn	4-5/7-8	F	Woodlands
1995	Cerura vinula	Puss Moth	5-7	L	Large; larva unusual and interesting
2139	Cerastis rubricosa	Red Chestnut	3-4	F	Comes to light and sugar
1724	Xanthorhoe spadicearia	Red Twin-spot Carpet	5-6/7-8	C	- very
2452	Catocala nupta	Red Underwing	8-9	F	Impressive! Comes readily to sugar
2323	Apamea sublustris	Reddish Light Arches	6-7	R	Willen & Lavendon records only
1760	Chloroclista siterata	Red-green Carpet	4-5	L	Woodlands
2263	Agrochola lota	Red-line Quaker	9-10	F	Comes to light, sugar & Ivy flowers
2039	Atolmis rubricollis	Red-necked Footman	6-7	R	Day & night flying; N. Pagnell only
1713	Idaea aversata	Riband Wave	6-8	C	Widespread
1802	Perizoma affinitata	Rivulet, The	5-7	L	Very few records
2342	Mesoligia literosa	Rosy Minor	7-8	R	Mostly coastal; here at Lavendon
2361	Hydraecia micacea	Rosy Rustic	8-10	F	Various habitats, often damp
2035	Thumatha senex	Round-winged Muslin	7-8	L	Marshy areas
2064	Phragmatobia fuliginosa	Ruby Tiger	4-6/8-9	F	Widespread and often comes to light
1735	Catarhoe rudibata	Ruddy Carpet	6-7	R	Beautiful; Hollington wood only
2338	Oligia versicolor	Rufous Minor	6-7	L	Woodlands
2382	Hoplodrina blanda	Rustic, The	6-8	C	Widespread
2334	Apamea sordens	Rustic Shoulder-knot	5-6	F	A variable species
2274	Xanthia icteritia	Sallow, The	9-10	C	Frequently recorded at light
1997	Furcula furcula	Sallow Kitten	5-6/8	F	Comes readily to light
1808	Perizoma flavofasciata	Sandy Carpet	6-7	L	Flies at dusk in various habitats
2256	Eupsilia transversa	Satellite, The	9-4	F	Woodlands; larvae eat other larvae
1940	Deileptenia ribeata	Satin Beauty	6-8	L	Coniferous woodland
1709	Idaea subsericeata	Satin Wave	6-7	R	Walton lake; very rare
1645	Falcaria lacertinaria	Scalloped Hook-tip	5-6/7-8	L	Woodlands with Silver Birch
1920	Odontopera bidentata	Scalloped Hazel	5-6	F	In most habitats
1921	Crocallis elinguaria	Scalloped Oak	7-8	C	Various habitats and colour forms
2400	Heliothis armigera	Scarce Bordered Straw		R	Immigrant; rare so far inland
2047	Eilema complana	Scarce Footman	7-8	F	Belies its name in being frequent
2421	Bena bicolorana	Scarce Silver-lines	6-8	F	Green; most often in Oak woods
1788	Rheumaptera cervinalis	Scarce Tissue	4-6	R	On Barberry in a few gardens
1933	Agriopis aurantiaria	Scarce Umber	10-11	L	Males to light; females $\pm$ wingless
1888	Ligdia adjustata	Scorched Carpet	5-6/8	L	Woodlands, hedges & bushy places
1904	Plagodis dolabraria	Scorched Wing	5-6	F	Woodlands
1915	Ennomos erosaria	September Thorn	7-10	L	Mainly in woodlands
1879	Lobophora halterata	Seraphim, The	5-6	F	Woodlands
2126	Xestia c-nigrum	Setaceous Hebrew Character	5-7/8-10	C	Widespread
1732	Scotopteryx chenopodiata	Shaded Broad-bar	7-8	C	Flies by day; meadows *etc.*
1840	Eupithecia subumbrata	Shaded Pug	6-7	L	Often in damp areas

2216	Cucullia umbratica	Shark, The	6-7	L	Comes to light; on railings
2147	Hada nana	Shears, The	5-7	R	Few records; Willen
2077	Nola cucullatella	Short-cloaked Moth	6-7	F	Prefers woodlands and hedgerows
1746	Anticlea badiata	Shoulder Stripe	3-4	F	Seen when few moths on the wing
2205	Mythymna comma	Shoulder-striped Wainscot	6-7	L	Attracted to flowers and light
2092	Agrotis puta	Shuttle-shaped Dart	4-10	F	Variable with interesting forms
2391	Chilodes maritimus	Silky Wainscot	6-8	R	Willen & Walton reedbeds at night
1727	Xanthorhoe montanata	Silver-ground Carpet	5-7	C	Common amongst nettles
2441	Autographa gamma	Silver Y	Sp-A		Regular immigrant; numbers vary
1708	Idaea dimidiata	Single-dotted Wave	6-8	C	Widespread
169	Zygaena filipendulae	Six-spot Burnet	6-8	L	Day flying
2133	Xestia sexstrigata	Six-striped Rustic	7-8	F	Often comes to light
2335	Apamea scolopacina	Slender Brindle	6-8	F	Attracted to light, sugar and flowers
1811	Eupithecia tenuiata	Slender Pug	6-7	F	Damp woodlands and marshy places
1859	Chloroclystis chloerata	Sloe Pug	5-6	F	Around Blackthorn and hedgerows
2305	Euplexia lucipara	Small Angle Shades	6-7	F	Woodlands and gardens
1690	Scopula imitaria	Small Blood-vein	7-8	F	Widespread
1925	Apocheima hispidaria	Small Brindled Beauty	2-3	R	Lavendon only; females wingless
2331	Apamea unanimis	Small Clouded Brindle	5-7	L	Has ill-defined markings
2345	Photedes minima	Small Dotted Buff	6-8	F	Males frequent at light; females not
1707	Idaea seriata	Small Dusty Wave	8-9	L	Rests on walls by day
1633	Eriogaster lanestris	Small Eggar	2-3	R	Lavendon, but not very recently
1673	Hemiostola chrysoprasaria	Small Emerald	6-8	L	Associated with Traveller's-joy
1948	Ectropis crepuscularia	Small Engrailed	5-6	F	Woodlands and bushy places
2492	Herminia grisealis	Small Fan-foot	6-8	F	Woodlands and bushy places
1702	Idaea biselata	Small Fan-footed Wave	6-8	C	Comes frequently to light
2385	Spodoptera exigua	Small Mottled Willow	7-10		Immigrant; very rare so far inland
1759	Ecliptopera silaceata	Small Phoenix	5-6	F	Woodlands
2182	Orthosia cruda	Small Quaker	3-4	F	Mainly Oak woodland
1803	Perizoma alchemillata	Small Rivulet	6-7	F	Flies at dusk (to mercury vapour)
2379	Coenobia rufa	Small Rufous	7-8	R	Willen; damp places just before dusk
1712	Idaea emarginata	Small Scallop	6-8	L	Damp woodlands
1882	Pterapherapteryx sexalata	Small Seraphim	5-6/7-8	L	In damp places
2123	Diarsia rubi	Small Square-spot	5-6/8-9	C	In a wide variety of habitats
2350	Photedes pygmina	Small Wainscot	8-9	F	Damp woodland and marshy areas
1781	Horisme vitalbata	Small Waved Umber	5-6/8	L	Woodlands; larva as above
1875	Asthena albulata	Small White Wave	4-7	L	Flies about 1 hour before dusk
2397	Panemeria tenebrata	Small Yellow Underwing	5-6	L	Day flying in meadows *etc.*
1876	Hydrelia flammeolaria	Small Yellow Wave	6-7	L	Woodlands
2198	Mythimna impura	Smoky Wainscot	6-8	C	- very
2477	Hypena proboscidalis	Snout, The	6-8	C	Widespread
2197	Mythimna straminea	Southern Wainscot	7-8	L	Reedbeds and wet ditches
2450	Abrostola triplasia	Spectacle, The	5-7	F	Appears to be 'wearing spectacles'
1757	Eulithis mellinata	Spinach, The	6-8	L	Mainly in gardens
2227	Brachionycha sphinx	Sprawler, The	11-12	F	Comes to light even when temp. low
1932	Agriopis leucophaearia	Spring Usher	2-3	L	Males on trunks; females wingless
1769	Thera britannica	Spruce Carpet	5-7	F	Woodlands and gardens
2134	Xestia xanthographa	Square-spot Rustic	7-9	C	A very variable species
2131	Xestia rhomboidea	Square-spotted Clay	8	R	Woodland; few records, Lavendon
2113	Spaelotis ravida	Stout Dart	7-9	L	Becoming less frequent
2474	Rivula sericealis	Straw Dot	6-7/8-9	C	A tiny moth; quite common
2303	Thalpophila matura	Straw Underwing	7-8	F	Often comes to light
1864	Chesias legatella	Streak, The	9-10	C	Most uncommon until recently
1747	Anticlea derivata	Streamer, The	4-5	F	Woods and bushy places
2298	Amphipyra berbera	Svensson's Copper Underwing	7-9	F	.Day rest under bark or hollow trees
2007	Pheosia tremula	Swallow Prominent	5-6/8	F	Often comes to light
1922	Ourapteryx sambucaria	Swallow-tail Moth	6-7	C	A lovely moth
2279	Acronicta aceris	Sycamore, The	6-8	F	Larva like a cog-wheel when rolled
2339	Oligia latruncula	Tawny Marbled Minor	5-7	C	Widespread
2235	Lithophane semibrunnea	Tawny Pinion	10-11	L	Seldom seen; may be on Ivy flowers
1893	Semiothisa liturata	Tawny-barred Angle	6-7	L	Coniferous woodland
1838	Eupithecia icterata	Tawny-spotted Pug	7-8	F	Very variable
1790	Triphosa dubitata	Tissue, The	4-5/7-8	L	Gardens, but rarely seen

No.	Species	Common name	Months	Status	Notes
1816	*Eupithecia linariata*	Toadflax Pug	7-8	R	Newport Pagnell & Lavendon only
1867	*Aplocera plagiata*	Treble-bar	5-6/8-9	L	Open areas of grass and waste-land
1711	*Idaea trigeminata*	Treble Brown Spot	7-8	R	Willen records, but rare
2380	*Charanyca trigrammica*	Treble Lines	5-7	L	Not often seen; Oak woods
2127	*Xestia ditrapezium*	Triple-spotted Clay	6-8	R	Few records; Willen & N. Pagnell
1826	*Eupithecia trisignaria*	Triple-spotted Pug	6-7	R	Damp woodland rides; marshy areas
2118	*Lycophotia porphyrea*	True Lover's Knot	6-8	R	Willen, but rarely seen
2087	*Agrotis segetum*	Turnip Moth	5-6	F	Resident; reinforced by immigration
1809	*Perizoma didymata*	Twin-spot Carpet	6-8	F	Males & females to light; latter rare
2189	*Orthosia munda*	Twin-spotted Quaker	3-4	L	Widespread locally
2370	*Archanara geminipuncta*	Twin-spotted Wainscot	8-9	L	Reedbeds and damp areas
2381	*Hoplodrina alsines*	Uncertain, The	6-8	C	Widespread
2026	*Orgyia antiqua*	Vapourer, The	7-9	F	Males fly by day; females wingless
2170	*Hadena compta*	Varied Coronet	6-7	L	50 years in Britain; now widespread
1897	*Semiothisa wauaria*	V-Moth, The	7-8	R	Gardens & allotments with currants
1858	*Chloroclystis v-ata*	V-Pug, The	5-6/7-8	F	Attractive green; often at moth traps
1821	*Eupithecia valerianata*	Valerian Pug	6-7	R	Damp woodland; Willen
1716	*Rhodometra sacraria*	Vestal, The			Immigrant; several records
2384	*Hoplodrina ambigua*	Vine's Rustic	5-10	F	Resident and suspected immigrant
2475	*Parascotia fuliginaria*	Waved Black	6-7	R	Wolverton; larva on bracket fungi
1936	*Menophora abruptaria*	Waved Umber	4-6	F	Widespread, but most often in woods
2373	*Archanara sparganii*	Webb's Wainscot	8-9	R	Reedbeds; Willen only
2060	*Spilosoma lubricipeda*	White Ermine	5-7	F	Widespread
2031	*Leucoma salicis*	White Satin Moth	7-8	L	Near Poplar trees
2081	*Euxoa tritici*	White-line Dart	7-8	L	Variable; rarely recorded locally
2140	*Cerastis leucographa*	White-marked	3-4	R	Comes to sallow; Shenley Wood
1957	*Lomographa bimaculata*	White-pinion Spotted	5-6	F	Woodlands & hedgerows; after dusk
1835	*Eupithecia tripunctaria*	White-spotted Pug	5-9	F	Woodlands, river banks, damp areas
1937	*Peribatodes rhomboidaria*	Willow Beauty	6-8	C	Tree trunks by day
1799	*Operophtera brumata*	Winter Moth	9-2	C	Males to light; females wingless
1739	*Epirrhoe rivata*	Wood Carpet	6-8	L	A woodland species
1830	*Eupithecia absinthiata*	Wormwood Pug	6-7	C	Widespread
1659	*Achlya flavicornis*	Yellow Horned	3-4	L	In woods where Birch present
1742	*Camptogramma bilineata*	Yellow Shell	6-8	C	Numbers seem to be dwindling
1883	*Acasis viretata*	Yellow-barred Brindle	5-6	L	Rests by day on lichen surfaces
2264	*Agrochola macilenta*	Yellow-line Quaker	9-11	L	On Ivy flowers & over-ripe Bramble
2030	*Euproctis similis*	Yellow-tail	7-8	C	Widespread

Micromoths

No.	Species	Common name	Months	Status
4	*Micropterix aruncella*		5-6/7-8	Uncommon
5	*Micropterix calthella*		5-6	Widespread and common
6	*Eriocrania subpurpurella*		4-6	Widespread
7	*Eriocrania chrysolepidella*		4	
9	*Eriocrania sparrmannella*		4	Uncommon
12	*Eriocrania sangii*		3-4	Common
22	*Etainia louisella*		5-6/7-10	Local and fairly common
23	*Ectoedemia argyropeza*		6	Widespread and common
25	*Ectoedemia intimella*		6	Widespread and common
42	*Ectoedemia septembrella*		5-6	Common
50	*Stigmella aurella*		5-6/8	Widespread and very common
67	*Stigmella plagicolella*		5-6/9	Common
75	*Stigmella floslactella*		5/8	Widespread and common
92	*Stigmella anomalella*	Rose Leaf Miner	5/8	Widespread and very common
99	*Stigmella hybnerella*		4-5	Common
100	*Stigmella oxyacanthella*		6-7	Widespread and very common
112	*Stigmella luteella*		5-7	Common
116	*Stigmella lapponica*		5	Fairly common
125	*Emmetia marginea*		5-9	Common
128	*Phylloporia bistrigella*		5-7	Uncommon
129	*Incurvaria pectinea*		4-5	
130	*Incurvaria masculella*		4-5	Common
132	*Incurvaria praelatella*		6	
140	*Nematopogon swammerdamella*		5-6	Common

No.	Species	Common Name	Flight	Status
148	Nemophora degeerella		5-6	Locally common
150	Adela reaumurella		5-6	Common
152	Adela rufimitrella		5-6	Uncommon
158	Antispila metallella		5	Uncommon
159	Antispila treitschkiella		6-7	Rare
186	Psyche casta		6-7	Common
196	Morophaga choragella		7-8	Local and scarce
216	Nemapogon cloacella	Cork Moth	5-8	Common
220	Nemapogon clematella		6-8	Local and scarce
229	Monopis obviella		5-10	Local and uncommon
240	Tinea pellionella	Case-bearing Clothes Moth	6	Local and uncommon
246	Tinea semifulvella		5-8	Common
247	Tinea trinotella		5-8	Widespread and common
263	Lyonetia clerkella	Apple Leaf Miner	5-10	Very common
264	Bedellia somnulentella		7-8	Scarce
266	Bucculatrix nigricomella		5-6/7-8	Local and uncommon
271	Bucculatrix albedinella		6	Local and uncommon
274	Bucculatrix ulmella		5-6/8	Common
284	Caloptilia rufipennella		8/10-5	Uncommon
287	Caloptilia robustella		5-7/9-10	Common
288	Caloptilia stigmatella		7-5	Widespread and common
293	Caloptilia syringella		4-5/7	Common
294	Aspilapteryx tringipennella		5-6/7-8	Local and uncommon
297	Eucalybites auroguttella		5/7-8	Common
301	Parornix betulae		5/8	Uncommon
303	Parornix anglicella		5/7-8	Common
304	Parornix devoniella		5-8	Common
308	Parornix finitimella		5/6-8	Widespread and common
315	Phyllonorycter harrisella		5-6/7-9	Common
320	Phyllonorycter quercifoliella		4-6/7-10	Very common
321	Phyllonorycter messaniella		6-10	Common
323	Phyllonorycter oxyacanthae		4-5/6-8	Very common
326	Phyllonorycter blancardella		5/8	Widespread and common
332a	Phyllonorycter leucographella	Firethorn Leaf Miner	5/7/9-10	1st British record 1991. Common in MK
333	Phyllonorycter salictella ssp. viminiella		5-8	Common
335	Phyllonorycter salicicolella		5/8	Common
342	Phyllonorycter coryli	Nut Leaf Blister Moth	5/8	Common
345	Phyllonorycter rajella		5/8	Fairly common
351	Phyllonorycter lautella		5/8	Local and uncommon
353	Phyllonorycter ulmifoliella		5/8	Common
354	Phyllonorycter emberizaepenella		5/8	Local and uncommon
359	Phyllonorycter nicellii		5/8	Local and uncommon
360	Phyllonorycter kleemannella		8	Local and common
361	Phyllonorycter trifasciella		5/8/11	Common
362	Phyllonorycter acerifoliella		5/8	Widespread and common
363	Phyllonorycter platanoidella		5/8	Local and uncommon
364	Phyllonorycter geniculella		5/8	Common
385	Anthophila fabriciana	Nettle Tap	5-11	Very common; day flying
391	Glyphipterix simpliciella	Cock's-foot Moth	5-6	Very common
411	Argyresthia goedartella		6-9	Very common
414	Argyresthia curvella		6-7	Local and uncommon
416	Argyresthia glaucinella		7-8	Fairly common; in Oak woodland
417	Argyresthia spinosella		6-7	Common
419	Argyresthia semifusca		8	Local and uncommon
420	Argyresthia pruniella	Cherry Fruit Moth	6-8	Locally common
421	Argyresthia bonnetella		6-9	Widespread and common
422	Argyresthia albistria		7-8	Widespread and common
424	Yponomeuta evonymella	Bird-cherry Ermine	7-8	Common
425	Yponomeuta padella	Orchard Ermine	7-8	Widespread and common
426	Yponomeuta malinellus	Apple Ermine	7-8	Scarce
427	Yponomeuta cagnagella	Spindle Ermine	7-9	Locally common
430	Yponomeuta plumbella		7-8	Scarce

436	Pseudoswammerdamia combinella		5-6	Fairly common
438	Swammerdamia pyrella		5/8	Common
440	Paraswammerdamia albicapitella		6-10	Common
441	Paraswammerdamia lutarea		6-8	Widespread and common
442	Cedestis gysseleniella		6-8	Local and uncommon
449	Prays fraxinella	Ash Bud Moth	6-7/8-9	Widespread and common
450	Scythropia crataegella	Hawthorn Moth	6-7	Local and uncommon
451	Ypsolopha mucronella		8-4	Local and uncommon
453	Ypsolopha dentella	Honeysuckle Moth	7-9	Fairly common
455	Ypsolopha scabrella		7-9	Widespread and common
460	Ypsolopha parenthesella		7-10	Common
462	Ypsolopha sequella		7-10	Widespread and fairly common
463	Ypsolopha vittella		7-8	Local and uncommon
464	Plutella xylostella	Diamond-back Moth	3-11	Migratory; seen most years
465	Plutella porrectella		5/7/9	Scarce
470	Orthotaelia sparganella		3/7-8	Local and uncommon
481	Epermenia falciformis		7-9	Scarce
491	Coleophora gryphipennella		6-7	Widespread and common
493	Coleophora serratella		6-8	Common
495	Coleophora spinella	Apple and Plum Case-bearer	6-8	Common
513	Coleophora potentillae		6	Scarce
516	Coleophora trifolii	Large Clover Case-bearer	6-7	Common
517	Coleophora frischella	Small Clover Case-bearer	5-9	Uncommon
522	Coleophora lineolea		6-8	Widespread and common
525	Coleophora solitariella		7	Local and uncommon
535	Coleophora ibipennella		7-8	Widespread and common
536	Coleophora betulella		7-8	Widespread and common
559	Coleophora peribenanderi		6-7	Fairly common
582	Coleophora glaucicolella		7-8	Locally common
587	Coleophora caespititiella		5-6	Locally common
606	Elachista humilis		5-7	Scarce
608	Elachista rufocinerea		4-6	Widespread and common
609	Elachista maculicerusella		5-9	Uncommon
610	Elachista argentella		5-7	Common
623	Elachista bisulcella		5-8	Local and uncommon
631	Cosmiotes freyerella		4-8	Local and uncommon
640	Batia lunaris		7-8	Widespread and common
642	Batia unitella		6-9	Common
647	Hofmannophila pseudospretella	Brown House-moth	1-12	Widespread and common
648	Endrosis sarcitrella	White-shouldered House-moth	1-12	Widespread and common
649	Esperia sulphurella		5-6	Common
658	Carcina quercana		7-9	Widespread and common
663	Diurnea fagella		3-5	Common
664	Diurnea phryganella		10-11	Common
665	Dasystoma salicella		4	Scarce
667	Semioscopis steinkellneriana		4-5	Local and uncommon
672	Depressaria pastinacella	Parsnip Moth	9-4	Widespread and common
688	Agonopterix heracliana		7-4	Widespread and common
689	Agonopterix ciliella		7-5	Uncommon
692	Agonopterix subpropinquella		8-4	Local and uncommon
695	Agonopterix alstromeriana		7-5	Widespread and common
696	Agonopterix propinquella		8-7	Local and uncommon
697	Agonopterix arenella		8-5	Common
709	Agonopterix liturosa		7-8	Local and uncommon
724	Metzneria lappella		6-7	Local and uncommon
731	Eulamprotes atrella		6-8	Common
757	Recurvaria nanella		6-7	Local and uncommon
762	Anthrips mouffetella		6-9	Local and uncommon
765	Teleiodes vulgella		6-7	Common
779	Bryotropha affinis		5-8	Widespread common; larvae on mosses
782	Bryotropha senectella		6-8	Locally common; larvae on mosses
787	Bryotropha terrella		6-8	Widespread and common
792	Mirificarma mulinella		7-8	Uncommon

819 Scrobipalpa costella		10-5	Common
822 Scrobipalpa acuminatella		5-6/8	Locally common
841 Sophronia semicostella		6-8	Scarce
853 Anacampsis populella		7-9	Locally common
862 Dichomeris marginella	Juniper Webber	6-8	Local and uncommon
866 Brachmia blandella		6-8	Common
868 Helcystogramma rufescens		6-8	Common
871 Oegoconia deauratella		6-8	Common
873 Blastobasis lignea		7-8	Locally common
874 Blastobasis decolorella		5-6/9-11	Common
878 Batrachedra praeangusta		7-8	Uncommon
883 Mompha raschkiella		5/8	Widespread and common
888 Mompha propinquella		6-8	Local and uncommon
892 Mompha subbistrigella		10-5	Local and uncommon
893 Mompha epilobiella		7-6	Widespread and common
905 Blastodacna hellerella		6-8	Common
924 Hysterophora maculosana		5-6	Uncommon
925 Phtheochroa rugosana		5-7	Widespread and fairly common
926 Phalonidia manniana		5-7	Scarce
936 Cochylimorpha straminea		5-7/8-9	Widespread and common
937 Agapeta hamana		5-9	Widespread and common
938 Agapeta zoegana		5-8	Widespread and common
947 Aethes smeathmanniana		5-8	Locally common
949 Aethes dilucidana		7-8	Local and uncommon
951 Aethes beatricella		6-8	Local and uncommon
954 Eupoecilia angustana			
ssp. angustana		6-9	Widespread and common
962 Cochylis roseana		5-8	Widespread and common
964 Cochylis dubitana		6/8-9	Common
965 Cochylis hybridella		7-8	Common
969 Pandemis corylana	Chequered Fruit-tree Tortrix	7-9	Widespread and common
970 Pandemis cerasana	Barred Fruit-tree Tortrix	6-8	Widespread and common
972 Pandemis heparana	Dark Fruit-tree Tortrix	6-9	Widespread and common
977 Archips podana	Large Fruit-tree Tortrix	6-9	Widespread and common
980 Archips xylosteana	Variegated Golden Tortrix	6-8	Widespread and common
983 Choristoneura hebenstreitella		6-7	Local and uncommon
985 Cacoecimorpha pronubana	Carnation Tortrix	4-10	Common; naturalised adventive
986 Syndemis musculana		5-7	Common
987 Ptycholomoides aeriferanus		6-9	Common
989 Aphelia paleana	Timothy Tortrix	6-8	Locally common
993 Clepsis spectrana	Cyclamen Tortrix	5-9	Common
994 Clepsis consimilana		6-9	Common
998 Epiphyas postvittana	Light-brown Apple-moth	1-12	Widespread; native to Australia!
1000 Ptycholoma lecheana		6-7	Widespread and common
1001 Lozotaeniodes formosanus		6-8	Locally common
1002 Lozotaenia forsterana		6-7	Fairly common
1010 Ditula angustiorana	Red-barred Tortrix	7-8	Widespread and common
1011 Pseudargyrotoza conwagana		5-9	Widespread and common
1014 Isotrias rectifasciana		6-7	Uncommon
1015 Eulia ministrana		5-6	Locally common
1020 Cnephasia stephensiana	Grey Tortrix	6-8	Widespread and common
1021 Cnephasia asseclana	Flax Tortrix	6-8	Widespread and common
1024 Cnephasia incertana	Light Grey Tortrix	6-7	Widespread and common
1025 Tortricodes alternella		2-3	Common
1033 Tortrix viridana	Green Oak Tortrix	6-8	Very common some years; on Oak
1035 Acleris bergmanniana		6-8	Widespread and common
1036 Acleris forsskaleana		7-9	Widespread and common
1037 Acleris holmiana		7-8	Local and uncommon
1038 Acleris laterana		8-10	Locally common
1039 Acleris comariana	Strawberry Tortrix	6-11	Local and uncommon
1041 Acleris sparsana		8-5	Local and uncommon
1042 Acleris rhombana	Rhomboid Tortrix	8-11	Widespread and common
1044 Acleris ferrugana		7/9-4	Local and uncommon

1048 Acleris variegana	Garden Rose Tortrix	7-11	Widespread and common
1053 Acleris hastiana		6-7/8-4	Widespread and common
1054 Acleris cristana		7-5	Widespread but not common
1061 Acleris literana		8-5	Local and uncommon
1062 Acleris emargana		7-9	Widespread but not common
1063 Celypha striana		7-9	Widespread and common
1076 Celypha lacunana	Dark Strawberry Tortrix	5-10	Widespread and very uncommon
1082 Hedya pruniana	Plum Tortrix	5-8	Widespread and common
1083 Hedya nubiferana	Marbled Orchard Tortrix	6-8	Widespread and common
1084 Hedya ochroleucana		6-8	Widespread and common
1086 Hedya salicella		6-8	Local and uncommon
1088 Pseudosciaphila branderiana		6-8	Local and uncommon
1091 Apotomis lineana		5-8	Scarce
1092 Apotomis turbidana		6-8	Locally common
1093 Apotomis betuletana		7-9	Locally common
1094 Apotomis capreana		7-8	Local and uncommon
1097 Endothenia gentianaeana		6-7	Widespread and common
1108 Lobesia abscisana		5/7-8	Locally common
1110 Bactra furfurana		6-8	Uncommon
1113 Eudemis profundana		7-8	Scarce
1115 Ancylis achatana		6-8	Widespread and common
1120 Ancylis mitterbacheriana		5-8	Widespread and fairly common
1122 Ancylis obtusana		5-7	Uncommon
1126 Ancylis badiana		4-6/7-8	Widespread and common
1133 Epinotia bilunana		6-8	Locally common
1134 Epinotia ramella		7-9	Locally common
1136 Epinotia immundana		4-6/8-9	Local and uncommon
1138 Epinotia nisella		7-9	Locally common
1139 Epinotia tenerana	Nut Bud Moth	7-10	Locally common
1150 Epinotia abbreviana		7-8	Widespread and common
1152 Epinotia maculana		8-10	Local and uncommon
1155 Epinotia brunnichana		7-9	Widespread and common
1159 Rhopobota naevana	Holly Tortrix	7-9	Widespread and common
1165 Zeiraphera isertana		7-9	Widespread and common
1167 Gypsonoma aceriana		7-8	Locally common
1169 Gypsonoma dealbana		6-8	Widespread and common
1170 Gypsonoma oppressana		6-7	Scarce
1171 Gypsonoma minutana		7	Uncommon
1174 Epiblema cynosbatella		5-7	Widespread and common
1175 Epiblema uddmanniana	Bramble Shoot Moth	6-8	Widespread and common
1178 Epiblema roborana		6-8	Widespread and common
1183 Epiblema foenella		7-8	Widespread and common
1184 Epiblema scutulana		5-7	Widespread and common
1184a Epiblema cirsiana		5-6	Common
1192 Eucosma conterminana		7-8	Local and uncommon
1197 Eucosma campoliliana		6-8	Widespread and common
1199 Eucosma pupillana		7-8	Scarce
1200 Eucosma hohenwartiana		6-8	Widespread and common
1201 Eucosma cana		6-8	Widespread and common
1205 Spilonota ocellana	Bud Moth	6-9	Widespread and common
1205a Spilonota laricana		6-9	
1207 Clavigesta purdeyi	Pine Leaf-mining Moth	7-9	Local and uncommon
1208 Pseudococcyx posticana		5-6	
1210 Rhyacionia buoliana	Pine Shoot Moth	6-8	Locally common
1211 Rhyacionia pinicolana		7-8	Scarce
1212 Rhyacionia pinivorana	Spotted Shoot Moth	5-7	Local and uncommon
1216 Enarmonia formosana	Cherry-bark Tortrix	6-7	Local and uncommon
1219 Lathronympha strigana		5-9	Widespread and common
1232 Pammene populana		7-8	Uncommon
1236 Pammene fasciana		5-7	Local and uncommon
1239 Pammene rhediella	Fruitlet Mining Tortrix	5-6	Local and uncommon
1272 Pammene aurana		6-7	Widespread and common
1241 Cydia compositella		5-6/8	Widespread and common

1245 Cydia janthinana		7-8	Widespread and common
1251 Cydia jungiella		4-6	Widespread and common
1257 Cydia nigricana	Pea Moth	5-7	Locally common
1260 Cydia splendana		7-9	Widespread and common
1261 Cydia pomonella	Codling Moth	5-9	Widespread and very common
1274 Dichrorampha alpinana		6-8	Locally common
1279 Dichrorampha acuminatana		5-6/8	Locally common
1288 Alucita hexadactyla	Twenty-plume Moth	8-7	Widespread and common
1290 Chilo phragmitella		6-8	Uncommon
1292 Calomotropha paludella		6-8	Local and uncommon
1293 Chrysoteuchia culmella		6-9	Widespread and very common
1294 Crambus pascuella		6-8	Widespread but uncommon
1301 Crambus lathoniellus		5-8	Widespread and common
1302 Crambus perlella		6-8	Very common
1304 Agriphila straminella		7-9	Very common
1305 Agriphila tristella		7-9	Very common
1306 Agriphila inquinatella		6-9	Local and uncommon
1309 Agriphila geniculea		7-9	Widespread and common
1313 Catoptria pinella		7-8	Widespread and fairly common
1316 Catoptria falsella		6-8	Common; larva on mosses on buildings
1329 Donacaula forficella		6-8	Local and uncommon
1330 Donacaula mucronellus		6-8	Scarce
1331 Acentria ephemerella	Water Veneer	6-9	May be in huge numbers at MV lamps
1332 Scoparia subfusca		6-8	Widespread and common
1333 Scoparia pyralella		6-8	Widespread and common
1334 Scoparia ambigualis		5-9	Widespread and common
1334a Scoparia basistrigalis		7-8	Scarce
1338 Dipleurina lacustrata		6-8	Common; larva feeds on mosses
1336 Eudonia pallida		6-8	Scarce; larva on mosses and lichens
1342 Eudonia angustea		6-10	Scarce; overwinters; larva on mosses
1344 Eudonia mercurella		6-9	Common; larva feeds on mosses
1345 Elophila nymphaeata	Brown China-mark	7-8	Larva feeds on aquatic plants
1348 Parapoynx stratiolatata	Ringed China-mark	6-9	Larva feeds on aquatic plants
1350 Nymphula stagnata	Beautiful China-mark	7-8	Found near water
1354 Cataclysta lemnata	Small China-mark	6-8	Uncommon; larva on duckweed
1356 Evergestis forficalis	Garden Pebble	5-10	Widespread and common
1358 Evergestis pallidata		6-8	Local and uncommon
1361 Pyrausta aurata		5-9	Common; day flying in sunshine
1362 Pyrausta purpuralis		5-8	Uncommon; day flying in sunshine
1368 Loxostege sticticalis		6-8	Scarce migrant/temporary resident
1371 Sitochroa verticalis		6-8	Locally uncommon
1376 Eurrhypara hortulata	Small Magpie	5-8	Widespread and common
1377 Perinephela lancealis		6-8	Scarce
1378 Phlyctaenia coronata		6-8	Widespread and common
1380 Phlyctaenia perlucidalis		6-7	Uncommon; spread from fens since1988
1385 Ebulea crocealis		6-8	Scarce
1388 Udea lutealis		7-9	Widespread and common
1390 Udea prunalis		6-8	Widespread and common
1392 Udea olivalis		6-8	Generally common in hedges
1395 Udea ferrugalis	Rusty Dot	any	Uncommon immigrant in Bucks
1398 Nomophila noctuella	Rush Veneer	5-9	Often common; breeding migrant
1405 Pleuroptya ruralis	Mother of Pearl	5-9	Usually very common
1413 Hypsopygia costalis	Gold Triangle	4-11	Common; larva in hay, old nests, thatch
1415 Orthopygia glaucinalis		7-8	Widespread and fairly common
1417 Pyralis farinalis	Meal Moth	6-9	Often common in grain stores *etc.*
1421 Aglossa pinguinalis	Large Tabby	6-8	Fairly common
1424 Endotricha flammealis		6-9	Widespread and common
1425 Galleria mellonella	Wax Moth	7-10	Uncommon; larva in bees' comb wax
1426 Achroia grisella	Lesser Wax Moth	6-10	Uncommon; larva in bees' comb wax
1428 Aphomia sociella	Bee Moth	5-8	Larvae in nests of bees and wasps
1436 Conobratha repandana		6-8	Locally common; usually near oaks
1437 Acrobasis consociella		7-8	Scarce
1439 Trachycera advenella		7-8	Widespread and common

1452	*Phycita roborella*		6-9	Widespread and common
1454	*Dioryctria abietella*		7-8	Local; with Pine and Norway Spruce
1458	*Myelois circumvoluta*	Thistle Ermine	6-8	Often common amongst thistles
1469	*Euzophera cinerosella*		7-9	Chiefly coastal; rare in Bucks
1470	*Euzophera pinguis*		7-9	Common; larvae under Ash bark
1481	*Homoeosoma sinuella*		6-8	Locally common
1483	*Phycitodes binaevella*		6-8	Widespread and common
1485	*Phycitodes maritima*		5-8	Chiefly coastal; rare in Bucks
1488	*Agdistis bennetii*		6/8	Coastal; one vagrant at Willen
1497	*Amblyptilia acanthadactyla*		8-5	Uncommon
1501	*Platyptilia gonodactyla*		5-9	Widespread; larva on Colt's-foot
1504	*Platyptilia pallidactyla*		6-8	Widespread but not common
1509	*Stenoptilia pterodactyla*		6-9	Common; near Germander Speedwell
1513	*Pterophorus pentadactyla*	White Plume-moth	6-8	Very common; with bindweeds
1514	*Pterophorus galactodactyla*		6-7	Scarce; larva on Greater Burdock
1517	*Adaina microdactyla*		5-8	Fairly common; difficult to detect
1524	*Emmelina monodactyla*		1-12	Very common; often disturbed

True Flies

True flies comprise a very large group where the hind wings have been modified to become halteres (balancing organs) so that only a single pair of wings remains. They occur nearly everywhere.

References & Further Reading

Colyer, C.N. and Hammond, C.O. (1951).   Flies of the British Isles. F. Warne & Co.

Stubbs, A.E. and Falk, S.J. (1993). British Hoverflies. British Entomological & Natural History Society.

Ablabesmyia monilis	a Midge	Common; larva aquatic in muddy sediments
Anopheles maculipennis	a Mosquito	Common near stagnant water; may bite man
Anthomyia procellaris	a Muscid	Common on umbels & Brambles, grey with black markings
Argyra leucocephala	a Long-headed fly	Uncommon, silvery in appearance, woods
Austrolimnophila ochracea	a Crane fly	Common in MK woods
Baccha elongata	a Hoverfly	Common in MK woods; densely shaded situations
Beris chalybata	a Soldier fly	Common in MK woods
Beris vallata	a Soldier fly	In low vegetation, black thorax
Bibio hortulanus	a Fever fly	Common in gardens
Bibio johannis	a Fever fly	Common in MK woods
Bibio marci	St Mark's fly	Swarms over short grass close to ground; late April
Bicellaria vana	an Empid fly	Common in MK woods
Bombylius major	a Bee fly	Commonly seen in Spring; furry with long proboscis
Calliphora vicina	a Bluebottle	Around houses; females attracted to meat
Calliphora vomitoria	a Bluebottle	Around houses; females attracted to meat and fish
Cerodontha denticornis	a Leaf-miner	
Cheilosia albitarsis	a Hoverfly	Common at buttercups in damp meadows, woods
Cheilosia pagana	a Hoverfly	Common; open grassland, waste ground
Cheilosia proxima	a Hoverfly	Local; woods, uncommon
Chironomus cingulatus	a Midge	Occasional; larva aquatic in muddy sediments
Chironomus plumosus	a Midge	Common; larva aquatic in muddy sediments
Chironomus riparius	a Midge	Occasional; larva aquatic in muddy sediments
Chloromyia formosa	a Soldier fly	Common in MK woods
Chorisops tibialis	a Soldier fly	Common in MK woods
Chrysops relictus	a Horse fly	Occasional in vegetation near water
Chrysotoxum bicinctum	a Hoverfly	Occasional; grassy places near scrub and trees
Chrysotoxum festivum	a Hoverfly	Occasional; grassy places near scrub and trees
Cladotanytarsus atridorsum	a Midge	Common; larva aquatic in muddy sediments
Cladotanytarsus nigrovittatus	a Midge	Common; larva aquatic in muddy sediments
Clusia flava	a Fungus fly	Common in MK woods
Clusiodes gentilis	a Fungus fly	Common in MK woods
Clusiodes ruficollis	a Fungus fly	Common in MK woods
Conops quadrifasciata	a Thick-headed fly	Occasional; ragwort, umbels; larva parasite of bees
Cricotopus intersectus	a Midge	Common; larva aquatic in muddy sediments
Cricotopus obnoxius	a Midge	Occasional; larva aquatic in muddy sediments
Cricotopus sylvestris	a Midge	Common; larva aquatic in muddy sediments
Cryptochironomus redekei	a Midge	Common; larva aquatic in muddy sediments
Cryptochironomus supplicans	a Midge	Occasional; larva aquatic in muddy sediments
Culex molestus	a Mosquito	Common near water
Culex pipiens	a Mosquito	Common in MK woods
Culiseta annulata	a Mosquito	Common in/near stagnant water; bites man
Dasyneura trifolii	a Gall midge	Gall on White Clover flowers
Dasyneura ulmariae	a Gall midge	Gall on Meadowsweet leaves
Dasyneura urticae	a Gall midge	Gall on Stinging Nettle leaves
Dasysyrphus abostriatus	a Hoverfly	Common; sunny margins of woods
Dasysyrphus tricinctus	a Hoverfly	Uncommon; sunny margins of woods
Dioctria atricapilla	a Robber fly	Common in MK woods
Dioctria hyalinipennis	a Robber fly	Common in MK woods
Diplophus febrilis	Fever fly	Similar to St Mark's fly in shape and habitat
Diplophus femoratus	a Fever fly	Common in MK woods
Dolichopus festivus	a Long-headed fly	Damp places
Dolichopus ungulatus	a Long-headed fly	Mostly near water
Einfeldia dissidens	a Midge	Occasional; larva aquatic in muddy sediments

Elachiptera cornuta	a Frit fly	Common in MK woods
Empis nigripes	an Empid fly	Common in MK woods
Empis nuntia	an Empid fly	
Endochironomus albipennis	a Midge	Occasional; larva aquatic in muddy sediments
Endochironomus albipennis	a Midge	Common; larva aquatic in muddy sediments
Epistrophe elegans	a Hoverfly	Common in spring on *Prunus* or Hawthorn blossom
Eristalis arbustorum	a Hoverfly	Common in MK woods and other sites
Eristalis intricarius	a Hoverfly	Occasional in marshy and woodland situations
Eristalis nemorum	a Hoverfly	Common in open habitats throughout the year
Eristalis pertinax	a Hoverfly	Abundant throughout the year; large; near flowers
Eristalis tenax	Drone fly	Common; large Hoverfly; larva is rat-tailed maggot
Episyrphus balteatus	a Hoverfly	Abundant throughout the year; distinctive pattern
Eumerus tuberculatus	a Hoverfly	Occasional in MK woods
Euribia cardui	a Gall fly	Gall on Creeping Thistle stems
Fannia armata	a Housefly	
Fannia canicularis	Lesser Housefly	Common indoors and out
Fannia serena	a Housefly	Around houses
Ferdinandea cuprea	a Hoverfly	Occasional in old woodlands; rare in MK
Geomyza balachowskyi	a Grass fly	
Geomyza tripunctata	a Grass fly	Common in MK woods
Graceus ambiguus	a Midge	Occasional; larva aquatic in muddy sediments
Haematopota pluvialis	Cleg fly	Occasional in MK woods
Helophilus hybridus	a Hoverfly	Common in wet areas; thorax yellow/black stripes
Helophilus pendulus	a Hoverfly	Common near and away from ponds
Helophilus trivittatus	a Hoverfly	Scarce by grassy ponds and ditches
Helina evecta	a Muscid	
Helina lasiophthalma	a Muscid	
Jaapiella veronicae	a Gall midge	Gall on Germander Speedwell terminal buds
Leptocera fontinalis	a Dung fly	
Leptogaster cylindrica	a Robber fly	Common in MK woods
Leucozona lucorum	a Hoverfly	Widespread; lush vegetation in damp woods
Limnia unguicornis	a Marsh fly	Common in MK woods
Limnochironomus nervosus	a Midge	Occasional; larva aquatic in muddy sediments
Limnophila ferruginea	a Crane fly	Common in MK woods
Limonia duplicata	a Crane fly	Common in MK woods
Limonia flavipes	a Crane fly	Common in MK woods
Limonia nubeculosa	a Crane fly	Common in MK woods
Limonia tripunctata	a Crane fly	Common in MK woods
Lonchaea fumosa	a Lonchaeid fly	Common in MK woods
Lonchoptera lutea	a Pointed-wing fly	Common in MK woods
Lucilia caesar	a Greenbottle	Common on carrion, dung & flowers; rarely indoors
Lyciella affinis	a Marsh fly	Common in MK woods
Lyciella decipiens	a Marsh fly	Common in MK woods
Lyciella platycephala	a Marsh fly	
Lyciella rorida	a Marsh fly	Common in MK woods
Lyciella 10-punctata	a Marsh fly	
Melanostoma mellinum	a Hoverfly	Very common in grassland and woods
Melanostoma scalare	a Hoverfly	Common in grass and damp margins of woods
Meliscaeva auricollis	a Hoverfly	Common in and around woods
Merodon equestris	Large Narcissus fly	Common in Bluebell woods; large hairy hoverfly
Metasyrphus corollae	a Hoverfly	Abundant wherever patches of flowers are found
Metasyrphus latifasciatus	a Hoverfly	Widespread; wet meadows
Metasyrphus luniger	a Hoverfly	Common on flowers throughout the year
Metriocnemus hygropetricus	a Midge	Occasional; larva aquatic in muddy sediments
Microchrysa polita	a Soldier fly	Common in MK woods
Microspecta lindrothi	a Midge	Occasional; larva aquatic in muddy sediments
Microtendipes chloris	a Midge	Occasional; larva aquatic in muddy sediments
Microtendipes pedellus	a Midge	Occasional; larva aquatic in muddy sediments
Minettia rivosa	a Marsh fly	Common in MK woods
Molophilus griseus	a Crane fly	Common in MK woods
Morellia simplex	a Muscid fly	
Musca domestica	Common Housefly	Familiar to all
Myathropa florea	a Hoverfly	Widespread; in wet woodlands, common in MK

Neoascia podagricas	a Hoverfly	Common in damp meadows & woodland margins
Nephrotoma appendiculata	a Crane fly	Common in damp woods; yellow & black markings
Nephrotoma quadrifaria	a Crane fly	Common in MK woods
Nycteribia sp.	a Bat fly	Occasional; parasitic on Daubenton's bat
Ocydromia glabricula	an Empid fly	Damp places, on waterside vegetation
Oedalia holmgrenii	an Empid fly	
Opetia nigra	an Aschizid fly	Common in MK woods
Opomyza germinationis	a Grass fly	Common in MK woods
Ormosia lineata	a Crane fly	Common in MK woods
Ormosia nodulosa	a Crane fly	Common in MK woods
Orthocladius consobrinus	a Midge	Common; larva aquatic in muddy sediments
Orthocladius obtexens	a Midge	Occasional; larva aquatic in muddy sediments
Oscinella hortensis	a Fruit fly	Grassland
Pachygaster atra	a Soldier fly	
Pachymeria femorata	an Empid fly	Common in MK woods
Pachymeria tessellata	an Empid fly	Common in MK woods
Palloptera umbellatarum	a Picture-wing fly	Common in MK woods
Parachironomus arcuatus	a Midge	Occasional; larva aquatic in muddy sediments
Parachironomus tenuicaudatus	a Midge	Occasional; larva aquatic in muddy sediments
Parachironomus varus	a Midge	Occasional; larva aquatic in muddy sediments
Paracladius conversus	a Midge	Occasional; larva aquatic in muddy sediments
Pararhamphomyia tarsata	an Empid fly	
Paratrichocladius rufiventris	a Midge	Occasional; larva aquatic in muddy sediments
Phaonia errans	a Muscid fly	Common in MK woods
Phaonia fuscata	a Muscid fly	Common in MK woods
Phaonia halterata	a Muscid fly	On tree trunks
Pherbellia dubia	a Marsh fly	Common in MK woods
Pipunculus campestris	an Aschizid fly	Common in MK woods
Platycheirus albimanus	a Hoverfly	Widespread; wood margins, hedgerows, etc
Platycheirus clypeatus	a Hoverfly	Widespread; wet meadows and marshes
Platycheirus manicatus	a Hoverfly	Common on dry open grassland
Platycheirus scutatus	a Hoverfly	Common; woodland margin
Platycheirus tarsalis	a Hoverfly	Uncommon; woodland edge
Platypalpus agilis	an Empid fly	
Platypalpus annulipes	an Empid fly	
Platypalpus calceata	an Empid fly	Common in MK woods
Platypalpus minuta	an Empid fly	Common in MK woods
Philygria stictica	a Shore fly	
Phytomyza aquilegiae	a Leaf-miner	Mines in leaves of Columbine
Phytomyza ilicis	Holly leaf-miner	Mines in Holly leaves
Phytomyza ranunculi	a Leaf-miner	Larva mines buttercup leaves
Poecilobothrus nobilitatus	a Long-headed fly	Common in MK woods
Polietes lardarius	a Muscid fly	Common in MK woods
Pollenia angustigena	a Cluster fly	
Polypedilum nubeculosum	a Midge	Common; larva aquatic in muddy sediments
Procladius choreus	a Midge	Occasional; larva aquatic in muddy sediments
Psectrocladius barbimanus	a Midge	Occasional; larva aquatic in muddy sediments
Psectrocladius obvius	a Midge	Occasional; larva aquatic in muddy sediments
Psectrocladius sordidellus	a Midge	Common; larva aquatic in muddy sediments
Psectrotanypus varius	a Midge	Occasional; larva aquatic in muddy sediments
Psila rosae	Carrot fly	Larva infests carrots and other umbellifers
Psilotanypus rufovittatus	a Midge	Occasional; larva aquatic in muddy sediments
Ptychoptera albimana	a Crane fly	Low vegetation, esp. by water or damp places
Rhabdophaga rosaria	a Gall midge	Camellia gall on Willow terminal buds
Rhagio lineola	a Snipe fly	Common in MK woods
Rhagio scolopacea	Snipe fly	Common; rests head down on tree trunks in woods
Rhamphomyia sulcata	an Empid fly	Common in MK woods
Rhaphium appendiculatum	a Long-headed fly	Common in MK woods
Rhingia campestris	a Hoverfly	Common; hedgerows, woods near cows
Sarcophaga carnaria	a Flesh fly	Feeds on carrion; common around houses
Sargus bipunctatus	a Soldier fly	Common in MK woods
Scaeva pyrastri	a Hoverfly	Large, conspicuous; often many immigrants
Scaptomyza pallida	a Fruit fly	Common in MK woods

Scatophaga furcata	a Dung fly	Common in meadows, woods
Scatophaga lutaria	a Dung fly	Common in meadows, woods
Sciara thomae	a Fungus Gnat	Common in houses and where mushrooms are grown
Sepsis fulgens	a Sepsid fly	Common in MK woods
Sepsis cynipsea	a Sepsid fly	Common in MK woods
Sicus ferrugineus	a Thick-headed fly	Wood margins, on umbels or brambles
Spelobia clunipes	a Dung fly	
Spaerocera curvipes	a Dung fly	Frequent on carrion and decaying matter
Sphaerophoria scripta	a Hoverfly	Abundant wherever patches of flowers are found
Suillia variegata	a Heleomyzid fly	Common in MK woods
Syritta pipiens	a Hoverfly	Common in MK woods
Syrphus ribesii	a Hoverfly	Abundant in gardens, hedgerows, *etc.*
Syrphus torvus	a Hoverfly	Common; woodland and especially at sallow catkins
Syrphus vitripennis	a Hoverfly	Common; a wide range of habitats
Tabanus autumnalis	a Horsefly	Scarce; Nationally Notable
Tanypus punctipennis	a Midge	Occasional; larva aquatic in muddy sediments
Tanypus vilipennis	a Midge	Occasional; larva aquatic in muddy sediments
Tanytarsus bathophilus	a Midge	Occasional; larva aquatic in muddy sediments
Tanytarsus gracilentus	a Midge	Occasional; larva aquatic in muddy sediments
Tanytarsus holochlorus	a Midge	Common; larva aquatic in muddy sediments
Tanytarsus lestagei	a Midge	Common; larva aquatic in muddy sediments
Tanytarsus pallidicornis	a Midge	Occasional; larva aquatic in muddy sediments
Tanytarsus veralli	a Midge	Occasional; larva aquatic in muddy sediments
Taxomyia taxi	a Gall midge	Artichoke gall on terminal buds of Yew
Tephritis cometa	a Tephritid fly	Common in MK woods
Tephritis neesii	a Tephritid fly	Occasional in MK woods
Tephrochlamys tarsalis	a Heleomyzid fly	
Thaumatomyia notata	a Frit fly	Common in MK woods
Thereva nobilitata	a Stiletto fly	Common in MK woods
Tipula oleracea	a Crane fly	Common in MK woods
Tipula paludosa	a Crane fly	Common in MK woods
Tipula scripta	a Crane fly	
Tipula vernalis	a Crane fly	
Tricholauxania pracusta	a Marsh fly	Common in MK woods
Volucella bombylans	a Hoverfly	Common in woods; a bumblebee mimic
Volucella inanis	a Hoverfly	Uncommon / local
Volucella inflata	a Hoverfly	Scarce; Nationally Notable
Volucella pellucens	a Hoverfly	Common in MK woods
Wachtiella persicariae	a Gall midge	Gall on Amphibious Bistort leaves
Xanthempis scutellata	an Empid fly	Common in MK woods
Xanthempis trigrammica	an Empid fly	Common in MK woods
Xylota segnis	a Hoverfly	Common in MK woods
Xylota sylvarum	a Hoverfly	Common in MK woods

Fleas

Fleas lost their wings during evolution to their parasitic habit on animals, have strong hind legs for jumping and are compressed laterally to facilitate movement through fur or feathers.

Ceratophyllus gallinae	a Bird flea	Occasional in nest boxes
Ctenocephalides canis	Dog flea	Parasite of domestic pets
Ctenocephalides felis	Cat flea	Parasite of domestic pets
Dasypsyllus gallinulae	a Bird flea	Occasional in nest boxes
Ischnopsyllus sp.	a Bat flea	Occasional; parasitic on Pipistrelle bat
Pulex irritans	Human flea	Found on Fox
Spilopsyllus cuniculi	Rabbit flea	Usually on ears; vector of myxomatosis

Sawflies, Ants, Bees and Wasps

This is another very large group comprising both solitary and social insects. Typically each has two pairs of membranous wings (with rather large squarish cells) and biting mouthparts although some have developed long tongues to reach nectar secreted in flowers. Sawflies may be distinguished by having no waist so that the abdomen joins the thorax across its full width. The name is derived from the saw-like ovipositors of most females. Ants, Bees and Wasps do have a waist and range in size from small, almost microscopic species, to relatively large Bumble and Carpenter bees and Social wasps.

References & Further Reading

Prys-Jones, O.E and Corbet, S.A. (1991). Bumblebees. Naturalists' Handbook 6. Richmond Publishing Company.

Redfern, M. and Askew, R.R. (1992). Plant Galls. Naturalists' Handbook 17, Richmond Publishing Company.

Richards, O.W. (1980). Scoliodea, Vespoidea and Sphecoidea (Hymenoptera, Aculeata). Handbooks for the Identification of British Insects. Royal Entomological Society.

Zahradnik, J. (1991). Bees, Wasps and Ants. Hamlyn.

Andrena fulva	Tawny Mining bee	Commonly nests in lawns
Andricus fecundator	a Gall wasp	Artichoke gall on Oak
Andricus kollari	a Gall wasp	Marble gall on Oak
Andricus quercuscalicis	a Gall wasp	Knopper gall on Oak
Anthophora plumipes	Hairy-footed Flower bee	Common in gardens visiting tubular flowers
Apis mellifera	Honey bee	Semi-domesticated; source of honey
Biorhiza pallida	a Gall wasp	Oak Apple gall on buds of Oak
Bombus hortorum	Large Garden Bumble bee	Common; very long tongue; nests near ground
Bombus lapidarius	Large Red-tailed Bumble	Very common in woods, fields, gardens, *etc.*
Bombus lucorum	White-tailed Bumble bee	Abundant; early flyer; nests underground
Bombus pascuorum	Common Carder bee	Common in gardens, woods, fields; nests on ground
Bombus pratorum	Early Bumble bee	Common; nests above ground
Bombus ruderarius	Red-tailed Carder bee	Common in open country; nests near ground
Bombus terrestris	Buff-tailed Bumble bee	Common everywhere; nests underground
Chrysis ignita	a Ruby-tailed wasp	Common; lays eggs in nests of Mason bees, *etc.*
Cynips divisa	a Gall wasp	Small gall on Oak leaves
Cynips quercusfolii	a Gall wasp	Cherry gall on Oak leaves
Diplolepis rosae	a Gall wasp	Robin's Pin-cushion (Bedeguar) on Dog Rose
Dolichovespula media	a Social wasp	Was rare but increasing; nests in hedges
Dolichovespula sylvestris	Tree wasp	Occasional; nest in bushes
Formica fusca	an Ant	Common; in shady places including gardens
Lasius flavus	Yellow Meadow ant	Common small yellow ant; nests in dry places
Lasius niger	Black Garden ant	Abundant; brown/black; nests under pavements
Liposthenus latreillei	a Gall wasp	Gall on Ground Ivy stems and leaves
Megachile centuncularis	Patchwork Leaf-cutter	Commonest leaf-cutter; attacks roses
Melecta albifrons	a Mason bee	Uncommon; cuckoo in nests of *Anthophora* sp.
Monomorium pharaonis	Pharaoh's ant	Occasional pest in heated buildings, very small
Myrmica rubra	a Red ant	Common everywhere; reddish-brown; sting painful
Myrmica ruginodis	a Red ant	Common in dry soils
Neuroterus numismalis	a Gall wasp	Silk Button Spangle gall on Oak
Neuroterus quercusbaccarum	a Gall wasp	Common Spangle and Currant galls on Oak
Osmia rufa	Red Mason bee	Common; nests in holes often in walls/gardens
Phymatocera aterrima	a Sawfly	In gardens, larva can defoliate Solomon's Seal
Pontania proxima	a Gall-forming sawfly	Bean gall on leaves of Crack Willow
Pontania viminalis	a Gall forming sawfly	Circular galls on willow leaves
Psithyrus bohemicus	a Cuckoo bee	Uncommon; can take over nest of *B. lucorum*
Psithyrus sylvestris	a Cuckoo bee	Widely distributed; takes over nest of *B. pratorum*
Tenthredo arcuata	a Sawfly	Larva feeds on Red Clover
Tenthredo scrophulariae	a Sawfly	Larva feeds on Figwort
Urocerus gigas	Wood wasp	Larva feeds on wood
Vespa crabro	Hornet	Largest wasp; reddish; nests in hollow trees/cavity
Vespula germanica	German wasp	Common; nests in holes in ground or buildings
Vespula vulgaris	Common wasp	Found everywhere; nests in ground or buildings

Beetles

7-spot Ladybird

Beetles are the most numerous group of animals on earth, with well over 350,000 species. They are readily recognised by their robust structure in which the front wings are tough and rigid whilst concealing the membranous hindwings beneath. Although almost all of them can fly, it is most usual in almost all habitats to find them among vegetation and on the ground where they move quite speedily.

This list comprises mostly those species recorded by Colin Plant in his survey of three ancient woodlands in Milton Keynes, with the addition of those identified by others.

References & Further Reading

Hodge, P.J. and Jones, R.A. (1995). New British Beetles; Species not in Joy's Practical Handbook. British Entomological & Natural History Society.

Joy, N.H. (1932). A Practical Handbook of British Beetles. E.W. Classey.

Majerus, M.E.N and Kearns, P.W.E. (1987). Ladybirds. Richmond Publishing Company.

Plant, C.W. (1996). A Survey of the Saproxylic Coleoptera at Howe Park Wood, Linford Wood and Shenley Wood. Ecological Studies in Milton Keynes, No. 133. Milton Keynes Parks Trust.

Abax parallelepipedus	a Ground beetle	Common in woods
Achenium humile	a Rove beetle	Common in woods/grassland
Acilius sulcatus	a Diving beetle	Common in ponds and still waters
Adalia 2-punctata	2-spot Ladybird	Abundant; very variable patterns; red/black
Adalia 10-punctata	10-spot Ladybird	Common; hedgerows, woods; v. variable; red/black
Agapanthea villosoviridescens	a Longhorn beetle	Nationally Notable B; on flowers in damp places
Agonum assimile	a Ground beetle	Common in woods
Agonum dorsale	a Ground beetle	Common in woods
Agriotes acuminatus	a Click beetle	Common in woods
Agriotes lineatus	a Click beetle	Common in grassland; larva is wireworm pest
Agriotes obscurus	a Click beetle	
Agriotes pallidulus	a Click beetle	Common in woods
Agriotes sputator	a Click beetle	
Aleochara bipustulata	a Rove beetle	
Aleochara ruficornis	a Rove beetle	Common in woods
Amara apricaria	a Ground beetle	
Amara familiaris	a Ground beetle	Common in woods
Amara ovata	a Ground beetle	
Amara plebeja	a Ground beetle	Common in dry grassy areas
Amphimallon solstitialis	Summer Chafer	Occasional; swarms round trees in dry places
Anacaena globulus	a Water beetle	Ponds, ditches
Anacaena limbata	a Water beetle	Ponds, ditches
Anaglyptus mysticus	a Longhorn beetle	Woodland, especially flowers of Hawthorn
Anaspis costae	a Scraptid beetle	Common in woods
Anaspis humeralis	a Scraptid beetle	Common in woods
Anaspis frontalis	a Scraptid beetle	Common in woods
Anaspis maculata	a Scraptid beetle	Common in woods
Anaspis regimbarti	a Scraptid beetle	Common in woods
Anobium punctatum	Furniture beetle	The Woodworm; saproxylic, common indoors/out
Anotylus rugosus	a Rove beetle	Common in woods
Anotylus sculpturatus	a Rove beetle	Common in woods
Anotylus tetrocrinatus	a Rove beetle	Common in woods/grassland
Anthicus antherinus	an Anthicid beetle	Common; compost heaps and other decaying veg
Anthrenus verbasci	Varied Carpet beetle	Adults visit flowers; larva eats woollens, feathers
Aphidecta obliterata	Larch Ladybird	Uncommon; in coniferous woodland
Aphthona euphorbiae	a Leaf beetle	Common in woods
Apion curtirostre	a Weevil	Common; in vegetation / leaf litter
Aridius nodifer	a Mould beetle	Very common in woods and grassland
Asaphidion curtum	a Ground beetle	Common in woods

Asaphidion flavipes	a Ground beetle	Banks of rivers, damp places
Atheta crassicornis	a Rove beetle	Common in woods
Atheta fungi	a Rove beetle	Common in woods
Atheta hepatica	a Rove beetle	
Atheta laticollis	a Rove beetle	
Atheta nigricornis	a Rove beetle	Common in woods
Athous bicolor	a Click beetle	Common in woods
Athous haemorrhoidalis	a Click beetle	Abundant in hedgerows and grassland
Athous hirtus	a Click beetle	
Athous vittatus	a Click beetle	On young trees
Atomaria fuscata	a Fungus beetle	
Atomaria nigrirostris	a Fungus beetle	
Badister bipustulatus	a Ground beetle	Common in woods
Batophila rubi	a Leaf beetle	
Barypeithes pellucidus	a Weevil	Common in woods
Bembidion biguttatum	a Ground beetle	Common in woods
Bembidion guttula	a Ground beetle	Common in woods
Bembidion harpaloides	a Ground beetle	Common in woods
Bembidion lunulatum	a Ground beetle	Common in woods
Bembidion obtusum	a Ground beetle	
Bembidion punctatum	a Ground beetle	Generally by river banks
Bembidion unicolor	a Ground beetle	
Brachypterus glaber	a Scavenging beetle	Common in woods
Brachypterus urticae	a Scavenging beetle	Common in woods; on nettles
Bradycellus verbasci	a Ground beetle	Common in woods
Bruchus atomarius	a Seed beetle	Common; Nationally Notable B; larva in seed
Byrrhus pilula	a Pill beetle	Common in spring among moss/grass
Byturus tomentosus	Raspberry beetle	Common; gnaws and lays eggs in raspberry buds
Calathus melanocephalus	a Ground beetle	Common in woods
Calathus piceus	a Ground beetle	Common in woods
Calvia 14-guttata	Cream-spot Ladybird	Uncommon; on shrubs and small trees
Cantharis cryptica	a Soldier beetle	Common among flowers on woodland margin
Cantharis decipens	a Soldier beetle	Common among flowers on woodland margin
Cantharis lateralis	a Soldier beetle	Common among flowers in woods
Cantharis lividia	a Soldier beetle	Common among flowers
Cantharis nigra	a Soldier beetle	Common among flowers in woods
Cantharis nigricans	a Soldier beetle	Common among flowers in woods
Cantharis pellucida	a Soldier beetle	Common among flowers in woods
Cantharis rufa	a Soldier beetle	Common among flowers in woods
Cantharis rustica	a Soldier beetle	Abundant among flowers
Carabus violaceus	Violet Ground beetle	Common in gardens, hedgerows, under stones
Cassida rubiginosa	a Tortoise beetle	On thistles
Cassida vibex	a Tortoise beetle	On knapweeds
Cerylon ferrugineum	a Cerylonid beetle	Under bark or saproxylic
Ceuthorhynchidius troglodytes	a Weevil	Common in woods
Ceuthorhynchidius pollinarius	a Weevil	Common in woods; on nettles
Ceuthorhynchidius quadridens	a Weevil	Common in woods
Chaetocnema concinna	a Leaf beetle	Common in woods
Chaetocnema hortensis	a Leaf beetle	Common in woods
Chalcoides aurata	a Leaf beetle	Common in woods
Chalcoides aurea	a Leaf beetle	Common in woods
Chalcoides fulvicornis	a Leaf beetle	Uncommon; on Aspen, brilliant golden green
Chalcoides plutus	a Leaf beetle	Rare, on poplars willows and Aspen
Chilocorus renipustulatus	Kidney-spot Ladybird	Common in sallow, Poplar & Birch woods
Choleva spadicea	a Leidid beetle	In vegetable refuse
Chrysolina polita	a Leaf beetle	Common on herbage of river banks / damp places
Cicindela campestris	Green Tiger beetle	Occasional; swift runner / flyer
Cidnopus minutus	a Click beetle	Common in woods
Cionus scrophulariae	a Weevil	Common in woods on Figwort
Cis bilamellatus	a Cissid beetle	Common in woods
Cis boleti	a Cissid beetle	Common in woods
Clivina fossor	a Ground beetle	Common; prefers cultivated land
Clytus arietis	Wasp beetle	Common; saproxylic

Coccinella 7-punctata	7-spot Ladybird	Found in almost every place where there are aphids
Coprophilus striatulus	a Rove beetle	
Corticaria impressa	a Mould beetle	Common in woods
Cortinicara gibbosa	a Mould beetle	Common in woods; on thistles
Crepidodera transversa	a Leaf beetle	Common in woods
Crioceris asparagi	Asparagus beetle	A pest of Asparagus; gardens
Cylindronotus laevioctostriatus	a Darkling beetle	Common in woods
Dasytes aerosus	a Scavenging beetle	Locally distributed
Denticollis linearis	a Click beetle	Common in woods; saproxylic
Deronectes elegans	a Diving beetle	Occasional; in ponds and still water
Donacia simplex	a Leaf beetle	Feeds on aquatic plants
Dorcus parallelipipedus	Lesser Stag beetle	Common in MK woods; saproxylic
Dorytomus dejeani	a Weevil	On willows, poplars, sallows & Aspen
Dorytomus tortrix	a Weevil	On willows
Dromius linearis	a Ground beetle	Common in woods
Dromius quadrimaculatus	a Ground beetle	Common in woods
Drusilla canaliculata	a Rove beetle	Common in woods
Dytiscus marginalis	Great Diving beetle	Relatively common in weedy ponds and still water
Enicmus transversus	a Mould beetle	Common in woods
Epuraea aestiva	a Scavenging beetle	Common in woods
Epuraea melanocephala	a Scavenging beetle	Common in woods
Epuraea melina	a Scavenging beetle	Common in woods
Ernobius mollis	a Woodborer	Common; saproxylic, outdoors
Euophryum confine	a Weevil	Common in woods; saproxylic
Eutrichapion loti	a Weevil	Common; ground living
Exochomus 4-pustulatus	Pine Ladybird	Common in coniferous woodlands
Galerucella lineola	a Leaf beetle	Common in woods
Gonodera luperus	a Darkling beetle	Saproxylic
Grammoptera ruficornis	a Longhorn beetle	Common in woods; saproxylic
Gymnetron pascuorum	a Weevil	Common in woods
Gymnetron villosulum	a Weevil	Forms gall on Water Speedwell fruits
Gyrinus spp.	Whirligig beetles	Common; whirl around on surface of water
Habrocerus capillaricornis	a Rove beetle	Common in woods
Haliplus flavicollis	a Water beetle	Common among blanketweed in ponds
Halyzia 16-guttata	Orange Ladybird	Uncommon; in mature woodlands
Harpalus affinis	a Ground beetle	Common in dry grassy areas and cultivated fields
Harpalus rufibarbis	a Ground beetle	Common in dry grassy areas and cultivated fields
Harpalus rufipes	a Ground beetle	The dominant carabid of cultivated fields
Helodes marginata	a Helodid beetle	Common; minute beetles found near ponds/streams
Helophorus aquaticus	a Water beetle	Common in still water, ditches
Hermaephaga mercurialis	a Leaf beetle	On Dog's Mercury
Hoplia philanthus	a Scarab beetle	On flowers
Hydrobius fuscipes	a Water beetle	Common in still water
Ilybius ater	a Diving beetle	Common in ponds and lakes
Ischnomera caerulea	a Flower beetle	RDB 3; dead wood indicator species
Laccobius minutus	a Water beetle	Common in ponds
Laccophilus minutus	a Diving beetle	Common in ponds and ditches
Laccophilus variegatus	a Diving beetle	Common in ponds and ditches
Lampyris noctiluca	Glow-worm	Occasional; females emit light; larva feeds on snails
Lathrimaeum atrocephalum	a Rove beetle	Very common in woods/grassland
Lathrobium brunnipes	a Rove beetle	Common in woods
Lathrobium fulvipenne	a Rove beetle	Common in woods
Lathrobium longulum	a Rove beetle	Common in woods
Leistus ferrugineus	a Ground beetle	Common in woods
Leistus fulvibarbis	a Ground beetle	Common in woods
Leistus rufomarginatus	a Ground beetle	
Leistus spinibarbis	a Ground beetle	Common in woods
Lema lichenis	a Leaf beetle	
Lesteva heeri	a Rove beetle	In wet moss
Lochmaea crataegi	a Leaf beetle	Common in woods; found on hawthorn
Longitarsus atricillus	a Leaf beetle	On leguminous plants
Longitarsus luridus	a Leaf beetle	Common in woods and on thistles
Longitarsus parvulus	Flax Flea beetle	Nationally Notable A, may damage flax crops

Loricera pilicornis	a Ground beetle	Common in woods
Malachius bipustulatus	Bladder beetle	Widespread; hunts other insects among flowers
Malachius viridis	a Scavenging beetle	Locally distributed; occasional in MK woods
Malthinus flaveolus	a Soldier beetle	Abundant on shrubs and grasses on wood margins
Malthodes minimus	a Soldier beetle	Common among flowers in woods
Malvapion malvae	a Weevil	Common in woods
Medon propinquus	a Rove beetle	Common in woods/grassland
Megarthrus sinuatocollis	a Rove beetle	Common in woods/grassland
Megasternum obscurum	a Hydrophilid beetle	Very common
Melanotus erythropus	a Click beetle	Common in woods
Meligethes aeneus	a Scavenging beetle	Common in woods
Meligethes flavimanus	a Scavenging beetle	Common in woods
Meligethes nigrescens	a Scavenging beetle	Common in woods
Metoecus paradoxus	a Rhipiphorid beetle	Nationally Notable B; rare; in wasp nests
Metopsia clypeata	a Rove beetle	Common in woods/grassland
Micraspis 16-punctata	16-spot Ladybird	Common in grassy places; yellow/black
Microcara testacea	a Scirtid beetle	
Micropeplus fulvus	a Rove beetle	Common in woods/grassland
Mycetoporus lepidus	a Rove beetle	Common in woods
Mycetoporus splendens	a Rove beetle	Common in woods/grassland
Mycetoporus splendidus	a Rove beetle	Common in woods/grassland
Nargus velox	a Leidid beetle	Very common in woods and grassland
Nebria brevicolis	a Ground beetle	Common in dry grassy areas and cultivated fields
Nedyus quadrimaculatus	a Weevil	Very common in woods; usually on Stinging Nettles
Noterus clavicornis	a Diving beetle	Occasional in densely vegetated ponds & lakes
Notiophilus biguttatus	a Ground beetle	Common in woodlands
Notiophilus palustris	a Ground beetle	Common in woodlands
Notiophilus substriatus	a Ground beetle	Common in areas with little vegetation
Oedemera lurida	a Flower beetle	Common on flowers
Oedemera nobilis	a Flower beetle	Common on flowers
Olibrus corticalis	a Phalacrid beetle	Rare, on mayweeds
Olophrum piceum	a Rove beetle	In damp places and moss
Omalium caesum	a Rove beetle	Common in woods
Omalium excavatum	a Rove beetle	Common in woods
Omalium italicum	a Rove beetle	Common in woods
Omalium rivulare	a Rove beetle	Common in woods
Omosita colon	a Scavenging beetle	Common in woods
Opilo mollis	a Clerid beetle	Nationally Notable B
Othius laeviusculus	a Rove beetle	In moss
Othius punctulatus	a Rove beetle	Common in woods/grassland
Otiorhynchus singularis	a Weevil	Common in woods
Otiorhynchus sulcatus	a Weevil	Common in woods
Oulema melanopa	a Leaf beetle	Common in woods; occasional on thistles
Oxypoda lividipennis	a Rove beetle	Common in woods
Oxystoma pomonae	a Weevil	Common in woods
Patrobus atrorufus	a Ground beetle	Common in woods
Perapion hydrolapathi	a Weevil	Common in woods
Phaedon tumidulus	a Leaf beetle	Common in woods
Philonthus cognatus	a Rove beetle	Common in woods
Philonthus decorus	a Rove beetle	Common in woods
Philonthus fuscipennis	a Rove beetle	Common in woods
Philonthus laminatus	a Rove beetle	Common in woods
Philonthus marginatus	a Rove beetle	Common in woods
Philonthus varius	a Rove beetle	Common in woods
Phyllobius argentatus	a Weevil	Common in woods
Phyllobius maculicornis	a Weevil	Common in woods
Phyllobius parvulus	a Weevil	On nettles
Phyllobius pomaceus	Green Nettle Weevil	Abundant, on nettles
Phyllobius pyri	a Weevil	Common in woods; on thistles
Phyllobius roboretanus	a Weevil	Common in woods; on thistles
Phyllobius viridiaeris	a Weevil	Common in woods; on thistles
Phyllodecta vulgatissima	a Leaf beetle	On willows, poplars, hibernate under bark
Phyllotreta atra	a Leaf beetle	Common in woods

Phyllotreta diademata	a Leaf beetle	Mostly on crucifers
Phyllotreta undulata	Lesser Striped Flea beetle	Pest of Turnip
Plagiodera versicolora	a Leaf beetle	Larva attacks willow leaf
Platambus maculatus	a Diving beetle	Common in running water
Plataraea brunnea	a Rove beetle	Common in woods
Platycis minuta	Net-winged beetle	Nationally Notable B; dead wood indicator species
Platypus cylindrus	Oak Pin-hole borer	Nationally Notable B; dead wood indicator species
Pogonochaerus hispidus	a Longhorn beetle	Saproxylic, on Ivy
Polydrusus cervinus	a Weevil	Common in woods
Polydrusus pterygomalis	a Weevil	
Polydrusus undatus	a Weevil	Common in woods
Potamonectes depressus	a Diving beetle	Common in lakes and rivers with gravelly beds
Pria dulcamarae	a Scavenging beetle	Common in woods
Prionychus ater	a Darkling beetle	Nationally Notable; found under loose bark
Propylea 14-punctata	14-spot Ladybird	Uncommon; on shrubs; yellow/black many patterns
Protapion apricans	a Weevil	Common in woods
Protapion dichroum	a Weevil	Common in woods
Protapion nigritarse	a Weevil	Common in woods
Protapion trifolii	a Weevil	Common in woods
Psylliodes chrysocephala	a Flea beetle	Larva in cauliflower stems, adult on leaves and flowers
Psylliodes napi	a Flea beetle	Common in woods
Psyllobora 22-punctata	22-spot Ladybird	Common in low vegetation; yellow with black spots
Pterostichus cupreus	a Ground beetle	Common in agricultural ground
Pterostichus macer	a Ground beetle	
Pterostichus madidus	Strawberry beetle	Common in gardens and other cultivated ground
Pterostichus melanarius	a Ground beetle	Common in agricultural ground
Pterostichus niger	a Ground beetle	
Pterostichus nigrita	a Ground beetle	
Pterostichus strenuus	a Ground beetle	Common in grassy areas and woodland edges
Pterostichus vernalis	a Ground beetle	
Ptilinus pectinicornis	Fan-bearing Woodborer	Common; saproxylic, mainly outdoors
Ptinus fur	White-marked Spider b.	In dry organic matter; pest of museums, in houses
Prionychus ater	a Darkling beetle	Rare; Nationally Notable B; dead wood indicator sp.
Pyrochroa serraticornis	Common Cardinal beetle	Common on flowers, tree stumps
Quedius curtipennis	a Rove beetle	Common in woods
Quedius fuliginosus	a Rove beetle	Common in woods
Quedius humeralis	a Rove beetle	Common in woods
Quedius maurorufus	a Rove beetle	Damp places
Quedius picipes	a Rove beetle	At grass roots, vegetable refuse
Quedius rufipes	a Rove beetle	At grass roots, vegetable refuse
Quedius scintillans	a Rove beetle	At grass roots, vegetable refuse
Quedius tristis	a Rove beetle	At grass roots, vegetable refuse
Rhagium mordax	a Longhorn beetle	Saproxylic
Rhagonycha fulva	Red Soldier beetle	Common on flowers; the children's 'bloodsucker'
Rhagonycha lignosa	a Soldier beetle	Common on flowers in woods
Rhinonchus castor	a Weevil	At roots of Knotgrass
Rhinonchus inconspectus	a Weevil	On Knotgrass and relatives
Rhizophagus parallelocollis	a Rhizophagid beetle	At sap, or decaying bodies underground
Rhynchites aequatus	an Attelabid beetle	Common in woods
Rhyzobius litura	a Coccinellid beetle	
Sciodrepoides fumatus	a Leidid beetle	
Scolytus intricatus	a Bark beetle	Common in woods; saproxylic
Scolytus scolytus	Elm Bark beetle	Common, pest of Elm; vector of Dutch Elm Disease
Semiris rigidicornis	a Rove beetle	Common in woods/grassland
Sepedophilus immaculatus	a Rove beetle	Common in woods/grassland
Sepedophilus marshami	a Rove beetle	Common in woods/grassland
Sepedophilus nigripennis	a Rove beetle	Common in woods/grassland
Simplocaria semistriata	a Pill beetle	Common; among moss and grasses
Sinodendron cylindricum	Rhinoceros beetle	Dead wood indicator species
Sitona lineatus	Pea Weevil	Very common in woods/grassland
Sphaeroderma testaceum	a Leaf beetle	Common in woods; on thistles
Staphylinus brunnipes	a Rove beetle	Common in woods/grassland
Staphylinus globulifer	a Rove beetle	Common in woods/grassland

Staphylinus olens	Devil's Coach Horse	Common in woods, gardens, hedges
Staphylinus siculus	a Rove beetle	Common in woods/grassland
Stenus impressus	a Rove beetle	Common in woods/grassland
Stilbus testaceus	a Phalacrid beetle	
Stilicus rufipes	a Rove beetle	Common in woods/grassland
Stomis pumicatus	a Ground beetle	
Strangalia maculata	a Longhorn beetle	Common; on flowers; larva in rotting tree stumps
Strophosomus melanogrammus	a Weevil	Common in woods
Strophosomus retusus	a Weevil	Under stones, leaves and refuse
Tachinus laticollis	a Rove beetle	Common in woods/grassland
Tachinus signatus	a Rove beetle	Very common in woods/grassland
Tachyporus chrysomelinus	a Rove beetle	Common in woods
Tachyporus hypnorum	a Rove beetle	Common in woods
Tachyporus nitidulus	a Rove beetle	Common in woods/grassland
Tachyporus solutus	a Rove beetle	Common in woods
Tetratoma fungorum	a Tetratomid beetle	Dead wood indicator sp.
Tetrops praeusta	a Longhorn beetle	Saproxylic
Trechus obtusus	a Ground beetle	Common in woods
Trechu quadristriatus	a Ground beetle	Common in woods
Trichapion simile	a Weevil	
Triplax russica	a Erotylid beetle	In tree fungi
Trixagus carinifrons	a Throscid beetle	Saproxylic
Trixagus dermestoides	a Throscid beetle	Saproxylic
Xantholinus jarrigei	a Rove beetle	Common in woods/grassland
Xantholinus linearis	a Rove beetle	Common in woods
Xylostiba monilicornis	a Rove beetle	Common in woods/grassland

Earthworms and Leeches

These are elongate soft-bodied segmented worms. Earthworms are familiar to all as inhabitants of our gardens and soil in general. Leeches are readily recognised by their prominent suckers, usually one anterior and one posterior, and are mostly found in freshwater.

Allolobophora longa	an Earthworm	Common in soil; forms casts on soil surface
Erpobdella testacea	a Leech	Common; in small weedy ponds
Helobdella stagnalis	a Leech	Common; feeds on snails and worms
Hemiclepsis marginata	a Leech	Common; on fish & amphibia or free-living
Lumbricus terrestris	Common Earthworm	Familiar and common species; casts within the soil
Piscicola geometra	a Fish leech	Common; parasitic on freshwater fish
Theromyzon tessulatum	a Leech	Feeds on blood of water birds

Rotifers

Rotifers are among the smallest and most common multi-celled organisms encountered in any sample of fresh water. Few exceed 0.5 mm in length and the body is divided into an anterior portion, the main body and a foot. The anterior end bears a ciliated corona by which the animals swim and cause currents to bring food into their mouths. It is this structure which gives the group its common name of wheel animalcules.

As these have no common names and no specific habitat information is given, the list extends over the 3 columns.

References & Further Reading
Koste, W. (1978). Rädertiere Mitteleuropas. 2 vols. Borntraeger, Berlin.

Albertia naidis	*Filinia longiseta*	*Monommata* sp.
Anuraeopsis fissa	*Keratella cochlearis*	*Mytilina mucronata*
Asplanchna girodi	*Philodina* sp.	*Mytilina ventralis*
Asplanchna priodonta	*Platyias quadricornis*	*Notholca acuminata*
Brachionus angularis	*Pleurotrocha petromyzon*	*Squatinella* sp.
Brachionus calyciflorus	*Polyarthra dolichoptera*	*Stephanoceros fimbriatus*
Brachionus leydigii	*Pompholyx sulcata*	*Synchaeta pectinata*
Brachionus urceolaris	*Rhinoglena frontalis*	*Synchaeta oblonga*
Cephalodella auriculata	*Keratella quadrata*	*Synchaeta tremula*
Cephalodella gibba	*Lecane bulla*	*Testudinella patina*
Colurella sp.	*Lecane lunaris*	*Trichocerca* sp.
Conochilus unicornis	*Lepadella patella*	*Trichotria pocillum*
Euchlanis dilatata	*Limnias ceratophylli*	